IN THE BEST INTERESTS OF CHILDREN AND YOUTH

STUDIA PAEDAGOGICA

New Series
42

Editorial Board
Prof. Dr. E. De Corte (Chairman)
Prof. Dr. A. De Munter
Prof. Dr. M. Depaepe
Prof. Dr. B. Maes
Prof. Dr. G. Vandemeulebroecke

Studia Paedagogica

IN THE BEST INTERESTS OF CHILDREN AND YOUTH

INTERNATIONAL PERSPECTIVES

Edited by Hans Grietens, Willy Lahaye,
Walter Hellinckx, & Lieve Vandemeulebroecke

In co-operation with:
Eddy Desmecht, Huguette Desmet & Jean-Pierre Pourtois

Leuven University Press
2005

Published with the support of the K.U.Leuven Commissie voor Publicaties

© 2005 Universitaire Pers Leuven / Leuven University Press / Presses Universitaires de Louvain
Blijde-Inkomststraat 5, B-3000 Leuven

All rights reserved. Except in those cases expressly determined by law, no part of this publication may be multiplied, saved in an automated datafile or made public in any way whatsoever without the express prior written consent of the publishers.

ISBN 90 5867 489 4

D / 2005 / 1869 / 50

NUR: 847

About the editors and contributors

Marc H. Bornstein is Senior Investigator and Head of Child and Family Research at the National Institute of Child Health and Human Development, USA.

Christine Cocker is Principal Lecturer – Social Work at the School of Health and Social Science, Middlesex University, Enfield, United Kingdom. At the time of preparing this paper, she was Service Development Director at NCH - The Bridge Child Care Development Service, London, United Kingdom.

Linda R. Cote is Research Scientist in Child and Family Research at the National Institute of Child Health and Human Development, USA.

Fiona Daly is Researcher in the Children's Research Centre, Trinity College, Dublin, Ireland.

Eddy Desmecht is Junior Researcher at the Département de Développement Familial et Communautaire, Université de Mons-Hainaut, Belgium.

Huguette Desmet is Professor at the Département de Développement Familial et Communautaire, Université de Mons-Hainaut, Belgium.

Jean E. Dumas is Professor at the Department of Psychological Sciences, Purdue University, West Lafayette, USA.

Israel Zvi Gilat, is Senior Lecturer at the Law School & School of Business and Management, Netanya Academic College, and Lecturer at the School of Education, Bar-Ilan University, Israel.

Robbie Gilligan is Professor of Social Work and Social Policy, Head of the Department of Social Studies and Associate Director (and co-founder) of the Children's Research Centre, Trinity College Dublin, Ireland.

Donald Gordon is Professor Emeritus at the Department of Psychology, Ohio University, Athens, OH, USA.

Hans Grietens is Professor at the Centre for Disability, Special Needs Education, and Child Care, Katholieke Universiteit Leuven, Belgium.

Walter Hellinckx is Professor at the Centre for Disability, Special Needs Education, and Child Care, Katholieke Universiteit Leuven, Belgium.

Henna J. Josias is Junior Researcher at the Department of Special Education and Youth Care, Leiden University, The Netherlands.

Erik J. Knorth is Professor at the Department of Special Education and Child Care, University of Groningen, The Netherlands.

Willy Lahaye is Junior Researcher at the Département de Développement Familial et Communautaire, Université de Mons-Hainaut, Belgium.

Marc J. Noom is Assistant Professor at the Department of Special Education and Youth Care, Leiden University, The Netherlands.

Ercilia Palacio-Quintin is Professor Emeritus at the Département de Psychologie, Université du Québec à Trois-Rivières, Canada.

Gérard Pithon is Professor at the Départment de Psychologie, Université Paul Valéry, Montpellier, France.

Jean-Pierre Pourtois is Professor at the Département de Développement Familial et Communautaire, Université de Mons-Hainaut, Belgium.

Shlomo Romi, is Senior Lecturer and Deputy Director of the School of Education, Bar-Ilan University, Israel.

Rudi Roose is Junior Researcher at the Department of Social Welfare Studies, University of Ghent, Belgium.

Marit Skivenes is Senior Researcher at the Institute for Labour and Social Research, Oslo, Norway.

Lieve Vandemeulebroecke is Professor at the Centre for Parenting Studies and Family Education, Katholieke Universiteit Leuven, Belgium.

Michel Vandenbroeck is Senior Researcher at the Resource and Training Centre for Child Care and the Department of Social Welfare Studies, University of Ghent, Belgium.

James K. Whittaker is Professor of Social Work, University of Washington, Seattle, USA.

Elisabeth Willumsen is Junior Researcher at the School of Health and Social Work Education, Stavanger University College, Stavanger, Norway.

Contents

About the editors and contributors   6

Table of contents   8

Introduction   11

Chapter 1
Serving the best interests of children and youth in a globalizing and diverse world: Some introductory thoughts - Grietens, H.   13

Part one   Modeling the complexity of parenting   25

Chapter 2
The dynamics of positive parenting: Psychological, social and cultural contexts - Dumas, J. E.   27

Chapter 3
Japanese American and South American immigrant mothers' perceptions of their own and their spouses' parenting styles - Cote, L. R. & Bornstein, M.   47

Chapter 4
Risk factors of child neglect and physical abuse – Palacio-Quintin, E.   77

Part two   The best interests principle in child and youth care practice   97

Chapter 5
Creating "prosthetic environments" for vulnerable children: Emergent cross-national challenges for traditional child and family services practice and research - Whittaker, J. K.   99

Chapter 6
An American training program for parent-child communication assisted by an interactive and evaluative CD-ROM adapted for French-speaking countries - Pithon, G. & Gordon, D.   119

Chapter 7
The dynamics of screening and setting indications for treatment in an integrated system of child and youth care - Noom, M. J., Knorth, E. J., & Josias, H. J.   131

Chapter 8
Selected aspects of education and contact with birth family amongst young people aged 13-14 years in long term foster care in Ireland - Gilligan, R. & Daly, F.   143

Chapter 9
User participation and child protection. A structural framework for collaboration in core groups - Skiveness, M. & Willumsen, E.   175

Part three Organizing child and youth care according to the best interests principle

195

Chapter 10
Respect for diversity in early childhood education - Vandenbroeck, M.

197

Chapter 11
Networking in youth care. Towards a common engagement - Roose, R.   215

Chapter 12
In the best interest of the child. Jewish and civic perspectives - Romi, S. & Gilat, I. Z.   231

Chapter 13
Child maltreatment. Learning from tragedy. Lessons from child deaths - Cocker, C.   251

INTRODUCTION

1

Serving the best interests of children and youth in a globalizing and diverse world: Some introductory thoughts

Hans Grietens

This book is entitled *In the best interests of children and youth. International perspectives*. The title sounds rather abstract and general, but a closer look learns that it can be read and interpreted in different ways. One can read it in a more or less neutral way and conclude that the book will be informative and tell about how people from different parts of the world think about children and youth and how they try to act in their best interests. Multiculturalists will assume an intercultural or culturally sensitive approach to child and youth care. Lawyers will associate the title with the Convention of the Children's Rights because of the phrase "in the best interests", whereas residential care workers perhaps will have in mind the works by Goldstein, Freud and Solnit. My interpretation of the title is a post hoc interpretation, since it has been inspired by the editorial work. Browsing through the manuscripts on child and youth care the contributors had submitted, two concepts came into my mind: globalization and diversity. In the following paragraph, I will give some thoughts about these concepts in relation to child and youth care. Next, the structure and the content of the book will be presented. I hope that my thoughts may inspire the reader to explore further the themes presented in the book.

Globalization and diversity in child and youth care

There can be no doubt that the globalized world we live in nowadays, has consequences for children and youth (see for instance Kaufman & Rizzini, 2002). Although the effects of globalization on the lives of children and youth have been addressed only recently by social scientists, it is clear that there are both positive and negative impacts. The possibilities globalization offers to improve children's lives are enormous and cannot be denied. The potentials are most visible at the macrolevel and in the political decision-making about children and youth, but they permeate all systems and spheres children and youth live in. At the moment when nearly all countries in the world have ratified the UN Convention on the Rights of the Child, the international rights of children and youth become a major topic binding all states, rich and poor (Freeman, 2004; Willems, 2002). Article three of the Convention ("In all actions concerning children, whether undertaken by public or private social welfare institutions, courts of law, administrative authorities or legislative bodies, the best interests of the child shall be a primary consideration") now is more than merely a statement. Policymakers are committed to do more than paying lip service to the Convention. They have to undertake systematic actions to prevent the violation of children's rights and to intervene when rights are violated. In many countries there is a children's rights commissioner. Furthermore, the issue of children's rights cannot be disentangled from children's development. Taking into account the rights of children and youth means taking into account their development and striving for an optimization of development. This is a major challenge to all professionals involved with children and youth, educators as well as policymakers. As Willems (2002) stated:

> "Children's rights by definition find themselves in the dimension of development, in the realm of the inherent right of every child to become an optimal person, regardless whether they specifically bear upon the child's development, his or her becoming a person, or relate to his or her autonomy, his or her being a person, a legal subject from birth on" (p. 71).

How an optimal development of children and youth can be described and what is needed to optimize development, is the object of developmental psychology, pedagogics and developmental psychopathology, disciplines which according to Willems (2002, p. 72) "are of important relevance to the international rights of the child." Here, it looks as if social and behavioral sciences can serve international law. However, every social and behavioral scientist knows how difficult it is to operationalize what an optimal development for children and youth means. Knowing that the development of children and youth is embedded in contexts and, more broadly, in cultures, and being aware of the bidirectional influences between individuals and contexts and the differences between contexts, it looks impossible to present to international fora what an optimal development may include. It is tempting to stress the importance of the family, the early mother-child relationship, attachment patterns, education or social networks. We know from research in the Western world that these are core elements on children's way to an optimal development, but can we implement our models and theories to children and families in Africa or the Islamic world? And what about the development of children and youth in countries and regions at war or in refugee camps? Research on resilience learns that at least some individuals living in unfavorable and even cruel conditions (e.g., maltreatment, war, homelessness) can survive, although the essential conditions for a normal development were lacking from the early beginning of their lives and risks were omnipresent (Friedman & Chase-Landsdale, 2002).

Often, in these debates on international fora, we hear the term "in the best interests of the child". This term, which is part of the title of this book and which is inscribed in the UN Convention on the Rights of the Child (article three), is popular among social scientists and lawyers. It even brings both disciplines closer together. At a first glance, serving "the best interests principle" seems to be more realistic and feasible than serving "the optimal development principle". The noun "interests" is vaguer than "development" and less subject of scientific research. The adjective "best" is used here to stress that in any situation the child should prevail and less to qualify the noun it precedes. But can the best interest principle be more than a slogan? As systems, cultures and traditions differ, how then can we define what acting in the best interests of children and youth should look like? There are no general standards to help us define what is in the best interests of children and youth. Again, we risk decontextualizing the problems we are faced with. For instance, in the domain of child and youth care, in general, placing children out-of-home is considered to be less in the child's interests than trying to keep the child in the family (except, of course, in cases of severe abuse or neglect). But trying to serve children's best interests by keeping them in their family is only an alternative if adequate services are available day and night. And what do we know about the outcomes these services produce? Do they produce better outcomes than out-of-home care? In particular, little is known about the long-term outcomes of these interventions. In a similar vein, one can pretend that foster care is to prefer to residential care, as it keeps children in family structures and enables them to maintain close ties with their biological parents. But again, can such statements be generalized? Are findings from studies conducted in the United States valid in populations of continental Europe, or vice versa? And what to think of countries, for instance in Southern Europe, in which residential care for children and youth takes a prominent place by tradition and foster care is underdeveloped? Systems of care differ between countries and are embedded in historical, cultural and political contexts. They cannot be reified and replaced by systems that work in other countries. This may be one of the main reasons why it is so difficult to draw feasible and take-home conclusions out of cross-national research on child and youth care issues (see Cocker & Grietens, 2004, for an example of the complexity of cross-national research on the issue of mental health problems among looked after children).

Is the best interests principle then worthless in our debates? Of course, it isn't. As mentioned before, the principle brings together social scientists and lawyers. Although both will have a different view and will concretize the principle differently according to the models and theories underlying their respective disciplines, there is a common background and even a common language, as the UN Convention on the Rights of the Child actually has become a concrete and objective tool for both social scientists and lawyers. Furthermore, the best interests principle is at the core of the interdisciplinary debate. In this volume, the reader will find several examples of communalities between disciplines and common vocabularies. One of the contributions for instance is entitled *In the best interest of the child: Jewish and civic perspectives*. It is written by an educational psychologist (Shlomo Romi) and a lawyer (Israel Zvi Gilat).

Only advocates of globalization who are blind to cultural, historical and contextual factors will be in favor of an *inclusive world child and youth care system* (by analogy with an inclusive world economy). Instead, it is our believe that policymakers and practitioners will always have to translate the models, knowledge and experiences they pick up in our globalized world into their cultures' or systems' frames of reference. *Think globally and act locally* has to be their motto (Dominelli, 2004). Taking this motto into account, we can learn much from each other and benefit from initiatives to improve children's and families' lives, undertaken in other countries and cultures.

Unfortunately, globalization has also negative impacts. Antiglobalistst use negative outcomes as arguments in their fight against globalization (Wiener, 2004). There are many negative outcomes and most of them also have an influence on the lives of children and youth (see Kaufman & Rizzini, 2002). Dominelli (2004), among others, argues that globalization has led to an internationalization of social problems:

> "These include features such as: the spread of poverty both between countries and within countries [ ]; the importation of social problems from one part of the globe to another, as in the sex trade in children; and the impact of migratory trends, including cross-country adoptions, asylum seekers and refugees." (p. 33).

In addition, children and youth are witnessing terrorist acts as well as war crimes and the excesses of religious fundamentalism and have easy access to pornography. At this moment, we are not able to evaluate what will be the long-term effects of the various problems globalization brings along, neither can we estimate whether the positive impacts will be longer-lasting than the negative ones. It is clear, however, that the mondialization poses new challenges to parents, educators and professionals.

Globalization also influences child and youth care work (Dominelli, 2004). Child and youth care workers can benefit from globalization in various ways. First, the internationalization of social problems makes them aware of the international dimensions of their work. It helps them appreciate the interdependent nature of the world and the problems marking the world's social landscape. Further, globalization may help child and youth care workers become more sensitive to the contexts they are faced with in their cases and undertake more context-specific interventions. One of the most tangible effects of globalization in the field of child and youth care is the increase of possibilities for networking. Further, globalization led to opportunities for students in child and youth care to broaden horizons. Dominelli and Bernard (2003) illustrated how young social workers learned about their professional self by international exchange oversea. Students participating at exchange programmes learn to know other professionals' contexts and other ways of coping with problems; sometimes the problems they face are new to them (e.g., extreme poverty) or embedded in political, religious and historical contexts that differ from the context in their home country. International exchange may also help them develop experience-based frameworks to consider the relationship between the local and the global.

The other side of globalization is that the impact of migration makes that diversity in child and youth care work has been increasing steadily. Today, child and youth care workers in Europe and North America are faced with clients from various cultures and very specific backgrounds. As borders between countries disappear, clients from all over the world enter child and youth care systems. The interculturalization of the care systems is high on the agenda of policymakers and curriculum developers in universities and high schools. Asylum seekers and unaccompanied young minors are target groups, bringing along new questions (Kohli, 2003). Do we have clear answers to the questions these clients pose? This question sounds somewhat rhetoric, as it looks like we even are not able to listen fully to the questions of ethnic minority clients and lack the basic skills for intercultural communication and the frameworks to make culturally sensitive interpretations of communications. Cultural competence has become an important issue in the field (see for instance Ewalt et al., 1999 and Webb, 2001). But until now, we know but little about the cultural sensitivity of interventions in child and youth care. How culturally sensitive are the interventions we do? Which conditions facilitate the cultural sensitivity of our work? Which factors are hampering? Research on these issues is still very scarce. A lot of studies have only been aimed at listing common problems in working with ethnic minority clients. Initiatives to enhance intercultural communication and work out sensitive practices are undertaken, but it will last at least some years before outcomes will be available and before we can define good practices in this field.

What are the limits of globalization in child and youth care? How far can universalism go? These questions are difficult to answer, as we yet do not know what the full consequences of globalization in the field are. Nevertheless, I agree with (Thomas, 2001), who wrote:

> "*Globalization will continue and it will accelerate* (my italics). Child and youth care practitioners will share more information with colleagues around the world, and will increasingly find it necessary to collaborate across national boundaries to accomplish the work. More children will spend more time in out-of-home care for part or all of the day. Families will face increasingly complex demands and tasks in raising their children, and pressures with industrialized and nonindustrialized societies alike will continue to destroy families, leaving children homeless, destitute, and in need of compassionate and competent care by others. These trends will produce a renewed emphasis within the child and youth care field on changing the systems that affect children and youths, rather than just impacting the individual child. Child and youth care practitioners will be expected more

than ever to use our skills to help families, communities, and child care environments to meet the needs of their children better." (http://cyc-net.org/Journals/jcycw-15-16-Thomas.htm)

What we can learn from each other, regardless of culture and context, are core skills and knowledge, or *metaprofessional* competences, necessary to plan activities for children and young people with problems, which address their needs in ways that are adequate. This will enable each of us to serve the best interests of children and youth in his/her own country, without loosing the unique identity of professions or the locality of systems. If what we learn from colleagues in the field helps us to diversify the services we provide, the famous motto *thinking globally and acting locally* will become true one day, to the benefit of all.

Structure and content of the book

I am aware that the thoughts developed in the previous paragraphs raise many questions, some of which will be discussed by the authors who contributed to this volume. I hope that they may add to a fruitful debate on globalization and diversity in child and youth care and that they may inspire many professionals in the field on their way to realize the aforementioned motto.

The body of this volume consists of twelve chapters, written by authors from nine countries: United States, Belgium, France, Israel, The Netherlands, Norway, Ireland, Canada, and United Kingdom. The chapters are grouped thematically into three parts.

Part one contains three chapters illustrating the search for theory-driven and empirically-based models to deal with the complexity of parenting. Nowadays, several models of parenting exist. Traditionally, models focussed on what went wrong between parent and child (e.g., in case of child maltreatment), but current models tend to be more comprehensive and integrative by taking into account aspects of positive parenting as well. Furthermore, researchers try to validate models of parenting across cultures.

In Chapter two, Dumas discusses the dynamics of positive parenting. In the French literature, positive parenting often is referred to as *bientraitance* (see Desmet, Pourtois, & Lahaye, 2005). What is *bientraitance*? It looks like the term is very difficult to translate and still more difficult to define. The author starts his quest for an answer to this question by confirming a fundamental assumption underlying research in the field of child psychopathology. The core of the assumption is that most of the disorders identified in children and youth are shared (Dumas, 2002). They cannot be restricted only to dysfunctions in the child but take place in a relationship or an interactive space. He applies this perspective to positive parenting. In the remainder of the chapter he outlines the characteristics of the interactive space, in particular the psychological, social and cultural context of positive parenting. Of particular interest is the dynamic model of positive parenting Dumas proposes. This model is based on synergics and focuses on relationships rather than on individuals. The approach is illustrated by an observational study on mother-child dyads (Dumas, Lemay, & Dauwalder, 2001).

In Chapter three, Cote and Bornstein report on a cross-cultural study among 34 Japanese American and 33 South American immigrant mothers of 5-to-20-month-old children. They compared the mothers' actual and ideal engagement in social, didactic, and limit setting as well as their perceptions of their spouses' interactions. The ethnic differences that were found in this study could be attributed to the mothers' cultural beliefs (in particular, collectivism). The authors concluded that cultural beliefs seemed to play a significant role in parenting. However, some findings in this study applied for both ethnic groups. Discrepancies between parents' ideal and actual behaviors, for instance, emerged in Japanese American and South American mothers for all three parenting domains. Similarly, both Japanse American and South American mothers reported differences between their own and their spouses' behaviors. At the end of the chapter, the authors point to some practical implications of their study. Can the discrepancies in mothers' reported actual and ideal childrearing practices not be interpreted as signals of parental dissatisfaction and stress? And, last but not least, every professional working with immigrant parents needs to be aware of the cultural values related to collectivistic beliefs and of the ways these values influence parenting practices.

Chapter four by Palacio-Quintin deals with the prevention of child maltreatment. The author is fully aware of the difficulties early prevention brings along and stresses that before preventive interventions are developed knowledge of risk factors is needed to identify target populations. She then offers the reader a detailed and up-to-date review of risk factors, related to child physical abuse and neglect. Adopting an ecological approach, we can discern risk factors in the different systems children and families are living in. Risk factors can be found in the social environment, the family, the parent and the child. It is well-known that there is not a single risk factor which leads to child physical abuse and neglect. Instead, risk factors interact with each other. The real danger is in the cumulative effects of risk factors. However, as Palacio-Quintin argues, we know too little about these interactions and cumulative effects. At the moment, we are not able to weigh the impact of risk factors. Further, we still know too little about the impact of protective factors and resilience mechanisms in children and families. Information about protective factors is necessary to help children and families break the intergenerational cycle of maltreatment. The author concludes by putting forward a research agenda, which includes the aforementioned and other issues still to be explored.

The common theme of the five chapters in *Part two* is the best interests principle in child and youth care practice.

Whittaker, in Chapter five, reflects on four key questions concerning children's mental health in the United States: 1) what are promising models?, 2) what are similarities and differences and how can they be assessed?, 3) taken together, do these promising interventions constitute something greater than the sum of their parts?, and 4) what challenges lie ahead in implementing effective child mental health services in the domains of policy, practice and evaluative research? Whittaker gives an overview of evidence-based interventions like multisystemic therapy, wraparound treatment and treatment foster care, most of which are based on systems-of-care thinking and ecological models to treatment. Most interventions create a specialized temporary environment within which and through which the treatment occurs. Whittaker calls this a *prosthetic environment* or a contextualized picture of person-in-environment which goes beyond the singular focus on the individual child or the family. The author is aware that more research is needed to evaluate these interventions and points to the need of cross-national research programs, as all interventions proposed were developed within the United States.

In Chapter six, Pithon and Gordon talk about the adaptation of an American training program on parent-child communication for French-speaking countries. The training program which is entitled *Parenting Wisely* consists of an interactive and evaluative CD-ROM in which educational problems have to be solved (Gordon, 1998). There is empirical evidence that the program produces positive effects in American users, with an increase of positive parent-child communications and a decrease of children's problem behaviors. The program has been used in different other countries as well, for instance in Australia. Pithon asks whether the program can be adapted and implemented in French-speaking countries, for instance Canada, France and the French-speaking part of Belgium. Being aware of the different traditions in the English-speaking and the French-speaking world with regard professional help in case of parent-child problems, this is a legitimate and very provoking question. Pithon does not answer this question himself and he is not making an analysis of the difficulties that may arise when Gordon's training program will be translated into French and implemented in the French-speaking world. Instead, he gives the word to Gordon by interviewing him and giving him the occasion to present his program and his doubts and worries about using the program outside the United States. It is up to the reader to draw conclusions about the usefulness of *Parenting Wisely* in his/her country.

In Chapter seven, Noom, Knorth and Josias report on the reorganization of the system of professional child and youth care in The Netherlands, which took place in the last decade. As in Flanders, a more integrated system has been strived for. The Youth Care Offices take a central place in the reformed system and are intended to be the first step in every youth care trajectory. The tasks of the Offices are standardized by means of a model or protocol, covering following topics: entry, screening, diagnosis, setting indications for treatment, assignment and placement. The authors present an empirical study on the dynamics of screening and setting indications for treatment. They analyzed 270 case files in six Youth Care Offices and learned a lot about the characteristics of clients and the relationships between clients' characteristics and proposed or authorized interventions. The wealth of information this study provides may help the offices to improve the efficacy of setting indications for treatment and may be of great interest to reformers in other countries, for instance in Belgium (Flanders).

In Chapter eight Gilligan and Daly report on the educational and social support experiences of young people aged 13-14 years in long term foster care in Ireland. The main reason for this study was a lack of information on young people's daily lives while in care, particularly those in long term foster care. In total, 205 foster carers were interviewed (this was about 90% of all young people aged 13-14 years in long term foster care in Ireland). Areas considered were young people's education and schooling and the nature of their contacts with birth families. The study is unique, not only for Ireland, as it offers a lot of information on the daily lives of foster children, data which are rather scarce. Gilligan and Daly concluded that there was an overall favourable educational progress among the foster children, although there were two areas of concern: educational needs with relatively high rates of remedial classes or being in a special class or school and bullying, the prevalence of which was higher than in the general population. Further, the study clearly showed the importance of family ties in the lives of young people. Measures that can strengthen family ties are placement of siblings together in the same foster family, placement in families of relatives and maintaining as much as possible the contacts between young people and their birth family members.

In Chapter nine by Skivenes and Willumsen we learn about user participation in the Norwegian child protection system. It is easily said that participation is in the best interests of the child but little is known about how to make participation function, its goals and the structural criteria needed. In their contribution, Skivenes and Willumsen try to answer some of these questions. They reflect on how to organize collaboration to ensure user involvement and to make legitimate decisions in child protection services. Four criteria should be met in deliberative processes handling normative questions, as for instance questions concerning out-of-home placement: affected parties must be involved in the decision-making process, availability of meeting places, differences in capabilities to present one's views and ability to deliberate must be compensated, public accessibility. The authors describe how in residential settings in Norway core group meetings are organized in order to fulfil these criteria. They discuss the methods and ethics of core group meetings and examined five cases. A thorough analysis of these cases showed what are strengths and weaknesses of core group meetings and enabled to provide recommendations to optimize user participation in the child protection system.

The major focus of the four chapters in *Part three* is on the organization of child and youth care systems according to the best interests principle.

Chapter ten by Vandenbroeck deals with diversity in early childhood education. The author analyzes how recent changes in the quality legislation influence our thinking on early childhood education and diversity. Further, he shows how actual societal changes create new forms of exclusion and stresses that nowadays certain groups have little access to this part of the social welfare system, in particular parents from lower socioeconomic groups. Diversity, for instance of parental perspectives, should be taken into account, when evaluating and monitoring quality of services. Indeed, good practices may differ from context to context. Vandenbroeck illustrates this by presenting the results of a small-scale study in day care settings in the inner city of Antwerp (Belgium). Parents from various cultural backgrounds participated at the study and had to comment on a videotaped toilet situation in the day care setting. Parents made sense out of the child's and the educator's behaviors and made very different comments, based on their own cultural frameworks, implicit theories and thoughts on what is good for children. The author concludes that such diversity in parental perspectives has important consequences for professionals. The professional is no longer an "expert" in education. Instead, he/she is challenged to co-construct the educational practice in a continuous dialogue with the parents. This can only be realized by a turn to radical reciprocity (Vandenbroeck, 2001).

In Chapter eleven, Roose discusses a central issue of the Strategic Youth Care Plan in Flanders (Belgium): networking in youth care. This plan which has the ambition to reform and restructure the child and youth care system in Flanders and strives for a more integrative approach of care, now is ready to be implemented. In order to examine and deepen the tenets of the plan, empirical research is needed. Strengthening the networks and better co-operation between caregivers is one of the core principles underlying the reforms. In his contribution, Roose presents the objectives and results of an action research directed in one region of Flanders (Waasland). This region received the status of a pilot region and was one of the first regions where networking has been realized according to the plan's principles (the Waasland Youth Care Networking). The central question of Roose's research was to find out which criteria networking needed to fulfil in order to increase the quality of care in the mind of the client. He interviewed 173 care providers. He concluded that not the improvement of the organization, but incorporation of committment and vision in the organization were valued as the most important issues. Further, care providers agreed that it is a major challenge to find a balance between a desire for control and a desire for involvement. Participative approaches are needed to tailor help to the clients' needs but have to be alternated with measures that are more controlling and power assertive.

Romi and Gilat, in Chapter twelve, describe the situation in Israel, where two different legal systems, a civic-state and a religious one, exist side by side. Both systems perceive the best interests of children differently. The civic interpretation of the best interests of children focusses on the physical and psychological needs in the here-and-now, whereas the Jewish religious interpretation is more future-oriented and stresses spiritual and ideological aspects of children as members of the community. The authors discuss the consequences living under a dual legal system has for children and parents. They describe how different views influence decisions when custody cases are brought before the court (either a civil or a religious court) and how the conflict between the civic liberal and the religious paternalistic approach permeates the current debates in Israel.

In Chapter thirteen, Cocker treats the issue of fatal child maltreatment. According to UNICEF (2003), each week in England and Wales two children die of abuse or neglect whilst in the care of their parents. Cocker discusses themes emerging from the research that reviews these serious cases. Can we predict such tragedies? The answer to this question is not simply yes or no. To avoid serious child maltreatment where possible, practitioners must have a good understanding of potential risk factors regarding parents and children, as well as know about common professional errors that can bias their work. Cross-cultural issues should also be taken into account, as is illustrated by two recent tragic cases of vulnerable children in the United Kingdom. Cocker argues that we can learn from tragedies and enhance our understanding of where processes have gone wrong. Competent professional involvement can make the necessary difference and may help prevent harm to other children, although there are no guarantees, as not all child deaths are predictable and preventable.

References

Cocker, C., & Grietens, H. (Eds.) (2004). Mental health in children in public state care: European perspectives. *International Journal of Child & Family Welfare, 7* (Nrs. 2-4, Special issues).

Desmet, H., Pourtois, J.-P., & Lahaye, L. (Eds.) (2005). *Culture et bientraitance.* Bruxelles: DeBoeck Université.

Dominelli, L. (2004). *Social work. Theory and practice for a changing profession.* Cambridge: Polity Press.

Dominelli, L., & Bernard, W. T. (Eds.) (2003). *Broadening horizons. International exchanges in social work.* Aldershot: Ashgate.

Dumas, J. E. (2002). *Psychopathologie de l'enfant et de l'adolescent (2ème édition).* Bruxelles: DeBoeck Université.

Dumas, J. E., Lemay, P., & Dauwalder, J.-P. (2001). Dynamic analyses of mother-child interactions in functional and dysfunctional dyads: A synergetic approach. *Journal of Abnormal Child Psychology, 29,* 317-329.

Ewalt, P. L., Freeman, E. M., Fortune, A. E., Poole, D. L., & Witkin, S. L. (Eds.) (1999). *Multicultural issues in social work. Practice and research.* Washington, DC: NASW Press.

Freeman, M. D. A. (Ed.) (2004). *Children's rights (Vols. 1 and 2).* Aldershot: Dartmouth Publishing Company.

Friedman, R. J., & Chase-Landsdale, P. L. (2002). Chronic adversities. In M. Rutter & E. Taylor (Eds.), *Child and adolescent psychiatry (4th edition)* (pp. 261-276). Malden, MA: Blackwell Science.

Gordon, D. A. (1998). *Parenting Wisely.* Athens (Ohio): Family Works, Inc.

Kaufman, N. E., & Rizzini, I. (Eds.) (2002). *Globalization and children: Exploring potentials for enhancing opportunities in the lives of children and youth.* New York: Kluwer Academic/Plenum Publishers.

Kohli, R. (Ed.) (2003). Child and family social work with asylum seekers and refugees. *Child & Family Social Work, 8* (Nr. 3, Special issue).

Thomas, D. (2000). Child and youth care workers to be replaced by robots in the future? *Journal of Child and Youth Care Work, 16* (available at http://cyc-net.org/Journals/jcycw-15-16-Thomas.htm).

UNICEF (2003). *A league table of child maltreatment deaths in rich nations. Innocenti Report Card No. 5, September 2003.* Florence: UNICEF Innocenti Research Centre.

Vandenbroeck, M. (2001). *The view of the Yeti. Bringing up children in the spirit of self-awareness and kindredship.* The Hague: Van Leer Foundation.

Webb, N. B. (Ed.) (2001). *Culturally diverse parent-child and family relationships. A guide for social workers and other practitioners.* New York: Columbia University Press Publishers.

Wiener, J. (2004). "Globalisation": The political function of ambiguity. In B. De Schutter & J. Pas (Eds.), *About globalisation. Views on the trajectory of mondialisation* (pp. 19-49). Brussels: VUB University Press.

Willems, J. C. M. (Ed.) (2002). *Developmental and autonomy rights of children: Empowering children, caregivers and communities.* Antwerp: Intersentia.

PART ONE

MODELING THE COMPLEXITY OF PARENTING

2

The dynamics of positive parenting: Psychological, social and cultural contexts

Jean E. Dumas

Introduction

Positive parenting is a relatively new concern among childhood professionals—be they psychologists, educators, psychiatrists, social workers or teachers. In all of Western societies there are indeed many more professionals specialized in people who are disturbed or doing evil, than in people who have a positive influence around them. As a consequence, we have accumulated more scientific data and practical knowledge over the past decades in the field of child maltreatment than in the field of positive parenting. There are at least two explanations for this imbalance.

First is the fact that people are much more concerned by disturbed or dangerous people than by positive and caring people. Social psychology has highlighted this fact in a number of research studies. For example, we find it easier to quickly notice the face of an angry or threatening person in a crowd of benevolent people than to locate a benevolent person in a neutral or non threatening crowd (Hansen & Hansen, 1988).

The imbalance between what is known about positive parenting and maltreatment is also explained by the fact that interest in these topics have been influenced by social changes that, in the Western world at least, have been as swift as they have been profound. Two lessons drawn from research on child abuse illustrate these changes and seem to me to be particularly important for people interested in the welfare of children in general and in positive parenting in particular. The first one comes from the fact that what is meant by treating children well or abusing them depends on rapidly changing and constantly evolving cultural standards. A few decades ago, many psychiatrists and psychologists of Freudian orientation maintained that sexual contacts between children and adults were often positive experiences that had a favorable impact on personality development:

> «The experience of the child in its sex relationship with adults does not seem always to have a traumatic

effect...The experience offers an opportunity for the child to test out in reality an infantile fantasy; it probably finds the consequences less severe, and in fact actually gratifying to a pleasure sense. The emotional balance is thus in favor of contentment...There was evidence that the child derived some emotional satisfaction from the experience» (Bender & Blau, 1937, p. 516-517).

This assertion was not published in a local professional bulletin that nobody read but in the *American Journal of Orthopsychiatry*, one of the United States' most prestigious professional publications in psychiatry. It is unimaginable that the editor of this journal would publish such an assertion today. To do so would immediately lead to a media uproar and loud words of condemnation from professional and child welfare associations. Yesterday's positive parenting is today's abuse.

A second lesson from the history of child maltreatment is that there is no typical abusing personality. When in 1962 Kempe and his colleagues published their now famous article on severe child abuse in the United States, they concluded that the phenomenon was rare and that only seriously disturbed parents would deliberately inflict the injuries they described:

«Psychiatric factors are probably of prime importance in the [origin of child maltreatment]...Parents who inflict abuse on their children do not necessarily have psychopathic or sociopathic personalities or come from bordeline socioeconomic groups, although most published cases have been in these categories. In most cases some defect of character structure is probably present» (Kempe, Silverman, Steele, Droegemueller, & Silver, 1962, p. 24).

This pioneering article in general and its conclusion in particular led to a series of scientific studies aimed at identifying the psychological characteristics of abusive parents. Twenty years of research or so did not yield a profile or profiles of abusive parents and throughout the 1980s a number of important reviews concluded that these parents are much more similar to average individuals than had been thought initially (see, for example, Wolfe, 1985).

Fundamental assumption

So what is positive parenting? There is no immediately obvious answer. As in the field of maltreatment, it is a reality in constant evolution and there are no lists of positive parenting characteristics anymore than there are lists of the personality characteristics of abusive parents. To start to answer the question, though, I believe that the current state of research in this area confirms the relevance of a fundamental assumption, namely that apart from some severe pathologies that are clearly ascribable to a known etiologic agent, most of the disorders identified by clinical or psychosocial diagnosis are always more or less "shared". They reflect a dysfunction that is less "in" the child or the parent than in their relationship or what I call their interactive space (Dumas, 2002; Fogel, 1993).

The interactive space

As Desmet, Pourtois and Lahaye (2005) emphasize, this assumption can be turned around and applied just as well to positive parenting, which is also a reality that is always more or less shared. Positive parenting does not amount to a set of emotional and behavioral characteristics that reside somewhere "in" the parent; rather, it is largely to be found in the evolving relationship that parent and child share. This means that positive parenting is locate d in the *interactive space* that connects them over time. This space is obviously not isolated. It is influenced by the different contexts of development of which it is a part, by what Bronfenbrenner (1979, 1999) calls *the mesosystem, the exosystem, the macrosystem,* and *the chronosystem.* These systems correspond roughly to the family's psychological, social, cultural and history contexts (see Figure 2.1).

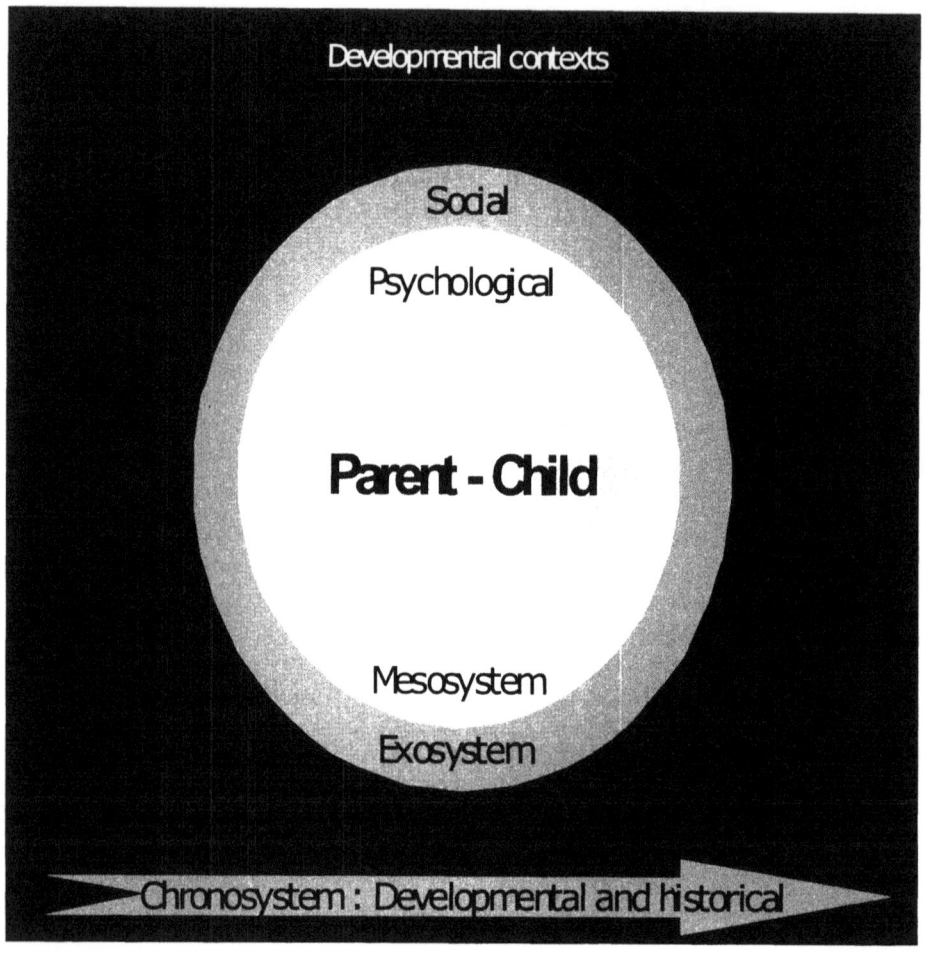

Figure 2.1
The interactive space of positive parenting (adapted from Bronfenbrenner, 1979, 1999).

The remainder of this chapter presents an outline of the characteristics of this interactive space and, particularly, of its psychological context. Before going on, it is however necessary to emphasize a point that should be obvious: child and parent both play active roles in this space. Developmental psychology has clearly established that, from birth, children have different temperaments that reflect amongst other things factors of a genetic and constitutional nature (Rothbart & Bates, 1998). Personality psychology has shown that the same applies to parents. In other words, the interactive space I will describe is itself in constant interaction with the personal contributions of the actors concerned, an essential point that I will not consider further here.

The psychological context of positive parenting

Emergence and co-regulation

Beyond the contribution of the temperament and personality of each actor to the interactive space, positive parenting is readily observable in the every-day small gestures that parents and children share and from which it emerges. I compare this *emergence* to a dripping faucet that, one drop at a time, eventually leaves an indelible mark at the bottom of a sink. To understand this emergence process it is essential to draw a distinction between *physical invariants* and *emotional invariants*.

Observations of newborn babies by Watson (1994) and Gergely and Watson (1999) have shown that, until 3 months of age, babies are mostly interested in perfect contingencies, that is in circumstances that involve *entirely foreseeable* changes in their environment. They find these contingencies mainly in the frequent limb movements they make when awake and that mobilize their entire attention and organization. When babies are comfortably seated or lying on their back, they spend a considerable amount of time making their arms and legs move in and out of their visual field, and smile or coo whenever an arm or leg enters or leaves that field. Repeated hundreds of times, these movements give babies reliable reference points, or physical invariants, that enable them to develop their first understanding of body and space, and of the distinction between themselves, others, and the world.

Babies' preference for perfect contingencies decreases from the age of 3 months on, to be gradually replaced by an interest in changes that *are not entirely foreseeable anymore*. This development is fundamental, although it usually goes unnoticed. It allows young children to become more and more interested in their social world, whose contingencies are very seldom as perfect as those of the physical world. These contingencies – such as a parent's tone of voice, smiles and caresses – are nevertheless foreseeable and give children their first *emotional invariants*. When they are generally positive and reliable, these invariants become essential psychological and social reference points that fully integrate children in the great dance of life.

Physical invariants stem from processes of sensory and motor self-regulation that depends almost entirely on the child. Emotional invariants are the result of a continuous process of co-regulation between the child and the immediate environment – between the child and in a majority of cases his/her parent(s). This co-regulation is an emerging phenomenon: it stems from and is guided by the dynamics of the actors' interactions, rather than by any behavioral plans or schemes that would be found somewhere inside the nervous or cognitive system of each one of them (Fogel, 1993).

Coping

For most children, the family is the setting that allows, or does not allow, them to find the emotional invariants they need to develop of a multitude of social, emotional and instrumental competencies (Dumas, 2000; Durning, 1995; Patterson, Reid & Dishion, 1992). These competencies are essential *to cope* with the many challenges that each day brings. These challenges are very diverse. They range from small frustrations – such as awaiting one's turn, sharing, and eating Brussels sprouts – to developmental demands and important life events – such as learning to walk, welcoming a young sibling, starting grade school, and much more. Whatever their nature, all these requirements put children's competencies to the test: they are beyond what they can easily do or entirely new; they tend to cause strong emotions; and they are stressful.

At any age, there are primarily three ways of coping: prosocial, antisocial, and asocial. One can seek to approach a challenge in a constructive manner, by listening to others, negotiating with them as necessary, and learning from them. Alternatively, one can do it in an aggressive or destructive manner, for example by attempting to impose a "solution" by force, by refusing to cooperate, or by accusing somebody else to be responsible of the state of affairs that frustrates us. Lastly, one can attempt to cope in a passive manner, by avoiding the situation, by not saying anything, or by denying the existence of the problem, in the false hope that it will disappear or that somebody else will take care of it.

In the family, these three ways of coping correspond to the different manners in which adults can treat children – from positive parenting to maltreatment:

- Prosocial coping corresponds to positive parenting
- Antisocial coping corresponds to abuse
- Asocial coping corresponds to neglect

From repeated practice to automaticity

As children and other family members must all cope with challenges every day, the manner in which they do so when they are together gives them a considerable amount of *practice* in their shared interactive space.

This practice goes largely unnoticed because here again it resembles a dripping faucet more than a tidal wave. Specifically, as I have argued elsewhere, with sufficient practice the ways in which family members relate to each other day after day become integrated into *shared behavioral patterns* that are typical of their relationship – into what I call *automatized transactional procedures* (ATPs) (Dumas, 1997). These procedures:
- are transactional
- require little or no conscious control or awareness
- are used as interactive guides
- provide continuity and stability in daily relationships
- are difficult to modify
- tend to generalize to other relationships

Social and cognitive psychology has demonstrated the importance of automatized processes in the organization of human behavior (Bargh & Chartrand, 1999; Bargh & Ferguson, 2000). These processes are to psychology what Bourdieu's habitus (1987) is to sociology. They do not lay down strict rules of individual or social behavior but provide dynamic strategies for coping with everyday challenges. Most of these strategies do not stem from conscious choices or rational decisions but from modes of coping that, through practice, have become customary and largely automatized. Within the family, these strategies determine each member's typical behavior while leaving him/her constantly free to act as he/she wishes. They also turn out to be more or less useful for the management of daily challenges and, in the long run, for the survival of family relationships and of the mesosystem of which they are a part.

The distinctive feature of ATPs is their transactive nature. They cannot be considered simply as the sum of the individual characteristics of the family members who enter repeatedly into the same patterns of interaction. Rather, they reflect the peculiar history of a relationship in which each member has acquired relationship-specific ways of feeling, attending, and behaving – of coping.

With time, ATPs can be performed with little or no conscious cognitive control or awareness. They become overlearned to such an extent that they give access to automatized emotions, cognitions, and actions that manifest themselves with little or no awareness and contribute directly to the maintenance of positive or aversive interactions, to their escalation over time, and to their generalization across settings. In particular, under conditions of stress characterized by high emotion and low attention, family members are most likely to rely on these overlearned patterns of interaction to manage each other's demands and, more generally, to respond to challenges.

The ATPs members of a family practice repeatedly in the course of living together are not only relationship-specific products of past interactions but essential guides to current and future interactions, both within the relationship and beyond. For example, the likelihood that a child will comply to a mother's command depends not only on the immediate stimuli that both of them exchange and on the presence of contextual events (e.g., child's involvement in a competing activity, maternal emotional distress). It depends also on the interactional history that child and mother have acquired over the years. Thus, even though the content of day-to-day interactions varies considerably across time and settings, ATPs provide a certain degree of continuity and stability in these interactions. When ATPs are dysfunctional, this continuity and stability tends to make relationship difficulties highly resistant to change, even though the protagonists – such as parents and children – may express a genuine desire to see their relationship improve.

Finally, with the passage of time, ATPs tend to generalize from the relationship in which they were acquired initially to other relationships, with each protagonist making use of skills that developed within a particular context (such as the disciplinary context of the parent-child relationship) in a variety of social settings. This is a positive outcome in most but not all circumstances. For example, at-risk youths who have acquired coercive skills in early childhood may later display the antisocial ways of coping they have acquired at home in other relationships and settings.

Towards a dynamic model of positive parenting: The synergetic approach

The evidence presented so far leads to a largely positive conclusion: positive parenting does not depend entirely on a set of fixed parental characteristics or on a limited number of positive life events, but rather on the dynamics of small daily exchanges that offer many opportunities for second chances and repairs. However, this immediately raises a new question: how do we study the processes of co-regulation that underlie this dynamic reality? Stated differently, how do we discover the ATPs that are generally observed in the relationships of parents who treat their children well and of children who treat their parents well?

Dynamic models are unfortunately rare in the social sciences in general and in psychology in particular. Traditional methods of psychological research consider individuals, rather than their relationships, as units of analysis. Going against this long tradition, however, a growing number of researchers make use of different dynamic approaches developed and successfully used in physics and biology to tackle important psychological questions. *Synergics* is one of those approaches.

Synergics is an interdisciplinary research field derived from chaos theory and interested in the behavior of complex systems. Its methods are based on the observation that, although this behavior is often chaotic at first sight, this behavior reflects a restricted number of parameters that can be isolated starting from repeated observations of these systems (Haken, 1992, 1999). In the field of family relations in general and positive parenting in particular, synergics focuses on relationships rather than individuals – on what Kantor called "inter-behavior" (Kantor & Smith, 1975) – and privileges dynamic statistical methods over more traditional parametric ones. Concretely, these methods make it possible to model the way a mother and her child behave with each other and, on the basis of repeated observations of their most frequent exchanges, to formulate assumptions on the nature of their relationship.

The synergetic approach applied to the study of mother-child relations

Research conducted by Dumas, Lemay, and Dauwalder (2001) illustrates the synergic approach. In this study we compared two groups of 11 dyads each, one of mothers and children in clinical consultation for serious relational conflicts and the other of mothers and children of the same socioeconomic background but without significant relationship difficulties. There were 7 boys and 4 girls in each group, on average 6 years old. Each dyad was observed in their home by trained observers using a standardized behavioral coding system for a total of 6 hours (at a rate of one hour 2 or 3 times per week during 2 or 3 weeks). These observations showed that children in the non-clinical group were much more compliant and affectionate, and less aggressive and disturbing than their counterparts in the clinical group. Likewise, mothers in the non-clinical group were more positive and affectionate and less aggressive and punitive toward their children than mothers in the clinical group. These differences were all significant, although none of the mothers of the clinical group were abusive or had been reported for abuse.

Once these parametric comparisons had been made, the study focused on the dynamic strategies used by the each group. In synergics terms, this consisted of establishing various *Karnaugh maps* for each dyad. These maps make it possible to take several mother and child variables in consideration simultaneously. Figure 2.2 illustrates a blank Karnaugh map representing four distinct behaviors: mother control and mother positive on the one hand, and child compliance and child positive of the other. This map defines an interactive space made up of 16 *states*. These states reflect all possible combinations of the four variables, which in each state can be either present or not (denoted by a 1 or 0). A Karnaugh map is always completed clockwise by sequentially joining with a line the states that are "visited" by the dyad during each minute of observation. As we conducted 6 hours of observation per dyad, each map in our study represents 360 transitions (60 min X 6 observations), either from one state to another, or within the same state (this occurred whenever the relationship remained within the same state for two consecutive minutes or more). By way of illustration, Figure 2.3 presents two completed charts, one based on the data of a non-clinical family and the other of a clinical one. As this figure shows, Karnaugh maps are difficult to interpret because the most frequent transitions observed in each dyad are hidden in the relatively chaotic matrix of all of their transactions.

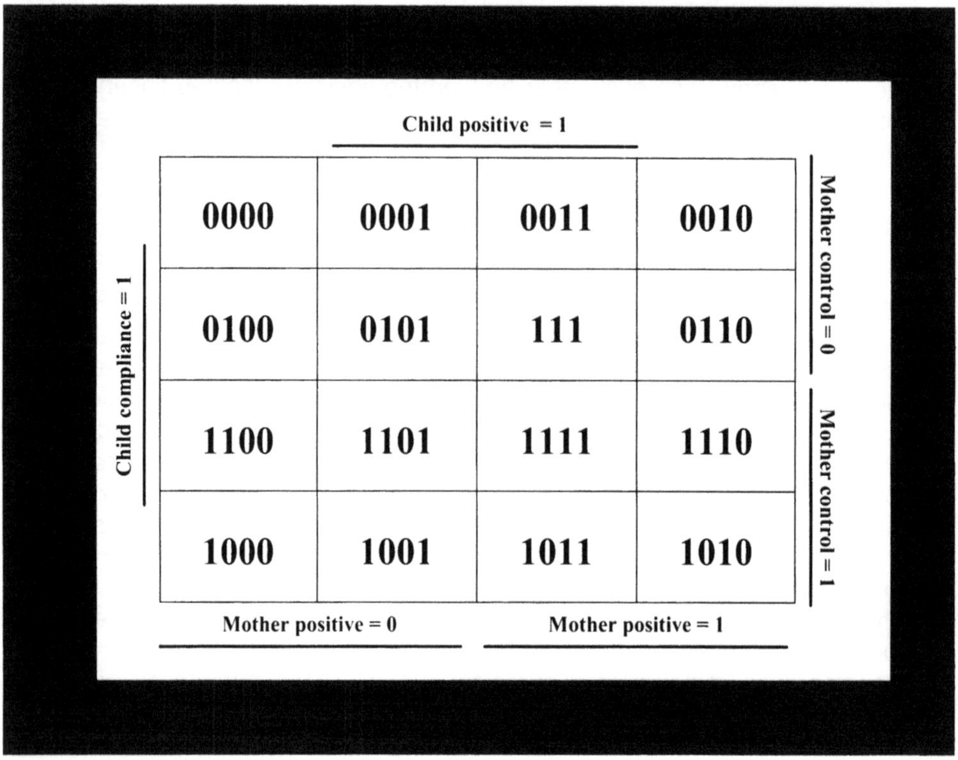

	Child positive = 1			
Child compliance = 1	0000	0001	0011	0010
	0100	0101	111	0110
	1100	1101	1111	1110
	1000	1001	1011	1010
	Mother positive = 0		Mother positive = 1	

Mother control = 0 (upper half) / Mother control = 1 (lower half)

Figure 2.2
Blank Karnaugh map representing four discrete mother and child behaviors: mother control, mother positive, child compliance, and child positive.

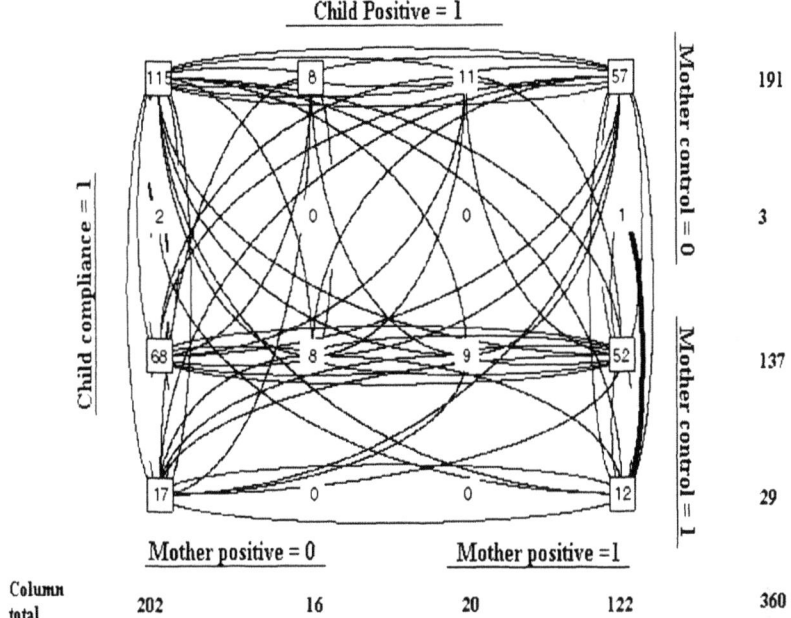

Figure 2.3
Karnaugh maps of a non-clinical family (average dyad) and of a clinical family (referred dyad).

To discover and compare the exchanges most frequently observed in the two groups, a synergic analysis requires a last step in which Karnaugh maps are drawn to represent only the most frequent transitions observed among the members from each group. Figure 2.4 presents two maps summarizing the positive transactions most frequently observed in the two groups. A visual comparison of these charts shows that transactions frequently go from various states to state 0000. This state represents the fact that, in each group, dyads were often engaged in other transactions than those that are summarized here. (It is always the case in this type of analysis, which can obviously account only for some elements of the large behavioral repertoire observed.) However, important group differences emerge when one considers the most frequent transactions towards states other than 0000. State 1100 was very often visited by non-clinical dyads. This state represents instances of child compliance to maternal requests, whether mothers accompanied their requests with positive or affectionate gestures or not. The fact that state 1000 frequently led to state 1100 indicated further that, when non-clinical children disobeyed their mothers, their noncompliance was quickly followed by compliance in later transactions. The situation was very different in the clinical group, where state 1000 was one of the most often visited. This state represents instances of repeated child noncompliance, whether mothers accompanied their requests with positive or affectionate gestures or not. Moreover, the fact that in the clinical group state 1100 frequently led to state 1000 indicates that when children in this group obeyed, their compliance was only momentary; it quickly led to new transactions in which their mothers' requests did not have their intended effect.

Positive parenting

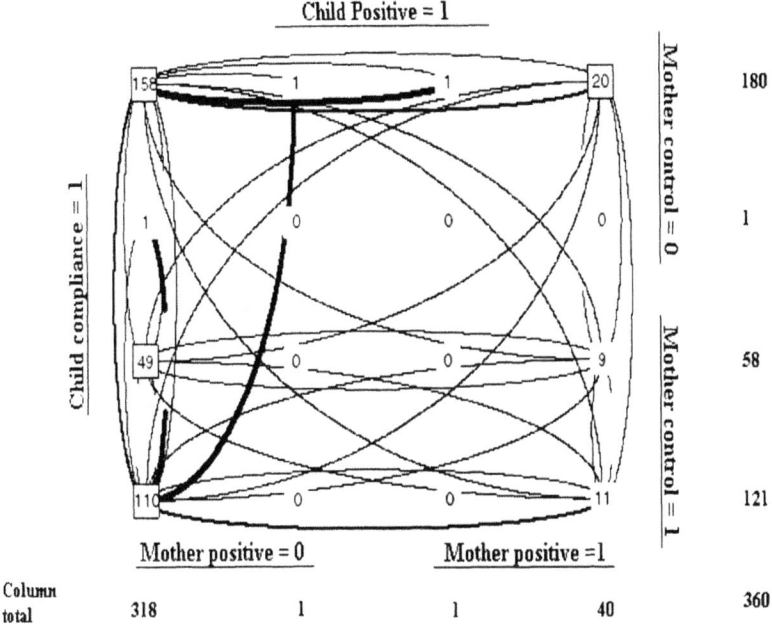

Figure 2.4
Karnaugh maps summarizing the most frequent transitions observed in the non-clinical group (top) and in the clinical group (bottom).

39

In short, this study shows that the synergic approach offers a tool for sequential analysis that, when applied to positive parenting, makes it possible to isolate the most frequent dynamic strategies mothers and children use in their daily relationships. This tool thus offers the possibility of studying the processes of co-regulation that are characteristic of well-functioning relationships and of more dysfunctional ones. More generally, this study supports the assumption that mothers and children develop their ATPs in the course of their daily transactions, not consciously so much as through repeated practice of similar exchanges. In many families these ATPs contribute to the physical and psychological well-being of children, but unfortunately threaten it on others.

The social context of positive parenting

The interactive space that connects parent and child and in which positive parenting is to be found extends well beyond the limits of the family (Gabel, Jésu, & Manciaux, 2000). I can give only one example here, which I take from my research on social insularity and, more particularly, from a study of very isolated mothers and their children, who were also observed on several occasions in the course of visits in their home (Dumas, 1986). These "insular" mothers, who all had an aggressive and disruptive child, were receiving psychological services to help them parent their children more positively. Several of them had been reported for abuse and all lacked social support and regularly had negative contacts with adults outside their family (e.g., with relatives, neighbors, social workers, and landlords). The study compared mother-child interactions at home on days when the mothers had had mostly positive, supportive social contacts with adults outside the home ("good days") and on days when they had not ("bad days"). Not surprisingly, the children's behavior did not differ much from day to day. However, their mothers were more likely to be harsh and inconsistent with them on "bad" than on "good" days. This shows that aggressive, antisocial children often manifest their disruptive behaviors in a family context in which their parents themselves are very lonely and lack adequate support and encouragement. More generally, this shows that the quality of the mother-child relationship and, therefore, the degree of positive parenting, reflects complex social circumstances that extend well beyond the confine of the home and that do not all involve the child directly.

The influence of the social context is also strongly apparent in the lively discussions that parents have in the parenting groups I have set up in recent years as part of a large-scale preventive effort to promote positive parenting and reduce risk of child maltreatment. These groups, which meet 2 hours per week for 8 weeks, are organized through preschools and daycare centers, and are open to all parents who have a child between the ages of 3 and 5. These groups follow a clearly established parenting program but actively solicit the contribution of all participants and give them many opportunities to share their experiences and the challenges they face as parents of young children. It is not possible to summarize the richness of their discussions in a few lines. However, many participants regularly stress how difficult it is for them to parent their children as positively as they would like. Parents explain this by saying, not only how challenging it is to be available, positive, and consistent day after day, but also how much more complicated their task is when they lack social, emotional, and material support or do not have close family members or friends on whom they can count. Many parents who attend these groups are very isolated. To make ends meet, they must work full-time or even longer by taking two or more jobs, and are often exhausted when they see their children at the end of the day. It is not surprising that they are not always able to be fully available for them under such circumstances.

More generally, these parenting groups highlight how difficult it is today for many mothers and fathers to parent their children positively. It would be obviously naive to believe that it was easy or even easier yesterday. However, I believe that the very rapid evolution of the family in the course of recent decades has made positive parenting very challenging because it must rely on an increasingly limited number of people. Western families are more nuclear and insular today than they were in earlier times, and children have fewer adults on average to take care of them and to guide them than their parents and their grandparents had. It is not always a bad thing, of course. But our parenting groups unfortunately show often the extent to which children lack in positive experiences and in positive parenting when they can only count on one or two parents who struggle with major challenges of their own.

The cultural context of positive parenting

Finally, the interactive space in which parents and children function daily also reflects our society's cultural understanding of positive parenting on the one hand and of maltreatment on the other hand. I already emphasized the evolving, dynamic nature of this understanding at the beginning of this chapter and will return to it now in closing.

Our growing awareness of the extent and severity of child maltreatment in many Western societies is a relatively recent phenomenon. This has not only led to the promulgation of laws to protect children. It has also contributed to major shifts in our understanding of what constitutes positive parenting and appropriate care of children by adults other than parents and close family members. These developments have had a considerable number of beneficial effects (Gabel et al., 2000; Wolfe, 1999). However, I believe that they have also had unintended effects that have left a number of children especially vulnerable. The most important one, in my eyes, lies in the fact that positive parenting has become increasingly defined as the almost exclusive responsibility of the child's parents. In Western societies in general and particularly in the United States where I work, parents and some close family members are the only adults who today have the right to openly express affection to children – to hug and kiss them, to comfort them, and to nurture them in caring and loving ways. Coupled with the rapid evolution of the nuclear family I discussed above, this exclusiveness leaves many abused and neglected children highly vulnerable because, when their parents fail to love and nurture them, they have nobody else to turn to – nobody to give them the affection they need to grow up in harmony with themselves and their environment.

Very few attentive and caring teachers dare go today beyond a strict definition of their professional responsibilities to reach to a student who is extremely unhappy in class or revolted, even when they and everybody else around know that the child has nobody to rely on at home. The same applies to concerned neighbors who have children themselves or are retired and see the child's often glaring needs. Those who dare go against the cultural prohibition to care for other people's children may find themselves accused of meddling or worse. The worthy aim of protecting children from a small number of dangerous pedophiles and criminals has led Western societies to adopt a highly restrictive definition of positive parenting. Concretely, this forces all children to put most of their eggs in the same basket—and to live in the hope that their family will be able to give them day after day the attention and affection they need. Unfortunately, for many children such as Toby this hope is futile.

Toby

The following story is true. It is the story of a teenager that my wife and I met when we worked as houseparents in a group home for delinquent girls in Tennessee.

Toby had just turned 15. Her brief stay in our group home was her 21st placement in an institution or foster home in less than three years. She remained only a few weeks in most places, usually because her belligerent behavior led to conflicts and she was sent away or because she was arrested for minor delinquency such as shoplifting. She also ran away from some placements to live in the streets of a large city she knew well. Toby had a long history of abuse and, for the past three years, one of prostitution as well. She prostituted herself mainly with an older man who, probably in large part thanks to his wealth, had long escaped prosecution. His name was Jack.

After about three weeks in the home, I asked Toby one evening to tell me about Jack. To my surprise, she did not hesitate. She told me with pride about the life of great luxury she had lived with him on different occasions and described with obvious pleasures the many places she had visited with him. I listened to her for a while before telling her that the man of whom she spoke in such a positive way was only interested by her body.

'I know. Everybody thinks he's a horrible man. But he isn't. He never hurt me, never.'

'Maybe he never hurt you but he pays you to have sex with him.'

Toby did not respond. She paused, visibly agitated. Her breathing was shallow. She was pressing her hands against her thighs. Her knuckles were white. Then her eyes and voice spoke with burning rage:

'My father, he would beat me and slap me and bruise me and beat me some more, and after he was done he'd still want to fuck the hell out of me! Now that's a horrible man. A bastard! DO YOU UNDERSTAND?

I ventured a sheepish yes that I was soon to regret.

'NO, YOU DON'T! You don't understand. Nobody does. You think that anybody who ever gets near a girl like me is a bastard, a child abuser, just because I'm underage. But not Jack, he's not like that.' Looking into the distance, much more calmly, she added almost with a smile: *'He's nice...'*

I became annoyed then.

'But Toby, wake up. This man may be nice but the only reason he wants you around is to have sex with him.'

'I know.'

'Well, that's abuse, Toby. There's no other word for it.'

She paused for a while, looking puzzled. And then slowly, almost kindly, with her hands emphasizing every word, she explained:

'You don't understand. He--yes, he wants sex. But he doesn't hurt me, he doesn't. He is nice and all along he holds me tight and he hugs me.' Toby had brought her arms tightly together, hugging herself, when she added softly, *'I think he loves me.'*

Now I understood. What I called abuse – still call abuse, will always call abuse – was experienced in a totally different manner by Toby. When you have never enjoyed as a child the delights of being hugged and loved and comforted by people who genuinely care for you, the physical advances of an old pedophile may actually be wonderful. When you've never tasted the real thing, something that comes close, in spite of ulterior motives, may fool you and make you believe that it is the real thing.

To conclude, let me be absolutely clear: I do not condone any form of abuse or believe that there are extenuating circumstances to abuse. However, Toby taught me that there are children who prefer the tenderness of a pedophile to no tenderness at all and who cannot see the difference because they were never loved appropriately. Her 21 placements in less than three years represent 21 missed opportunities to give her some of the affection she craved for, largely because our child welfare system forbids all expressions of affection to children like her. So is there any surprise that Toby sought it often elsewhere? A major challenge for Western societies today is to invent new, creative ways of caring for children like Toby in a healthy manner; to discover substitutes for truly positive parenting for children who do not have parents able or willing to care for them as they need and deserve to be cared for.

Acknowledgement

Preparation of this manuscript was supported by grant R21 HD40079 from the United States National Institute of Child Health and Human Development and by grant R49/CCR 522339 from the United States Centers for Disease Control and Prevention. This support is gratefully acknowledged.

References

Bargh, J. A., & Chartrand, T. L. (1999). The unbearable automaticity of being. *American Psychologist, 54,* 462-479.

Bargh, J. A., & Ferguson, M. J. (2000). Beyond behaviorism: On the automaticity of higher mental processes. *Psychological Bulletin, 126,* 925-945.

Bender, L., & Blau, A. (1937). The reaction of children to sexual relations with adults. *American Journal of Orthopsychiatry, 7,* 500-518.

Bourdieu, P. (1987). *Choses dites.* Paris : Editions de Minuit.

Bronfenbrenner, U. (1979). *The ecology of human development: Experiments by nature and design.* Cambridge, MA: Harvard University Press.

Bronfenbrenner, U. (1999). Environments in developmental perspective: Theoretical and operational models. In S. L. Friedman & T. D. Wachs (Eds.), *Measuring environment across the life span* (pp. 3-28). Washington, DC: American Psychological Association.

Desmet, H., Pourtois, J.-P., & Lahaye, W. (Eds.) (2005). *Culture et bientraitance.* Bruxelles: DeBoeck Université.

Dumas, J. E. (1986). Indirect influence of maternal social contacts on mother-child interactions: A setting event analysis. *Journal of Abnormal Child Psychology, 14,* 205-216.

Dumas, J. E. (1997). Home and school correlates of early at-risk status: A transactional perspective. In R. F. Kronick (Ed.), *At-risk youth: Theory, practice, reform* (pp. 97-117). New York: Garland Publishing.

Dumas, J. E. (2000). *L'enfant violent. Le connaître, l'aider, l'aimer.* Paris : Bayard.

Dumas, J. E. (2002). *Psychopathologie de l'enfant et de l'adolescent.* 2ème édition. Bruxelles: De Boeck Université.

Dumas, J. E., Lemay, P., & Dauwalder, J.-P. (2001). Dynamic analyses of mother-child interactions in functional and dysfunctional dyads: A synergetic approach. *Journal of Abnormal Child Psychology, 29,* 317-329.

Durning P. (1995), *Éducation familiale. Acteurs, processus et enjeux,* Paris : PUF.

Fogel, A. (1993). *Developing through relationships. Origins of communication, self, and culture.* Chicago, IL: University of Chicago Press.

Gabel, M., Jésu, F., & Manciaux, M. (Eds.) (2000). *Mieux traiter familles et professionnels.* Paris: Fleurus.

Gergely, G., & Watson, J. S. (1999). Early socio-emotional development: Contingency perception and the social-biofeedback model. In P. Rochat (Ed.), *Early social cognition: Understanding others in the first months of life* (pp. 101-136). Mahwah, NJ: Lawrence Erlbaum.

Haken, H. (1992). Synergetics in psychology. In W. Tschacher, G. Schiepek, & E. J. Brunner (Eds.), *Self-organization and psychology. Empirical approaches to synergetics in psychology* (pp. 32-54). Berlin: Springer.

Haken, H. (1999). Synergetics and some applications to psychology. In W. Tschacher & J.-P. Dauwalder (Eds.), *Dynamics, synergetics, autonomous* agents. Nonlinear systems approaches to cognitive psychology and cognitive science (pp. 3-12). Singapore: World Scientific.

Hansen, C. H., & Hansen, R. D. (1988). Finding the cope in the crowd: An anger superiority effect. *Journal of Personality and Social Psychology, 54*, 917-924.

Kantor, J. R., & Smith, N. W. (1975). *The science of psychology: An interbehavioral survey*. Chicago, IL: Principia Press.

Kempe, C. H., Silverman, F. N., Steele, B. F., Droegemueller, W., & Silver, H. K. (1962). The battered-child syndrome. *Journal of the American Medical Association, 181*, 105-112.

Patterson G. R., Reid J. B., & Dishion T. J. (1992), *Antisocial boys*, Eugene, OR: Castalia.

Rothbart, M. K., & Bates, J. E. (1998). Temperament. In W. Damon & N. Eisenberg (Eds.), *Handbook of child psychology. Social, emotional, and personality development* (Vol. 3, pp. 105-176). New York: Wiley.

Watson, J. S. (1994). Detection of self: The perfect algorithm. In S. T. Parker, R. W. Mitchell, & M. L. Boccia (Eds.), *Self-awareness in animals and humans* (pp. 131-148). New York: Cambridge University Press.

Wolfe, D. A. (1985). Child-abusive parents: An empirical review and analysis. *Psychological Bulletin, 97*, 462-482.

Wolfe, D. A. (1999). *Child abuse: Implications for child development and psychopathology*. Thousand Oaks, CA: Sage.

3

Japanese American and South American immigrant mothers' perceptions of their own and their spouses' parenting styles

Linda R. Cote & Marc H. Bornstein

Introduction

Culture shapes one's beliefs and behaviors toward others, and this is particularly true with respect to childrearing (Bornstein, 1980, 1991; Garcia Coll, Meyer, & Brillon, 1995; Greenfield & Suzuki, 1998). Previous research has frequently pointed to differences in parenting beliefs and parenting behaviors across cultures as well as among different ethnic groups within pluralistic societies, like the United States (see, e.g., Bornstein, 1991; Garcia Coll & Pachter, 2002; Harkness & Super, 1996; LeVine, 1982; Parke & Buriel, 1998).

The present study focuses on intracultural differences in *parenting style*, which we define here as the degree to which parents emphasize or engage in each of three domains of behavior with their children – social exchange, didactic interaction, and limit setting. Social exchanges consist of physical and verbal strategies parents use to engage their young in affective interpersonal dyadic interchanges (e.g., Bornstein, 1985, 2002; Kaye, 1982; Stern, 1979). Rocking, kissing, tactile comforting, smiling, vocalizing, and playful facetoface contact are illustrative of social exchange, which focuses on the dyad. Social parenting also includes the regulation of affect and emotions. Didactic interactions are ones in which the caregiver attempts to stimulate the infant's attention to objects, properties, or events in the environment (Bornstein, 1985, 2002; Papoušek & Bornstein, 1992) and consists of the variety of strategies parents employ in stimulating their infants to engage and understand the environment outside the dyad. Didactics include introducing, mediating, and interpreting the external world; describing and demonstrating; as well as provoking or providing opportunities to observe, to imitate, and to learn. Education of the young is a vital and critically cultural human parenting function. Limit setting can be defined as the parents' attempt to inculcate self-control in their children (Emde, 1992). Of all the parenting behaviors psychologists study, limit setting has received the most attention (Maccoby & Martin, 1983) because it is believed that the particular types of limit setting strategies parents employ have differential effects on children (e.g., authoritative parenting styles are thought to have positive effects, Baumrind, 1991; harsh physical discipline and other power-assertive techniques are thought to have negative effects, Deater-Deckard & Dodge, 1997; Maccoby & Martin, 1983; Sears, Maccoby, & Levin, 1957). We adopt the term limit setting rather than discipline for several reasons. First, discipline connotes punishment, yet our measure sought to embody ways that parents guide their children's behavior, which is not necessarily punitive. Second, while all punishment would be inappropriate for an infant, many forms of limit setting are culturally sanctioned and appropriate. For example, putting an infant on a sleep/wake or feeding schedule or regulating a child's access to areas that may be dangerous by "child proofing" are examples of ways U.S. parents set limits on their young children. Alongside the cross-cultural universality of social, didactic, and limit setting domains of parenting, ethnic differences exist across cultures in the degree to which parents stress the importance of social, didactic, and limit setting behaviors (e.g., Bornstein et al., 1996; Caudill & Frost, 1972; MacPhee, Fritz, & Miller-Heyl, 1996). Thus, these parenting behaviors were the focus of the current study.

Japanese American and South American parents

It is important for researchers in pluralistic societies (like the United States) to investigate intracultural parenting goals and practices so that teachers, clinicians, and parent educators can work effectively with ethnically diverse families (e.g., American Psychological Association, 1998; Greenfield & Suzuki, 1998; Sue, 1991). Although practitioners and researchers may believe that, once immigrants have been in a country for a time, their beliefs and behaviors come to resemble those of the dominant group in that country, investigators who study the process of acculturation have demonstrated that this is an unfounded assumption, and that beliefs about the family and parenting in particular may resist change (e.g., Berry, 1990; LeVine, 1982). Moreover, research on ethnic groups in most multiethnic societies has not kept pace with the influx of immigrants (see Bean, Crane, & Lewis, 2002, for a review). In an attempt to redress this information void, we studied one Asian American and one Latino American ethnic group in the United States.

Asian American and Latino American cultural groups present an interesting comparison in their own right because they are reported to be collectivist groups acculturating to the United States, a highly individualistic society (e.g., Hofstede, 1991; Markus & Kitayama, 1991; Parke & Buriel, 1998). *Collectivism* is defined as the extent to which individuals view themselves as inextricably connected to others and are motivated by the norms and values of their cultural or social group; by contrast, *individualism* refers to the extent to which individuals view themselves as independent and motivated by their own preferences, goals, and rights (e.g., Harwood, Handwerker, Schoelmerich, & Leyendecker, 2001; Markus & Kitayama, 1991; Triandis, 1995). Although some have questioned an overly rigid interpretation of this dichotomy (Oyserman, Coon, & Kemmelmeier, 2002; Raeff, 1997), we have found in our samples (Bornstein & Cote, 2001), as have others (e.g., Hofstede, 1991; Marín & Marín, 1991; Markus & Kitayama, 1991; Parke & Buriel, 1998), that Asian and Latino Americans stress collectivist beliefs more than individualist ones. In turn, individualist and collectivist cultural values are believed to underlie observed differences in parenting (e.g., Caudill & Schooler, 1973; Cote & Bornstein, 2000; Greenfield & Suzuki, 1998; Harwood, Schoelmerich, Schulze, & Gonzalez, 1999; Tamis-LeMonda, Bornstein, Cyphers, Toda, & Ogino, 1992).

Because "Asian Americans" and "Latino Americans" demonstrate within-group diversity in terms of socioeconomic status (Smith, 1999), language, culture, generational level, reasons for immigrating to the United States (Parke & Buriel, 1998), and most importantly childrearing (Field & Widmayer, 1981; Parke & Buriel, 1998; Uba, 1994), we focused on a specific subgroup of each. Japanese American and South American families in particular were the subject of this study because they are demographically similar. Both were immigrants to the United States (as contrasted with refugees; Berry & Sam, 1997), and both groups immigrated from modern relatively industrialized countries-of-origin which espouse female education, a high level of literacy, low birth rate, small family size, and nuclear family structure (e.g., Wilson & Pan, 2000). We thus compared childrearing practices and goals among demographically comparable ethnic groups both of which possessed a collectivist orientation.

Moreover, we chose to study Japanese American and South American mothers because previous research has shown differences in the parenting behavior of these mothers. With respect to social, didactic, and limit setting domains, the following cultural differences were hypothesized. Because *observational* studies have shown that South American mothers engage in more social exchange but equivalent levels of didactic interaction as Japanese American mothers (Bornstein & Cote, 2001), we hypothesized that these same patterns would emerge for mothers' reports of their behavior. Because the Japanese mother-child relationship tends to be indulgent during the early years (in comparison to European American parenting; e.g., Hara & Minagawa, 1996; Lanham & Garrick, 1996), and because mothers in South America (Argentina specifically) emphasize obedience in their childrearing strategies (e.g., Bornstein et al., 1992; Bornstein et al., 1996), we hypothesized that South American immigrant mothers would engage in more limit setting than Japanese American immigrant mothers in the United States.

Discrepancies between actual and ideal parenting behaviors

Mothers' ideal behaviors reflect their goals or aspirations – how they *wish* they would parent. These ideals are believed to guide parenting strategies (McGillicuddy-De Lisi & Sigel, 1995). We asked mothers to report about their actual and ideal behavior with their infants and toddlers because

49

the disparity between mothers' actual and ideal behavior allows us to glimpse areas of dissatisfaction with parenting (Cohen, Dibble, & Grawe, 1977). Moreover, such dissonance between actual and ideal behavior may provoke emotional distress (including anxiety) or stress in the individual (Alexander & Higgins, 1993; Lawton & Coleman, 1983; Lawton et al., 1983). Cohen et al. (1977) and Gfellner (1990) reported that, generally, European American parents report that they deviate from their ideals. Other researchers have found discrepancies in some areas of parenting but not others. For example, in their study of parents of young children, Lawton, Schuler, Fowell, and Madsen (1984) found the most agreement between parents' actual and ideal social behavior. Ethnic differences in the actual-ideal disparity have also been reported (e.g., Gfellner, 1990). For example, Bornstein et al. (1996) found that Argentine mothers displayed greater dissonance between actual and ideal engagement in social exchange than U.S. mothers, and Argentine mothers displayed the most dissonance for didactic interaction, but none for limit setting. Because previous research has found that Japanese American mothers tend to be less satisfied with their parenting than South American mothers (Bornstein et al., 1998; Cote & Bornstein, 2003), and more self-critical of their parenting (Shwalb, Kawai, Shoji, & Tsunetsugu, 1995), we expected that they, like South American mothers, would report discrepancies in their social and didactic parenting, but not limit setting, by rating their ideal behavior higher than their actual behavior.

Maternal perceptions and fathering

Mothers' perceptions of their parenting behavior were chosen as the focus of study because we wished to make the design of this study comparable to previous research in this area (e.g., Bornstein et al., 1996), and because mothers are still typically the primary caregivers of their children during the early years (e.g., Barnard & Solchany, 2002; Bornstein, 2002; Parke, 2002). However, as recent reviews of fathering underscore, fathers play a significant role in their children's development but are still understudied (Cabrera, Tamis-LeMonda, Bradley, Hofferth, & Lamb, 2000; Parke, 2002). Because mothers influence fathering both directly (e.g., Belsky, 1979) and indirectly (e.g., Parke, 2002), and because discrepancies between spouses with respect to childrearing may affect children's development (e.g., Block, Block, & Morrison, 1981), we studied mothers' perceptions of their husbands' parenting. By studying women's perceptions of their spouses' actual and ideal parenting, we could evaluate mothers' perceptions of the fathers' role, which have been shown to differ by cultural group (Bornstein et al., 1996), and whether their own husbands live up to their expectations.

Researchers have reported differences in the ways mothers and fathers engage their infants. For example, Galejs and Pease (1986) found no differences between European American mothers' and fathers' behavior with their 3-month-old children, but the two parents of 3-year-old children did differ. Mothers emphasized the expression of feelings, for example, whereas fathers assumed disciplinary functions and emphasized taking turns, being polite, sharing, and being responsible. Because theirs was a cross-sectional and not a longitudinal study, it is unclear whether these parenting differences developed over time or were due to a cohort effect; nor can we say whether these effects would be similar with a culturally diverse sample. Julian, McKenry, and McKelvey (1994) found among a culturally diverse sample of U. S. parents (inlcuding Latin and Asian American parents) that mothers reported that they praise and hug their young children more frequently than fathers do. Argentine mothers have reported that they engage in more social and didactic behavior with their toddlers than do their spouses, but ideally they would engage in more didactic behavior and less limit setting than their husbands (Bornstein et al., 1996); we predicted that our South American immigrant mothers would follow this pattern. Also, because it is the responsibility of mothers (and not fathers) in Japan to "create" successful children (Kojima, 1996), we hypothesized that the Japanese American immigrant mothers in our sample would rate themselves as engaging in more parenting behavior of all kinds (social, didactic, and limit setting) with their infants and young children than their spouses.

Continuity and stability in parenting

In this study, we also assessed the basic developmental functions of continuity and stability of parenting behaviors from infancy to toddlerhood in these two immigrant groups. Continuity has been defined as consistency in the group mean level of a phenomenon through time (Bornstein & Suess, 2000; Wohlwill, 1973), and is distinct from stability, which is defined as consistency in the relative ranks of individuals in a group with respect to some phenomenon over time (e.g., Bornstein & Suess, 2000; McCall, Eichorn, & Hogarty, 1977). Research into which parenting orientations are stable and which are changeable is still scant (e.g., Holden & Miller, 1999; Okagaki & Divecha, 1993).

Enormous developmental differences exist between 5- and 20-month-old children, and so, if parenting behavior is responsive to children's developmental level, we might expect it to be discontinuous. On the other hand, if parental perceptions of childrearing styles are adopted from the culture, as some have suggested (e.g., McGillicuddy-De Lisi, 1992; Sigel & Kim, 1996), then we might expect childrearing styles to be continuous (constant) over time. Previous research with Japanese American and South American immigrant families has found that some parenting cognitions (i.e., attributions, self-perceptions) are largely continuous over the transition from infancy to toddlerhood (Cote & Bornstein, 2003), which is consistent with Rubin and Mills's (1992) finding of consistency in European American mothers' cognitions over the transition from early to middle childhood. We predicted that social behaviors would be continuous among mothers who highly value interdependence (e.g., Bornstein & Cote, 2001). Because children's interest in object play increases during infancy (e.g., Bornstein &

Tamis-LeMonda, 1990; Cohn & Tronick, 1987; Fogel, 1993), however, we hypothesized that mothers might respond to these changes in their infants, such that they would engage in more didactic interactions with older infants, resulting in discontinuity in didactic interactions. Likewise, we hypothesized that limit setting would be discontinuous from infancy to toddlerhood because infants become increasingly able to act on the environment and then become more goal-directed (e.g., McCall et al., 1977; Piaget, 1952; U_giris, 1983), and so "call" for more of these kinds of interactions from parents. Previous researchers have found that parents report that they engage in more limit setting with older children which supports the idea that parents are responsive to children's developmental level (e.g., Volling, 1997).

Previous research on European American mothers' reported behaviors – including social exchange and limit setting – has found that they are normally stable over time (Roberts, Block, & Block, 1984; Sears et al., 1957). Although the stability of ethnically diverse parents' reports of their behaviors has not been assessed, some Japanese American and South American mothers' parenting cognitions have been found to be stable over a 15-month period (Cote & Bornstein, 2003). Thus, we predicted that all of the parenting behaviors we examined would be stable (i.e., mothers would be consistent within themselves over time).

Overview

We investigated cultural contributions to parenting behavior, discrepancies between reported behaviors and goals, mothers' observations and expectations for their spouses' parenting behavior, and the continuity and stability of parenting behaviors from infancy to toddlerhood among immigrant Japanese American and South American families living in the United States.

Method

Participants

Thirty-four Japanese American and 33 South American mothers of young children (30 females, 37 males) participated. Mothers were primiparous at the time of the first visit, and all were from maritally intact families. All infants were term and healthy at birth and at the times of each of two research visits to the home. Participants were primarily from the Washington, DC, metropolitan area, and were recruited from mass mailings, hospitals, newspaper advertisements, and personal contacts. Table 3.1 (see Appendix) contains sociodemographic information about the participants, including generation and acculturation level. Our samples are demographically representative of immigrants from Japan and South America living in the metropolitan Washington, DC, area (Whoriskey & Cohen, 2001; Wilson & Pan, 2000), and they are representative of Japanese and South American immigrants to the United States (who for the past 20 years have been well-educated, from the urban middle-class, and primarily immigrating for economic reasons; Levinson & Ember, 1997; U.S. Census Bureau, 2001).

South American mothers' countries of ancestral origin were: Argentina ($n = 6$), Colombia ($n = 8$), and Peru ($n = 6$), with some from Bolivia ($n = 2$), Chile ($n = 3$), Ecuador ($n = 4$), Paraguay ($n = 1$), Uruguay ($n = 1$), and Venezuela ($n = 2$). These South American countries (like the United States) are ethnically heterogenous, and influenced by European immigration (Winn, 1992). Just as one could choose to study one cultural group within the United States (e.g., middle-class European Americans), participating mothers represented a specific segment of the South American population (i.e., middle-class urbanites from Spanish-speaking countries). Furthermore, all mothers were ethnically Latina and not indigenous peoples. In areas of the United States where there are several Latino groups and not a large concentration of one particular Latino group, as there are in the Washington, DC, metropolitan area (Whoriskey & Cohen, 2001; Wilson & Pan, 2000), people tend to identify themselves as Latinos or by their regional affiliation rather than by their country of origin (Winn, 1992). Mothers participating in this study *self-identified* as South American by responding to an advertisement for "South American families"/"familias de origen Sud Americano" – an important methodological issue for research with Latino participants (Marín & Marín, 1991) – and empirically there were no reliable differences within the South American immigrant group on either the sociodemographic or dependent variables (comparing Argentine, Peruvian, Colombian, and the remaining mothers). Thus, much like research that groups European American mothers together, and for both empirical and theoretical reasons, we adopted the common practice of grouping South American immigrants from different nations together (see, e.g., Escovar & Escovar, 1985; Field & Widmayer, 1981; Frisbie & Bean, 1995; Marín & Marín, 1991). We use the term "South American" rather than South American American throughout this paper because the latter term is cumbersome and redundant; moreover, Central and South Americans do not equate the term "American" with inhabitants of the United States as North Americans do (Winn, 1992).

Procedure

Mothers completed the Parental Style Questionnaire, an acculturation scale, an individualism/collectivism scale, and a sociodemographic questionnaire about their family when their children were 5½ and 20 months of age. They also completed a questionnaire that assessed their tendency to make socially desirable responses.

Measures

Several steps were taken to promote the validity and cultural appropriateness of the instruments for we aimed to arrive at translations that had "adapted" equivalence across cultures from a psychological perspective (van de Vijver & Leung, 1997). The questionnaires, originally constructed and written in English, were first translated into Japanese and Spanish and then backtranslated by bilingual bicultural Japanese and Argentine natives using standard backtranslation techniques (see Brislin, 1980, 1986). The translated instruments were next checked for preservation of meaning and cultural appropriateness by professional collaborators from each country. Then, professionals and bilingual mothers from each culture who lived in the United States and were not participants in the study were interviewed regarding the comprehensibility and cultural validity of items in the instruments and appropriate adjustments were made. Finally, pilot testing was undertaken to ensure that the instruments were comprehensible and ethnographically valid (see van de Vijver & Leung, 1997). Participants chose the language in which they completed the questionnaires (i.e., English, Spanish, or Japanese).

The *Parental Style Questionnaire* (PSQ; Bornstein et al., 1996) is a maternal report measure of parenting behavior. This 16-item questionnaire asks mothers to rate on a 5-point Likert-type scale (from 1 *hardly at all* to 5 *all the time*) how frequently they *actually* engage in specific parenting behaviors (e.g., "I provide my child with independent time to explore and learn on his/her own") Mothers were then asked to rate the same 16 items again, but this time with respect to their *ideal* parenting behavior. Additionally, mothers were asked to rate their spouses' actual and ideal behavior for the same 16 items. The 16 items form 3 domains – social (5 items), didactic (9 items), and limit setting (2 items). Mean scores for each of these 3 domains were calculated separately for mothers' ratings of their own actual and ideal behavior, and for mothers' ratings of their husbands' actual and ideal parenting behavior, thus generating 12 subscale scores at each time period (5 and 20 months). A comparison of two of the 24 subscales (mothers' reports of their actual social and didactic behavior at 5 months) appears in Cote and Bornstein (2000); however, in that paper social and didactic behavior were compared to each other. Construct validity and internal reliability of the PSQ have been established in previous research (Bornstein et al., 1996). Specifically, the social subscale related positively and significantly to interpersonal affect and self-esteem in maternal personality; the didactic scale related positively and significantly to SES and maternal education and the maternal personality variables energy level, self-esteem, innovation, and breadth of interest; and the limit setting subscales related negatively and significantly to SES and maternal education, and positively and significantly to organization, responsibility, and value orthodoxy in maternal personality (Bornstein et al., 1996). Cronbach's alpha scores for the 12 subscales ranged from .52 to .86 in the present samples (with all but one subscale – mother's rating of their ideal limit setting – above .65); these alpha coefficients are comparable to previous studies of mothers in the United States and other cultures (Bornstein et al., 1996), and they suggest good internal reliability for the majority of the subscales (DeVellis, 1991).

The *Japanese American Acculturation Scale (JAAS)* and *South American Acculturation Scale (SAAS)* (Cote & Bornstein, 2000) are 21-item measures that were adapted from the Suinn-Lew Asian Self-identity Acculturation Scale (Suinn & Lew, 1987) in order to specifically evaluate Japanese and South American immigrants. These acculturation scales embody a bicultural perspective on acculturation, whereby identification with the cultures of origin and destination are seen as balancing, rather than opposing, each other (see Ward, 1999). The JAAS and SAAS items are identical and cover topics such as language, identity, friendship, behavior, generation, and attitudes. Example items include: "How do you identify yourself?" and "Do you participate in Japanese/South American occasions, holidays, traditions, etc.?" Participants rated each item on the JAAS from 1 (*Japanese*) to 5 (*U.S. American*); the SAAS scale ranged from 1 (*South American*) to 5 (*U.S. American*). Acculturation level was calculated by taking the mean of mothers' ratings on all 21 items. Both the JAAS and SAAS had high internal reliability scores (α = .90 to .96). In addition, these measures demonstrated good construct validity: for immigrant mothers, age at time of immigration, $r(24) = -.41$, $p < .05$, and $r(28) = -.33$, $p < .10$, and number of years mothers had lived in the U.S. at the time of the study, $r(24) = .71$, $p < .001$, and $r(28) = .43$, $p < .05$, correlated with acculturation level on the JAAS and SAAS, respectively; these correlation coefficients are similar in direction and magnitude to those found in other studies (e.g., Ownbey & Horridge, 1998).

The *Individualism/Collectivism Scale* (INDCOL; Triandis, 1995) asks participants to rate on a 9-point Likert-type scale from 1 (*strongly disagree*) to 9 (*strongly agree*) how much they agree with 32 statements reflecting individualist and collectivist values. Example items include: "Without competition it is not possible to have a good society." and "It is my duty to take care of my family, even when I have to sacrifice what I want." The items form 2 subscales: individualism (16 items) and collectivism (16 items; 5 of which were omitted from the current analyses in order to increase Collectivism subscale reliability, as recommended by Triandis, 1995, and Ward & Kennedy, 1999, and ecological validity). Individualism and collectivism scores were calculated by taking the mean of mothers' ratings on the items that comprised the individualism and collectivism subscales, respectively. The INDCOL subscales have demonstrated construct validity (Triandis, 1995) and internal reliability (Cote & Bornstein, 2003; Triandis, 1995). Reliabilities for the INDCOL individualism and collectivism subscales, respectively, were acceptable (α = .54 to .76, with all but one subscale above α = .60).

We collected information on mothers' acculturation level and levels of individualism and collectivism and used them as covariates in our study because previous researchers have suggested that underlying cultural beliefs are crucial to understanding cultural differences in beliefs and behaviors (e.g., Berry, Trimble, & Olmedo, 1986; Markus & Kitayama, 1991; Triandis, 1989), and because acculturation, individualism, and collectivism in particular have been implicated in cultural variation in childrearing (e.g., Caudill & Schooler, 1973; Cote & Bornstein, 2000; Farver & Lee-Shin, 2000; Greenfield & Suzuki, 1998; Harwood et al., 1999, 2001; Li-Repac, 1982; Nakagawa, Teti, & Lamb, 1992; Strom, Daniels, & Park, 1986; Tamis-LeMonda et al., 1992).

The *Marlowe-Crowne Social Desirability Scale* (SDS; Crowne & Marlowe, 1960) is a 33-item scale that assesses an individual's tendency to answer questions in a socially desirable way. This scale has good test-retest reliability, internal consistency, and construct validity (Crowne & Marlowe, 1960). The SDS demonstrated good internal reliability in the current samples (α = .66 for Japanese American mothers; α = .72 for South American mothers). Because there may be cross-cultural differences in self-serving bias (e.g., Markus & Kitayama, 1991), this scale was used to control potential self-serving bias in mothers' responses to the PSQ.

Results

Preliminary analyses

Prior to data analysis, univariate and multivariate distributions of the dependent variables and covariates were examined for normalcy, homogeneity of variance, outliers, and influential cases (Fox, 1997; Tabachnick & Fidell, 1996). Transformations were applied where applicable to meet the assumptions of parametric statistical testing. Additionally, one mother was identified as having scores on her own and her spouse's ideal limit setting that were both univariate and multivariate outliers at 20 months; therefore, all analyses involving these DVs were performed with and without the outlier, and differences between the analyses are reported.

Analytic plan

We wished to explore the role of cultural background in group differences; thus, we empirically controlled several potentially confounding sociodemographic factors. Specifically, maternal (education level, SES, number of hours per week of work, age, social desirability) and child (gender) sociodemographic and cultural variables (acculturation level, individualism score, collectivism score) were screened as covariates. No child gender differences were found at any level (main effects or interactions). All covariates reported below correlated meaningfully (i.e., explained at least 5% of the variance) and independently with the DV, and the main effect of the covariate in the multivariate analysis of variance (MANOVA) was significant. Due to space limitations, analyses involving covariate(s) are only reported if the results differed from the analyses without the covariate(s). Wilks' lambda is reported for all multivariate tests. Significant interactions were decomposed using single-*df* univariate tests of the simple effects; because there were only two levels for all of the between- and within-subjects factors, pairwise comparisons of marginal means were unnecessary (see Keppel, 1991).

Social exchange

A mixed design multivariate analysis of variance (MANOVA) with one between factor (Cultural Group) and three within factors (Child Age, Parent, Situation) was conducted first: there were 2 levels of Cultural Group (Japanese American, South American), 2 levels of Child Age (5 months, 20 months), 2 levels of Parent (mothers' ratings of their own social exchange, mothers' ratings of their husbands' social exchange), and 2 levels of Situation (ratings of actual and ideal social exchange with their own children). Mothers' collectivism scores were significantly positively related to 7 of the 8 DVs in this analysis, rs = .25 to .40, $ps < .05$; therefore, they were used as covariates in follow-up analyses of between-group differences. Four significant interactions emerged. First, there was a significant Cultural Group x Situation interaction, $F(1, 65) = 6.38$, $p < .05$, $\eta^2_p = .09$. Analysis of simple effects revealed that South American mothers reported that they and their spouses actually engaged in more social exchange with their children than Japanese American parents, $F(1, 65) = 5.30$, $p < .05$, $\eta^2_p = .08$. This difference attenuated to nonsignificance when cultural variables were controlled (i.e., mothers' level of collectivism at 5 and 20 months, separately). Moreover, South American and Japanese American parents reported that they would ideally engage in more social exchange with their children than they do: $F(1, 65) = 43.39$, $p < .001$, $\eta^2_p = .40$, and $F(1, 65) = 105.80$, $p < .001$, $\eta^2_p = .62$, respectively.

Second, there was a significant Cultural Group x Parent interaction, $F(1, 65) = 7.13$, $p = .01$, $\eta^2_p = .10$. Analysis of simple effects showed that South American mothers reported that they engaged in significantly more social exchange with their children than Japanese American mothers, $F(1, 65) = 8.58$, $p < .01$, $\eta^2_p = .12$. This difference attenuated to nonsignificance when cultural variables (i.e., mothers' levels of collectivism at 5 and 20 months, separately) were controlled. South American mothers also reported that they engaged in significantly more social exchange with their infants than did their spouses, $F(1, 65) = 25.49$, $p < .001$, $\eta^2_p = .28$.

Third, the Situation x Parent interaction was significant, $F(1, 65) = 15.17$, $p < .001$, $\eta^2_p = .19$. Analysis of simple effects showed that mothers reported that they would ideally engage in more social exchange with their children than they actually do, $F(1, 65) = 110.43$, $p < .001$, $\eta^2_p = .63$, and that their spouses would also ideally engage in significantly more social exchange with their children than they actually do, $F(1, 65) = 99.07$, $p < .001$, $\eta^2_p = .60$. Furthermore, mothers reported that they engaged in more (actual) social exchange with their children than their husbands, $F(1, 65) = 22.69$, $p < .001$, $\eta^2_p = .26$.

Finally, there was a significant Cultural Group x Child Age interaction, $F(1, 65) = 4.56$, $p < .05$, $\eta^2_p = .07$. Analysis of simple effects showed that South American mothers reported that they and their spouses engaged in more social exchange with their infants when their infants were 20 months old than Japanese American parents, $F(1, 65) = 5.96$, $p < .05$, $\eta^2_p = .08$. This difference attenuated to nonsignificance when cultural variables (i.e., mothers' levels of collectivism at 5 and 20 months, separately) were controlled (Table 3.2 in Appendix). No Child Age effects were significant, suggesting that parents' reports of social exchange are continuous from infancy to toddlerhood.

Didactic interaction

A MANOVA with one between factor (Cultural Group) and three within factors (Child Age, Parent, Situation) was conducted to examine didactic interaction. Mothers' collectivism scores were significantly positively related to 5 of the 8 DVs in this analysis, $rs = .27$ to $.40$, $ps < .05$; therefore, they were used as covariates in follow-up analyses of between-group differences. Although several 2-way interactions emerged, there were two significant 3-way interactions that superseded and included all of the 2-way interactions. First was a significant interaction of Cultural Group x Situation x Parent, $F(1, 65) = 5.78$, $p < .05$, $\eta^2_p = .08$. Analysis of the simple effect of Cultural Group showed that South American mothers reported that they actually engaged in more didactic interaction with their children than Japanese American mothers, $F(1, 65) = 16.70$, $p < .001$, $\eta^2_p = .20$. This difference attenuated to nonsignificance when cultural variables (i.e., mothers' levels of collectivism at 5 and 20 months, separately) were controlled. Analysis of the simple effect of Situation showed that Japanese American and South American mothers each reported that they, $F(1, 65) = 279.92$, $p < .001$, $\eta^2_p = .81$, and $F(1, 65) = 115.09$, $p < .001$, $\eta^2_p = .64$, respectively, and their husbands, $F(1, 65) = 105.98$, $p < .001$, $\eta^2_p = .62$, and $F(1, 65) = 96.79$, $p < .001$, $\eta^2_p = .60$, respectively, would ideally engage in more didactic interaction with their infants than they actually do. Analysis of the simple effect of Parent indicated that South American mothers reported that they engaged in more actual, $F(1, 65) = 21.43$, $p < .001$, $\eta^2_p = .25$, and ideal, $F(1, 65) = 6.04$, $p < .05$, $\eta^2_p = .09$, didactic interaction than their husbands.

There was also a Cultural Group x Parent x Child Age interaction, $F(1, 65) = 8.06$, $p < .01$, $\eta^2_p = .11$. Analysis of the simple effects of Cultural Group revealed that South American mothers reported that they engaged in more didactic interaction with their infants than Japanese American mothers at both 5 and 20 months, $F(1, 65) = 4.07$, $p < .05$, $\eta^2_p = .06$, and $F(1, 65) = 13.57$, $p < .001$, $\eta^2_p = .17$, respectively. These differences attenuated to nonsignificance when cultural variables (i.e., mothers' levels of collectivism at 5 and 20 months, separately) were controlled. Analysis of the simple effects of Parent showed that South American mothers reported that they engaged in more didactic interaction with their children at both 5, $F(1, 65) = 15.63$, $p < .001$, $\eta^2_p = .19$, and 20 months, $F(1, 65) = 15.18$, $p < .001$, $\eta^2_p = .19$, than did their husbands; in contrast, Japanese American mothers reported that their husbands engaged in significantly more didactic interaction with their children at 5 months than they did, $F(1, 65) = 4.77$, $p < .05$, $\eta^2_p = .07$. Analysis of the simple effects of Child Age revealed that South American mothers reported that they engaged in more didactic interaction with their children at 20 months than at 5 months, $F(1, 65) = 4.46$, $p < .05$, $\eta^2_p = .06$, whereas Japanese American mothers reported that their husbands engaged in significantly more didactic interaction with their children at 5 months than at 20 months, $F(1, 65) = 6.99$, $p = .01$, $\eta^2_p = .10$ (Table 3.2 in Appendix).

Limit setting

A MANOVA with one between factor (Cultural Group) and three within factors (Child Age, Parent, Situation) was conducted to examine limit setting. Mothers' collectivism scores were significantly positively related to 6 of the 8 DVs in this analysis, $rs = .37$ to $.51$, $ps < .01$, their individualism scores were significantly positively related to 2 of the 8 DVs in this analysis, $rs = .37$ to $.39$, $ps < .01$, and their acculturation scores were significantly positively related to 2 of the 8 DVs in this analysis, $rs = .24$ to $.25$, $ps < .05$; therefore, these variables were used as covariates in follow-up analyses of between-group differences. Four significant two-way interactions emerged. First, there was a significant Cultural Group x Parent interaction, $F(1, 65) = 5.78$, $p < .05$, $\eta^2_p = .08$. Analysis of simple effects revealed that South American mothers reported that they and their husbands engaged in more limit setting with their children than Japanese American mothers, $F(1, 65) = 34.24$, $p < .001$, $\eta^2_p = .35$, and fathers, $F(1, 65) = 12.88$, $p = .001$, $\eta^2_p = .17$, respectively. These differences attenuated to nonsignificance when mothers' 5- (i.e., levels of individualism and collectivism) and 20-month (i.e., acculturation level, individualism, and collectivism) cultural variables and mothers' social desirability scores were controlled. Japanese American mothers also reported that their husbands engaged in more limit setting with their children than they did, $F(1, 65) = 17.26$, $p < .001$, $\eta^2_p = .21$.

Second, there was a significant Cultural Group x Child Age interaction, $F(1, 65) = 9.94$, $p < .01$, $\eta^2_p = .13$. Analysis of simple effects showed that South American mothers reported that they and their spouses engaged in more limit setting than Japanese American parents when their children were both 5 and 20 months old, $F(1, 65) = 8.54$, $p < .01$, $\eta^2_p = .12$, and $F(1, 65) = 36.82$, $p < .001$, $\eta^2_p = .36$, respectively. These differences attenuated to nonsignificance when cultural variables (i.e., levels of individualism and collectivism at 5 months; acculturation level, individualism, and collectivism at 20 months) and mothers' social desirability scores were controlled. Moreover, South American mothers reported that they and their spouses engaged in more limit setting when their infants were 20 months old than when they were 5 months old, $F(1, 65) = 22.66$, $p < .001$, $\eta^2_p = .26$.

Third, there was a significant Situation x Child Age interaction, $F(1, 65) = 12.92$, $p = .001$, $\eta^2_p = .17$. Analysis of simple effects indicated that mothers reported that they and their spouses actually engaged in more limit setting at 20 months than at 5 months, $F(1, 65) = 22.85$, $p < .001$, $\eta^2_p = .26$. Moreover, at both 5, $F(1, 65) = 62.53$, $p < .001$, $\eta^2_p = .49$, and 20 months, $F(1, 65) = 58.90$, $p < .001$, $\eta^2_p = .48$, mothers reported that they would like themselves and their spouses ideally to engage in more limit setting with their children than they actually do.

Finally, there was a significant Parent x Child Age interaction, $F(1, 65) = 4.53$, $p < .05$, $\eta^2_p = .07$. Analysis of the simple effects revealed that mothers reported that they, $F(1, 65) = 16.17$, $p < .001$, $\eta^2_p = .20$, and their spouses, $F(1, 65) = 5.99$, $p < .05$, $\eta^2_p = .08$, engaged in more limit setting at 20 months than at 5 months. In addition, mothers reported that they engaged in significantly less limit setting than their husbands when their children were 5 months old, $F(1, 65) = 17.81$, $p < .001$, $\eta^2_p = .22$. When this MANOVA was conducted again without the outlying case, the Child Age x Parent interaction effect became marginally significant; however, the results of the simple effects were the same as those reported above. When the outlying case was excluded, the effect of acculturation and social desirability as covariates were no longer significant; analyses without these covariates and without the outlying case produced the same outcome as reported.

Stability of social exchange, didactic interaction, and limit setting

One-tailed Pearson correlations tested the stability of mothers' reported parenting in the three domains from 5 to 20 months. Maternal sociodemographic and cultural variables were screened and used as covariates as necessary. For Japanese American mothers, social exchange and didactic interaction, but not limit setting, were significantly positively correlated across 5 to 20 months, even when sociodemographic factors were controlled (Table 3.3 in Appendix). For South American mothers, all correlations between social exchange, didactic interaction, and limit setting at 5 and 20 months were significantly positively correlated, even when covariates were controlled (Table 3.3). Overall, these results indicate that mothers' reported parenting behaviors in these two immigrant groups were highly stable over a 15-month period. No differences in the magnitude of correlations for Japanese American and South American mothers were found (evaluated using two-tailed z tests).

Discussion

The goal of this study was to investigate similarities and differences in mothers' beliefs about their own and their husbands' parenting, and discrepancies between their actual and ideal parenting, in three domains – social exchange, didactic interaction, and limit setting. We also assessed continuity and stability in parents' styles over the transition from parenting an infant to parenting a toddler in two underresearched immigrant groups to the

United States: Japanese Americans and South Americans. The results of our study suggest that many of the initial cultural differences found in mothers' reported parenting behaviors and goals appeared to be attributable specifically to mothers' levels of collectivism. Actual/ideal discrepancies and parent gender differences were found for social, didactic, and limit setting behaviors. Discontinuities in parenting behaviors emerged, particularly for South American parents; mothers' reported parenting behaviors were largely stable.

Japanese American and South American parenting styles

Although initial cultural group differences were found in mothers' social exchange and didactic interaction, these differences attenuated to nonsignificance when mothers' reported levels of collectivism were controlled, suggesting that these differences were specifically attributable to cultural beliefs that underlie cultural affiliation. This suggests that, with respect to maternal perceptions of both social and didactic behaviors in these immigrant groups, individual variability in levels of collectivism are better predictors than is cultural group affiliation. In an observational study of maternal behaviors, however, mothers' levels of collectivism were not found to relate to or mitigate differences between Japanese American and South American mothers' social and didactic behaviors (Bornstein & Cote, 2001). This suggests that maternal perceptions, but not mothers' actual behaviors with their infants, are influenced by individual variation in cultural beliefs and that those who study parenting (i.e., maternal reports of their parenting behavior, as well as their parenting cognitions) among ethnically diverse samples ought also to measure mothers' cultural cognitions (e.g., collectivism, individualism, acculturation). These findings are important because previous researchers have suggested that more research that explicitly links parenting to general cultural values is needed in order to explain *why* cultural differences in parenting exist (e.g., Greenfield & Suzuki, 1998; Okagaki & Divecha, 1993). Our finding that mothers with higher levels of collectivism reported that they would engage in more social and didactic behavior suggests that mothers who are more collectivist have a stronger drive to socialize their children in ways valued by their country-of-origin (social exchanges) *and* by the country to which they immigrated (didactic interactions), whereas mothers who are less collectivist are less inclined to socialize their children according to the social norms of either cultural group (i.e., culture of origin or destination).

As with social and didactic behaviors, initial cultural group differences in parents' limit setting behaviors seem to be attributable to mothers' level of collectivism; however, limit setting was also influenced by mothers' levels of individualism, acculturation, and social desirability. Specifically, mothers who were more collectivist or individualist, or more acculturated to U.S. society, or who wished to appear more socially desirable reported that they more frequently set limits with their children. The positive relations between limit setting and both acculturation and social desirability suggest that these mothers recognize limit setting as an American parenting goal (e.g., regulating the infants' sleep/wake and feeding by putting the infant "on a schedule") and that more collectivist mothers are more likely to adopt this mainstream U.S. parenting norm. The positive relation between individualism and limit setting suggests that mothers who are more individualist set more limits with their children possibly in the hope that they will internalize the social norms of their community and learn to function independently while exercising self-control.

Discrepancies between actual and ideal parenting style

Discrepancies between parents' actual and ideal behaviors emerged for each of the three domains of behavioral style we examined. Namely, parents' actual behaviors fall short of their ideals. For example, South American and Japanese American parents each reported that they would *ideally* engage in more social exchange with their children than they *actually* do, and that they would like their spouses also ideally to engage in more social exchange with their children than they actually do. Moreover, the finding that both groups of mothers reported that they and their husbands should ideally engage in more social exchange replicates research that has found high rates of social interactions among mothers in Japan and Argentina (Bornstein, Azuma, Tamis-LeMonda, & Ogino, 1990; Bornstein, Haynes, Pascual, Painter, & Galperín, 1999) and attests to the high value placed on social exchanges with children in these cultural groups.

Discrepancies between parents' actual and ideal didactic interactions with their children also emerged. Namely, Japanese American and South American mothers each reported that they and their husbands should ideally engage in more didactic interaction with their infants than they actually do. This across-the-board interest in engaging in more didactics with their children, regardless of parents' cultural background or gender, suggests that parents may be responding to the move from social to object play that infants and parents transit (perhaps universally) around middle infancy (e.g., Bornstein & Tamis-LeMonda, 1990; Cohn & Tronick, 1987; Fogel, 1993).

Discrepancies between mothers' actual and ideal limit setting also emerged. Namely, at both 5 and 20 months, mothers reported that they and their spouses would ideally like to engage in significantly more limit setting than they actually do. Thus, discrepancies between parents' actual and ideal behavior emerged for each of the behaviors we examined. Overall, the picture that develops is that Japanese American and South American parents have higher expectations for their parenting style than they reach. That this same pattern has been found for European American parents (e.g., Cohen et al., 1977; Gfellner, 1990) suggests that it may be part of a larger cultural syndrome afflicting U.S. middle-class parents, or parents in general.

Maternal perceptions and fathering style

Some parent gender differences emerged. Notably, South American mothers reported that they engage in more social exchanges with their children than do their husbands, and, moreover, this difference is accounted for by their actual behavior rather than their ideal behavior. No differences between Japanese American mothers' and fathers' social exchange emerged. Thus, South American mothers see themselves as more involved in social exchanges with their children than their husbands, but Japanese American mothers feel that their own and their husbands' social exchanges with their children are equitable.

Similar to previous research with mothers living in South America proper (Bornstein et al., 1996), South American mothers living in the United States reported that they engaged in significantly more actual and ideal (assessed separately) didactic interactions with their children than did their husbands; moreover, this was true at both 5 and 20 months. In contrast, Japanese American mothers reported that their husbands engaged in significantly more didactic interactions with their children at 5 months than they did. Thus, South American mothers see themselves as more involved in didactic interactions with their infants and toddlers than their husbands, but Japanese American mothers see their husbands as more involved in didactic interactions with their infants than they are. Thus, it may be that South American mothers view stimulating their children's social and cognitive development as their parenting tasks, whereas Japanese American mothers view stimulating their children's social development as their primary parenting task and stimulating their children's social and cognitive development as part of the father's role.

Parent gender differences in limit setting also emerged: Japanese American mothers reported that their husbands engaged in significantly more limit setting with their children than they did. Additionally, mothers reported that they engaged in less limit setting than their husbands when their children were 5 months old. This suggests that mothers may see it as the father's job to set limits with children, whereas their job is to nurture their children.

The overall picture that emerges is of South American immigrant mothers taking more responsibility for engaging their children socially and didactically than their husbands, which mirrors Argentine mothers' reports of their and their husbands' actual behavior (Bornstein et al., 1996). In contrast, Japanese American mothers seem to share responsibility with their husbands for engaging in social exchanges with their infants (perhaps because they see it as their role to nurture their children), and they expect fathers to be more responsible for didactic interactions and setting limits with their infants (perhaps because they see it as their spouse's role to teach their children). The differences between Japanese mothers' and fathers' social behavior replicates research that has found high rates of social interactions among mothers in Japan (Bornstein, Azuma, Tamis-LeMonda, & Ogino, 1990), and the findings for limit setting are also consistent with previous work that suggests that the Japanese mother-child relationship tends to be indulgent during the early years (compared to European American parenting; e.g., Hara & Minagawa, 1996; Lanham & Garrick, 1996), and apparently, in comparison to the father-child relationship in Japan. Our finding that Japanese American fathers engage in more didactic behaviors with their children than do their wives is consistent with the traditional Japanese view that teaching is one of the primary tasks of fatherhood (although in the past half century this teaching function of father-child interactions has been supplemented by a companionate relationship; Hara & Minagawa, 1996).

Continuity and discontinuity in parenting style

Mothers' reported actual and ideal social exchange, and those of their spouses, were found to be continuous from 5 to 20 months of age in these samples. This again may reflect the strong value placed on social exchanges among these relatively more collectivist parents. Unlike social exchange, parents' didactic interactions was discontinuous from infancy to toddlerhood. As predicted, South American mothers reported that they engaged in more didactic interactions with their children at 20 months than at 5 months, which may reflect children's increasing interest in object play. Contrary to our expectations, however, Japanese American mothers reported that their husbands engaged in significantly more didactic interactions with their children at 5 than at 20 months. It may be that Japanese American fathers wish to stimulate this behavior in their young infants, and hence engage in it more frequently when their infants are 5 months old, but see less of a need to stimulate this behavior with toddlers, perhaps because by this age children engage in these behaviors on their own. Like didactic interaction, parents' limit setting was discontinuous over time, particularly among South American parents: South American mothers reported that they and their spouses engaged in significantly more limit setting when their infants were 20 months old than when they were 5 months old. Moreover, increases in parents' limit setting from infancy to toddlerhood appeared with respect to actual, but not ideal behavior. We expected, and found, that limit setting behavior would be discontinuous because from 5 to 20 months of age children increasingly act on the environment and become more goal-directed (e.g., McCall et al., 1977; Piaget, 1952; U_giris, 1983) and therefore require more limit setting over time for their own safety.

Stability and instability of parenting style

Overall, mothers' reported social and didactic behaviors were highly stable over this 15-month period regardless of cultural group; Japanese American mothers' limit setting behavior was unstable, whereas South American mothers' limit setting was stable. The findings of stability for maternal reports of parenting behavior for both cultural groups mirrors what has been found for other parenting cognitions among Japanese American and South American middle-class mothers in the United States (Cote & Bornstein, 2003), and is consistent with reports of parenting beliefs and behaviors among European American middle-class mothers in the United States (Roberts et al., 1984; Sears et al., 1957). The finding that limit setting was unstable for Japanese American mothers, however, suggests that these mothers may feel confused with respect to imposing limits on their children's behavior, perhaps as a result of conflicting value systems in their country-of-origin and country-of-adoption. Specifically, the cultural norm for mothers in Japan is to be very permissive and indulgent with young infants (e.g., Hara & Minagawa, 1996; Lanham & Garrick, 1996) because it is believed that infants are born spiritually pure and are gradually corrupted (or "spoiled") by general exposure to adults (whose characters have been corrupted by daily living); in contrast (European) Americans believe that spoiling is caused by parental indulgence (Hara & Minagawa, 1996).

Conclusions

The findings from the current research point to several practical implications. First, discrepancies in mothers' reported actual and ideal childrearing practices emerged in each of the parenting domains we examined for themselves and for their husbands, which could signal areas of dissatisfaction with parenting and potentially cause stress in the parent (Lawton & Coleman, 1983; Lawton et al., 1983). As Lawton has suggested, with the continuing isolation of the nuclear family, American parents do not have access to the resources that they once had to solicit childrearing advice and support, and this may be doubly true for immigrant mothers. Moreover, this may reflect the pressure that Japanese American and South American mothers put on themselves and the importance they attach to the maternal role (Bornstein et al., 1998; Kojima, 1996; Lebra, 1976). Second, that cultural differences stand in proxy for belief systems (i.e., levels of collectivism) in the present study points to the need for researchers, clinicians, and parent educators to be aware of the cultural value of collectivism and the ways it influences parenting practices. As Greenfield and Suzuki (1998) pointed out, for many recent immigrants the culture of the country of origin can be very different from the culture of the country of adoption, and it is the responsibility of the professional community to understand the values and goals that underlie apparent cultural differences so that they can better serve these families.

References

Alexander, M. J., & Higgins, E. T. (1993). Emotional trade-offs of becoming a parent: How social roles influence self-discrepancy effects. *Journal of Personality and Social Psychology, 65,* 1259-1269.

American Psychological Association. (1998). *APA Resolution on immigrant children, youth, and families.* Retrieved May 10, 2000 from http://www.apa.org/pi/cyf/cyfres.html.

Barnard, K. E., & Solchany, J. E. (2002). Mothering. In M. H. Bornstein (Ed.), *Handbook of parenting: Vol. 3. Being and becoming a parent* (2nd ed., pp. 3-25). Mahwah, NJ: Erlbaum.

Baumrind, D. (1991). Rearing competent children. In W. Damon (Ed.), *The Jossey-Bass Social and Behavioral Science Series: Child development today and tomorrow* (pp. 349-378). San Francisco: Jossey-Bass.

Bean, R. A., Crane, D. R., & Lewis, T. L. (2002). Basic research and implications for practice in family science: A content analysis and status report for U.S. ethnic groups. *Family Relations, 51,* 15-21.

Belsky, J. (1979). The interrelation of parental and spousal behavior during infancy in traditional nuclear families: An exploratory analysis. *Journal of Marriage and the Family, 41,* 749-755.

Berry, J. W. (1990). Psychology of acculturation: Understanding individuals moving between cultures." In R. W. Brislin (Ed.), *Applied cross-cultural psychology: Cross-cultural research and methodology series* (pp. 232-253). Newbury Park, CA: Sage.

Berry, J. W., & Sam, D. L. (1997). Acculturation and adaptation. In J. W. Berry, M. H. Segall, & C. Kagitçibasi (Eds.), *Handbook of cross-cultural psychology: Vol. 3. Social behavior and applications* (2nd ed., pp. 291-326). Boston: Allyn and Bacon.

Berry, J. W., Trimble, J. E., & Olmedo, E. L. (1986). Assessment of acculturation. In W. J. Lonner & J. W. Berry (Eds.), *Field methods in cross-cultural research. Cross-cultural research and methodology series* (vol. 8, pp. 291-324). Beverly Hills, CA: Sage Publications.

Block, J. H., Block, J., & Morrison, A. (1981). Parental agreement-disagreement on child-rearing orientations and gender-related personality correlates in children. *Child Development, 52,* 965-974.

Bornstein, M. H. (1980). Crosscultural developmental psychology. In M. H. Bornstein (Ed.), *Comparative methods in psychology* (pp. 231281). Hillsdale, NJ: Erlbaum.

Bornstein, M. H. (1985). How infant and mother jointly contribute to developing cognitive competence in the child. *Proceedings of the National Academy of Sciences, 82,* 74707473.

Bornstein, M. H. (Ed.). (1991). *Cultural approaches to parenting.* Hillsdale, NJ: Erlbaum.

Bornstein, M. H. (2002). Parenting infants. In M. H. Bornstein (Ed.), *Handbook of parenting: Vol. 1. Children and parenting* (2nd ed., pp. 3-43). Mahwah, NJ: Erlbaum.

Bornstein, M. H., Azuma, H., TamisLeMonda, C., & Ogino, M. (1990). Mother and infant activity and interaction in Japan and in the United

States: I. A comparative macroanalysis of naturalistic exchanges. *International Journal of Behavioral Development, 13*, 267287.

Bornstein, M. H., & Cote, L. R. (2001). Mother-infant interaction and acculturation I: Behavioral comparisons in Japanese American and South American families. *International Journal of Behavioral Development, 25*, 549-563.

Bornstein, M. H., Haynes, O. M., Azuma, H., Galperín, C., Maital, S., Ogino, M., et al. (1998). A cross national study of selfevaluations and attributions in parenting: Argentina, Belgium, France, Israel, Italy, Japan, and the United States. *Developmental Psychology, 34*, 662676.

Bornstein, M. H., Haynes, O. M., Pascual, L., Painter, K. M., & Galperín, C. (1999). Play in two societies: Pervasiveness of process, specificity of structure. *Child Development, 70*, 317331.

Bornstein, M. H., & Suess, P. E. (2000). Child and mother cardiac vagal tone: Continuity, stability, and concordance across the first 5 years. *Developmental Psychology, 36*, 54-65.

Bornstein, M. H., & Tamis-LeMonda, C. S. (1990). Activities and interactions of mothers and their firstborn infants in the first six months of life: Covariation, stability, continuity, correspondence, and prediction. *Child Development, 61*, 1206-1217.

Bornstein, M. H., Tal, J., Rahn, C., Galperín, C. Z., Pêcheux, M., Lamour, M., Toda, S., Azuma, H., Ogino, M., & TamisLeMonda, C. S. (1992). Functional analysis of the contents of maternal speech to infants of 5 and 13 months in four cultures: Argentina, France, Japan, and the United States. *Developmental Psychology, 28*, 593603.

Bornstein, M. H., Tamis-LeMonda, C. S., Pascual, L., Haynes, O. M., Painter, K. M., & Galperín, C.Z. (1996). Ideas about parenting in Argentina, France, and the United States. *International Journal of Behavioral Development, 19*, 347-367.

Brislin, R. W. (1980). Translation and content analysis of oral and written material. In H. C. Triandis & J. W. Berry (Eds.), *Handbook of cross-cultural psychology* (Vol. 1, pp. 389-444). Boston: Allyn & Bacon.

Brislin, R. W. (1986). The wording and translation of research instruments. In W. J. Lonner & J. W. Berry (Eds.), *Field methods in cross-cultural research* (pp. 137-164). Newbury Park, CA: Sage.

Cabrera, N. J., Tamis-LeMonda, C. S., Bradley, R. H., Hofferth, S., & Lamb, M. E. (2000). Fatherhood in the twenty-first century. *Child Development, 71*, 127-136.

Caudill, W., & Frost, L. (1972). A comparison of maternal care and infant behavior in JapaneseAmerican, American, and Japanese Families. In U. Bronfenbrenner (Ed.), *Influences on human development* (pp.329342). Hinsdale, IL: Dryden.

Caudill, W. A., & Schooler, C. (1973). Child behavior and child rearing in Japan and the United States: An interim report. *The Journal of Nervous and Mental Disease, 157*, 323338.

Cohen, D. J., Dibble, E., & Grawe, J. M. (1977). Parental style: Mothers' and fathers' perceptions of their relations with twin children. *Archives of General Psychiatry, 34*, 445-451.

Cohn, J. F., & Tronick, E. Z. (1987). Mother infant face-to-face interaction: The sequence of dyadic states at 3, 6, and 9 months. *Developmental Psychology, 23,* 68-77.

Cote, L. R., & Bornstein, M. H. (2000). Social and didactic parenting beliefs and behaviors among Japanese American and South American mothers of infants. *Infancy, 1,* 363-374.

Cote, L. R., & Bornstein, M. H. (2003). Cultural and parenting cognitions in acculturating cultures: I. Cultural comparisons and developmental continuity and stability. *Journal of Cross-Cultural Psychology, 34,* 323-349.

Crowne, D. P., & Marlowe, D. (1960). A new scale of social desirability independent of psychopathology. *Journal of Consulting Psychology, 24,* 349-354.

Deater-Deckard, K. & Dodge, K. A. (1997). Externalizing behavior problems and discipline revisited: Nonlinear effects and variation by culture, context, and gender. *Psychological Inquiry, 8,* 161-175.

DeVellis, R. F. (1991). *Applied social science research methods series: Vol. 26. Scale development: Theory and applications* (L. Bickman & D. J. Rog, Series Eds.). Newbury Park, CA: Sage.

Emde, R. N. (1992). The infant's relationship experience: Developmental and affective aspects. In A. J. Sameroff & R. N. Emde (Eds.), *Relationship disturbances in early childhood: A developmental approach* (pp. 33-51). New York: Basic Books.

Escovar, L. A., & Escovar, P. L. (1985). Retrospective perception of parental child-rearing practices in three culturally different college groups. *International Journal of Intercultural Relations, 9,* 31-49.

Farver, J. M., & Lee-Shin, Y. (2000). Acculturation and Korean-American children's social and play behavior. *Social Development, 9,* 316-336.

Field, T. M., & Widmayer, S. M. (1981). Motherinfant interactions among lower SES Black, Cuban, Puerto Rican and South American immigrants. In D. S. Palermo (Series Ed.) & T. M. Field, A. M. Sostek, P. Vietze, & P. H. Leiderman (Vol. Eds.), *Child psychology: Cultural and early interactions* (pp. 4162). Hillsdale, NJ: Erlbaum.

Fogel, A. (1993). *Developing through relationships: Origins of communication, self, and culture.* Chicago, IL: University of Chicago Press.

Fox, J. (1997). *Applied regression analysis, linear models, and related methods.* Thousand Oaks, CA: Sage.

Frisbie, W. P., & Bean, F. D. (1995). The Latino family in comparative perspective: Trends and current conditions. In P. W. Cookson, Jr. (Series Ed.) & C. K. Jacobson (Vol. Ed.), *Garland library of sociology. American families: Issues in race and ethnicity* (pp. 2971). New York: Garland.

Galejs, I., & Pease, D. (1986). Parenting beliefs and locus of control orientation. *The Journal of Psychology, 120,* 501-510.

Garcia Coll, C. T., Meyer, E. C., & Brillon, L. (1995). Ethnic and minority parenting. In M. H. Bornstein (Ed.), *Handbook of parenting: Vol. 2. Biology and ecology of parenting* (pp. 189209). Hillsdale, NJ: Erlbaum.

Garcia Coll, C. T., & Pachter, L. M. (2002). Ethnic and minority parenting. In M. H. Bornstein (Ed.), *Handbook of Parenting: Vol. 4. Social conditions and applied parenting* (2nd ed., pp. 1-20). Mahwah, NJ: Erlbaum.

Gfellner, B. M. (1990). Culture and consistency in ideal and actual child-rearing practices: A study of Canadian Indian and white parents. *Journal of Comparative Family Studies, 21*, 413-423.

Greenfield, P. M., & Suzuki, L. K. (1998). Culture and human development: Implications for parenting, education, pediatrics, and mental health. In W. Damon (Series Ed.), & I. E. Sigel & K. A. Renninger (Vol. Eds.), *Handbook of child psychology: Vol. 4. Child psychology in practice* (5th ed., pp.1059-1109). New York: Wiley.

Hara, H. & Minagawa, M. (1996). From productive dependents to precious guests: Historical changes in Japanese children. In S. Harkness & C. M. Super (Series Eds.) & D. W. Shwalb & B. J. Shwalb (Vol. Eds.), *Culture and human development. Japanese childrearing: Two generations of scholarship* (pp. 930). New York: Guilford.

Harkness, S., & Super, C. (1996). *Parents cultural belief systems: Their origins, expressions, and consequences.* New York: The Guilford Press.

Harwood, R. L., Handwerker, W. P., Schoelmerich, A., & Leyendecker, B. (2001). Ethnic category labels, parental beliefs, and the contextualized individual: An exploration of the individualism-sociocentrism debate. *Parenting: Science and practice, 1*, 217-236.

Harwood, R. L., Schoelmerich, A., Schulze, P. A., & Gonzalez, Z. (1999). Cultural differences in maternal beliefs and behaviors: A study of middleclass Anglo and Puerto Rican mother infant pairs in four everyday situations. *Child Development, 70*, 1005-1016.

Hofstede, G. (1991). *Cultures and organizations: Software of the mind.* London: McGraw-Hill.

Holden, G. W., & Miller, P. C. (1999). Enduring and different: A meta-analysis of the similarity in parents' child rearing. *Psychological Bulletin, 125*, 223-254.

Hollingshead, A. B. (1975). *The fourfactor index of social status.* Unpublished manuscript, Yale University.

Julian, T. W., McKenry, P. C., & McKelvey, M. W. (1994). Perceptions of Caucasian, African-American, Hispanic, and Asian-American parents. *Family Relations, 43*, 30-37.

Kaye, K. (1982). *The mental and social life of babies.* Brighton: Harvester Press.

Keppel, G. (1991). *Design and analysis* (3rd ed.). Englewood Cliffs, NJ: Prentice Hall.

Kojima, H. (1996). Japanese childrearing advice in its cultural, social, and economic contexts. *International Journal of Behavioral Development, 19*, 373-391.

Lanham, B. B., & Garrick, R. J. (1996). Adult to child in Japan: Interaction and relations. In S. Harkness & C. M. Super (Series Eds.) & D. W. Shwalb & B. J. Shwalb (Vol. Eds.), *Culture and human development. Japanese childrearing: Two generations of scholarship* (pp. 97124). New York: Guilford.

Lawton, J. T., & Coleman, M. (1983). Parents' perceptions of parenting. *Infant Mental Health Journal, 4,* 352-361.

Lawton, J., Coleman, M., Boger, R., Pease, D., Galejs, I., Poresky, R., et al. (1983). A Q-sort assessment of parents' beliefs about parenting in six midwestern states. *Infant Mental Health Journal, 4,* 344-351.

Lawton, J. T., Schuler, S. G., Fowell, N., & Madsen, M. K. (1984). Parents' perceptions of actual and ideal child-rearing practices. *Journal of Genetic Psychology, 145,* 77-87.

Lebra, T. S. (1976). *Japanese patterns of behavior.* Honolulu: The University Press of Hawaii.

LeVine, R. A. (1982). *Culture, behavior, and personality: An introduction to the comparative study of psychosocial adaptation* (2nd ed., pp. 15-39). New York: Aldine.

Levinson, D., & Ember, M. (Eds.) (1997). *American immigrant cultures: Builders of a nation. Vols. 1, 2.* New York: Macmillan.

Li-Repac, D. C. (1982). *The impact of acculturation on the child-rearing attitudes and practices of Chinese-American families: Consequences for the attachment process.* (Doctoral dissertation, University of California, Berkeley, 1982). Ann Arbor, MI: University Microfilms International.

Maccoby, E. E., & Martin, J. A. (1983). Socialization in the context of the family: Parent-child interaction. In P. H. Mussen (Series Ed.) & E. M. Hetherington (Vol. Ed.), *Handbook of child psychology: Vol. 4. Socialization, personality, and social development* (pp. 1-101). New York: Wiley.

MacPhee, E., Fritz, J., & Miller-Heyl, J. (1996). Ethnic variations in personal social networks and parenting. *Child Development, 67,* 3278-3295.

Marín, G., & Marín, B. V. (1991). *Applied social research methods series: Vol. 23. Research with Hispanic populations.* Newbury Park, CA: Sage.

Markus, H. R., & Kitayama, S. (1991). Culture and the self: Implications for cognition, emotion, and motivation. *Psychological Review, 98,* 224253.

McCall, R. B., Eichorn, D. H., & Hogarty, P. S. (1977). Transitions in early mental development. *Monographs of the Society for Research in Child Development, 42* (3, Serial No. 171).

McGillicuddy-De Lisi, A. V. (1992). Parents' beliefs and children's personal-social development. In I. E. Sigel, A. V. McGillicuddy-DeLisi, & J. J. Goodnow (Eds.), *Parental belief systems: The psychological consequences for children* (2nd ed., pp. 115-142). Hillsdale, NJ: Erlbaum.

McGillicuddy-De Lisi A. V. & Sigel, I. E. (1995). Parental beliefs. In M. H. Bornstein (Ed.), *Handbook of parenting: Vol. 3. Status and social conditions of parenting* (pp. 333-358). Mahwah, NJ: Erlbaum.

Nakagawa, M., Teti, D. M., & Lamb, M. E. (1992). An ecological study of childmother attachments among Japanese sojourners in the United States. *Developmental Psychology, 28,* 584592.

Okagaki, L., & Divecha, D. J. (1993). Development of parental beliefs. In T. Luster & L. Okagaki (Eds), *Parenting: An ecological perspective* (pp. 35-67). Hillsdale, NJ: Erlbaum.

Ownbey, S. F., & Horridge, P. E. (1998). The Suinn-Lew Asian Self-Identity Acculturation Scale: Test with a non-student, Asian-American sample. *Social Behavior and Personality, 26,* 57-68.

Oyserman D., Coon, H., & Kemmelmeier, M. (2002). Rethinking individualism and collectivism: Evaluation of theoretical assumptions and meta-analyses. *Psychological Bulletin, 128*, 3-72.

Papoušek, H., & Bornstein, M. H. (1992). Didactic interactions. In H. Papoušek, U. Jurgens, & M. Papoušek (Eds.), *Nonverbal vocal communication: Comparative and developmental approaches* (pp. 209-220). Cambridge: Cambridge University Press.

Parke, R. D. (2002). Fathers and families. In M. H. Bornstein (Ed.), *Handbook of parenting: Vol. 3. Being and becoming a parent* (2nd ed., pp. 27-73). Mahwah, NJ: Erlbaum.

Parke, R. D., & Buriel, R. (1998). Socialization in the family: Ethnic and ecological perspectives. In W. Damon (Series Ed.) & N. Eisenberg (Vol. Ed.), *Handbook of child psychology: Vol. 3. Social, emotional, and personality development* (5th ed., pp. 463-552). New York: Wiley.

Piaget, J. (1952). *The origins of intelligence in children* (M. Cook, Trans.). New York: International Universities Press.

Raeff, C. (1997). Individuals in relationships: Cultural values, children's social interactions, and the development of an American individualistic self. *Developmental Review, 17*, 205-238.

Roberts, G. C., Block, J. H., & Block, J. (1984). Continuity and change in parents' child-rearing practices. *Child Development, 55*, 586-597.

Rubin, K. H., & Mills, R. S. L. (1992). Parents' thoughts about children's socially adaptive and maladaptive behaviors: Stability, change, and individual differences. In I. E. Sigel, A. V. McGillicuddy-De Lisi, & J. J. Goodnow (Eds.), *Parental belief systems: The psychological consequences for children* (2nd ed., pp. 41-69). Hillsdale, NJ: Erlbaum.

Sears, R. R., Maccoby, E. E., & Levin, H. (1957). *Patterns of child rearing*. Evanston, IL: Row, Peterson, and Company.

Shwalb, D. W., Kawai, H., Shoji, J., & Tsunetsugu, K. (1995). The place of advice: Japanese parents' sources of information about childrearing and child health. *Journal of Applied Developmental Psychology, 16*, 629-644.

Sigel, I. E., & Kim, M. (1996). The answer depends on the question: A conceptual and methodological analysis of a parent belief-behavior interview regarding children's learning. In S. Harkness & C. Super (Series & Vol. Eds.), *Culture and human development. Parents' cultural belief systems: Their origins, expressions, and consequences* (pp. 83-120). New York: Guilford.

Smith, J. P. (1999, February). *Health and economic outcomes of new immigrants*. Paper presented at the NIH Director's Wednesday Afternoon Lecture Series, National Institutes of Health, Bethesda, MD.

Stern, D. N. (1979). *The first relationship*. London: Fontana.

Strom, R., Daniels, S., & Park, S. (1986). The adjustment of Korean immigrant families. *Educational and Psychological Research, 6*, 213-227.

Sue, S. (1991). Ethnicity and culture in psychological research and practice. In J. D. Goodchilds (Ed.), *Psychological perspectives on human diversity in America. The Master Lectures* (pp. 5185). Washington, DC: American Psychological Association.

Suinn, R. M., & Lew, S. (1987). *Suinn-Lew Asian Self-identity Acculturation Scale.* Unpublished manuscript, Colorado State University, Department of Psychology.

Tabachnick, B. G., & Fidell, L. S. (1996). *Using multivariate statistics* (3rd ed.). New York: Harper Collins.

TamisLeMonda, C. S., Bornstein, M. H., Cyphers, L., Toda, S., & Ogino, M. (1992). Language and play at one year: A comparison of toddlers and mothers in the United States and Japan. *International Journal of Behavioral Development, 15,* 1942.

Triandis, H. C. (1989). The self and social behavior in differing cultural contexts. *Psychological Review, 96,* 506-520.

Triandis, H. C. (1995). *Individualism and collectivism.* Boulder, CO: Westview Press.

Uba, L. (1994). *Asian Americans: Personality patterns, identity, and mental health.* New York: Guilford.

U. S. Census Bureau. (2001). *Profile of the foreign-born population in the United States: 2000* (Current Population Reports, Series P23-206) [Electronic version]. Washington, D.C.: Government Printing Office.

U_giris, I. _. (1983). Organization of sensorimotor intelligence. In M. Lewis (Ed.), *Origins of intelligence* (2nd ed., pp. 135-189). New York: Plenum.

van de Vijver, F., & Leung, K. (1997). *Methods and data analysis for cross-cultural research.* Thousand Oaks, CA: Sage.

Volling, B. L. (1997). The family correlates of maternal and paternal perceptions of differential treatment in early childhood. *Family Relations, 46,* 227-236.

Ward, C. (1999). Models and measures of acculturation. In W. J. Lonner, D. L. Dinnel, D. K. Forgays, & S. A. Hayes (Eds.), *Merging past, present, and future in cross-cultural psychology* (pp. 221-230). Lisse, Netherlands: Swets & Zeitlinger.

Ward, C., & Kennedy, A. (1999). The measurement of sociocultural adaptation. *International Journal of Intercultural Relations, 23,* 659-677.

Whoriskey, P., & Cohen, S. (2001, November 23). Immigrants arrive from far and wide: Suburbs see surge from range of areas. *The Washington Post,* p. B01.

Wilson, S., & Pan, P. P. (2000, January 23). A diverse, growing population. *The Washington Post,* p. A18.

Winn, P. (1992). *Americas: The changing face of Latin America and the Caribbean.* Berkeley, CA: University of California Press.

Wohlwill, J. F. (1973). *The study of behavioral development.* New York: Academic Press.

Appendix

Table 3.1
Sociodemographic information for mothers

Demographic Variables	Cultural Groups				
	Japanese American (n = 34)		South American (n = 33)		Group Difference
Mother	M	SD	M	SD	
Acculturation level at 5 months[a]	2.31	.80	2.40	.53	t (65) = -0.51, ns
Acculturation level at 20 months[a]	2.33	.84	2.42	.55	t (57.14) = -0.48, ns
Generation level[a]	1.26	.79	1.21	.48	t (65) = 0.33, ns
Nativity (immigrant:U.S. born)[b]	29:5		29:4		χ^2 (1, N = 67) = 0.10, ns
Age at immigration[b]	27.92	3.66	21.09	10.57	t (37.02) = 3.31, p < .01
Years in U.S. at 5 month visit[b]	5.48	3.13	9.67	6.76	t (42.43) = -3.03, p < .01
Level of individualism at 5 months[c]	5.87	.92	6.03	1.02	t (65) = -0.69, ns
Level of individualism at 20 months[c]	5.60	1.26	6.07	.95	t (65) = -1.74, ns
Level of collectivism at 5 months[c]	6.88	1.02	7.36	.73	t (65) = -2.21, p < .05
Level of collectivism at 20 months[c]	6.75	.92	7.37	.72	t (65) = -3.07, p < .01
Age at 5 months	31.80	3.75	31.83	5.31	t (65) = -0.02, ns
Age at 20 months	33.02	3.76	33.08	5.33	t (65) = -0.05, ns
Hollingshead SES	57.81	8.27	48.50	13.12	t (53.68) = 3.46, p = .001
Education[d]	5.76	.78	5.94	.86	t (65) = -0.87, ns
Hours of work/week at 5 months[e]	9.24	16.38	16.73	17.06	t (65) = -1.83, ns
Social Desirability Scale	17.76	4.38	20.79	4.74	t (64) = -2.70, p < .01

Child					
Age at 5 months (days)	173.15	13.68	167.67	12.61	$t(65) = 1.70$, ns
Age at 20 months (days)	616.94	19.95	623.82	22.16	$t(65) = -1.34$, ns
Birth weight (grams)	3257.47	408.97	3528.36	674.21	$t(52.45) = -1.98$, ns
Gender (female:male)	15:19		15:18		$\chi^2(1, N = 67) = 0.01$, ns

Note. Sample sizes for some analyses vary due to missing data.
[a] Scale ranges from 1 to 5; on average, mothers were bicultural and between first- and second-generation;
[b] Includes only mothers who are first-generation Americans (i.e., mothers who were not born in the United States and immigrated to the United States during their lifetimes);
[c] Scale ranges from 1 to 9;
[d] Hollingshead (1975) education scale ranges from 1 to 7 and was adjusted by bicultural researchers to account for differences between countries in the duration, quality, and content of schooling; [e] Includes homemaker mothers.

Table 3.2
Cultural differences, parent gender differences, situational discrepancies, and continuity in parenting style

Domain	Japanese American (n = 34)				South American (n = 33)			
	Mother		Father		Mother		Father	
	Actual	Ideal	Actual	Ideal	Actual	Ideal	Actual	Ideal
	4.35 (.35)	4.74 (.32)	4.17 (.66)	4.82 (.27)	4.61 (.34)	4.79 (.28)	4.20 (.60)	4.65 (.41)
	4.32 (.36)	4.74 (.30)	4.10 (.63)	4.68 (.39)	4.62 (.31)	4.84 (.23)	4.32 (.46)	4.76 (.28)
	3.49 (.54)	4.35 (.45)	3.64 (.72)	4.48 (.49)	3.88 (.55)	4.42 (.47)	3.48 (.70)	4.32 (.58)
	3.58 (.37)	4.38 (.36)	3.44 (.52)	4.29 (.48)	4.01 (.41)	4.55 (.36)	3.64 (.59)	4.44 (.49)
	2.73 (.80)	3.43 (.81)	3.15 (.97)	3.99 (.85)	3.29 (1.33)	4.15 (.91)	3.52 (1.24)	4.24 (.79)
	3.12 (1.05)	3.31 (.93)	3.24 (.85)	3.81 (.90)	4.24 (.71)	4.55 (.64)	4.14 (.91)	4.61 (.67)

Note. All values denote M (SD).

Table 3.3
Stability of mothers' parenting behavior from 5 to 20 months

Cultural cognitions	Cultural groups	
	Japanese American (n = 34)	South American (n = 33)
Social exchange	.67***/.63***[a]	.63***/.61***[d]/.65***[a]
Didactic interaction	.56***/.54***[b]/.50***[c]	.49**/.37*[e]/.44**[a]
Limit setting	.28	.51***/.42**[f]/.47**[e]/.35*[g]

Note. Only theoretically expected relations were tested; all tests are Pearson's one-tailed correlations.
[a] Controlling cultural variables (collectivism);
[b] Controlling mother sociodemographic variables (number of hours per week of work, SES);
[c] Controlling cultural variables (acculturation, collectivism);
[d] Controlling mother sociodemographic variables (education level, number of hours per week of work, social desirability score);
[e] Controlling mother sociodemographic variables (age, education level, social desirability score);
[f] Controlling mother sociodemographic variables (age, SES, social desirability score);
[g] Controlling cultural variables (acculturation level, individualism, collectivism).
*$p \leq .05$; **$p \leq .01$; ***$p \leq .001$.

4
Risk factors of child neglect and physical abuse

Ercilia Palacio-Quintin

Introduction

It is well-known that children suffering from neglectful and abusive caregiving may encounter serious difficulties in successfully resolving early developmental tasks and may be vulnerable to later deviations or delays in all development areas (Palacio-Quintin & Jourdan-Ionescu, 1994; Urquiza, Wirtz, Peterson, & Singer, 1994). Behavioral and adaptive problems appear also in most cases (Eckenrode, Laird & Doris, 1993; Salsinger, Feldman, Hammer & Rosario, 1993). Abuse and neglect have not only negative effects on the child but also long lasting deleterious effects over the life-span. Considering this, preventive interventions with at risk families before the maltreatment develops are crucial and knowledge of risk factors for child abuse and neglect is needed to identify populations.

From the seventies up to now a lot of retrospective studies have been carried around factors related to child abuse and neglect. On the contrary, the number of prospective studies about risk factors are limited. Thus, the prospective studies are the only ones that can prove that a factor is really a risk for child abuse and neglect and not simply a consequence of maltreatment. Several problems are common to both kinds of studies. First, factors chosen to define risk samples vary widely throughout the studies and comparisons are not easy. Secondly, some methodological problems have to be mentioned. In the majority of studies the practice of aggregating physical abuse and neglect into one category of child maltreatment is current. Also mothers of physically abused children, even if they are not abusing, are integrated in abusive mothers samples. Now, in a sample of physically abused and neglected children (Palacio-Quintin, 1995) we found that several cases of abused children were cases where the violence comes from the father and neglect from the mother. Neglect is characterized by a chronic lack of care and the absence of parenting while abuse is a voluntary or involuntary act of physical or emotional aggression. Also, although each type of maltreatment is likely to present a risk to a child's future functioning, there are differential effects and different processes underlying each type of maltreatment (Erickson Egeland & Pianta, 1989; Palacio-Quintin & Ethier, 1993; Polansky Chambers, Buttenwieser, & Williams, 1981). Neglect is the most frequent form of maltreatment and its effects the most deleterious

(Jourdan-Ionescu & Palacio-Quintin, 1997; Lafont, 1997; Palacio-Quintin & Jourdan-Ionescu, 1994). Because neglect is more frequent, we find in studies with mixed samples of maltreated children a majority of cases of neglect. The same situation is found in prospective studies. For example, Kotch, Browne, Dufort, and Winsor (1999) have recruited a sample of 708 at risk mothers during pregnancy and made a follow-up during four years after childbirth. During this time, there were 290 reports of child maltreatment involving 172 children. Neglect alone constituted 83 % of the total reports, neglect and abuse 8 percent and only 9 percent abuse alone. That's why some factors recognized in many writings as related to child abuse and neglect are in fact more representative of neglectful families.

The majority of the studies had taken in account only maternal characteristics, so, in spite of the great number of studies, knowledge about abusive and neglectful fathers and their role in the phenomena is a major gap in the field.

The aim of this chapter is to make a wide analysis of risk factors for child neglect and physical abuse taking in account social, familial, parents and child factors and paying special attention to some issues frequently neglected in the studies and the reviews. So, we will pay special attention to paternal characteristics and we will try to differentiate risk factors for neglect and risk factors for physical abuse when possible.

At this point, it is important to remember that risk factors for child abuse and neglect are not causes but rather factors indicating a greater probability of abuse and neglect. Going through the description of abuse and neglect risk factors we have also to keep in mind that maltreatment is not the outcome of any single factor but the outcome of a multiple combination of factors (Corbillon, Augain, Durning, Fablet, & Fablet, 1997; Woodward & Fergusson, 2002). The multifactorial perspective of maltreatment is well recognized nowadays (Belsky, 1993; Cicchetti & Carlson, 1989; Garbarino & Sherman, 1980) and simplistic notions of unidirectional influences must be put aside. This means that multiple factors interact to produce circumstances that can trigger abusive or neglectful parenting. Multiple factors operate cumulatively and interactively and many have also multiple paths of influence and may serve to modify or improve the impact of other factors. Finally, the quality of parental care is determinated by the balance of a multitude of stressors (risk, potentiating or vulnerability factors) and supports (compensatory, protective or resiliency factors) that exist within and outside the family. These factors act in combination to determine better or worst parenting and at the extreme, risk of child abuse and neglect.

We will consider three types of risk factors: social or environmental factors, familial and parental factors and child factors.

Social or environmental factors

A large number of studies have found that children from disadvantaged home environments are at increased risk of child abuse and neglect. This disadvantaged social environment is characterized by several demographic indicators as low income (Chamberland, Bouchard, & Beaudry, 1986; Garbarino & Sherman, 1980), both parents unemployed and depending of the public assistance (Svedin, Wadsby, & Sdysjö, 1996) and parent's low educational level (Sidebottham, Golding, & the ALSPAC Study Team, 2001). These sociodemographic indicators are particularly related to child neglect (Drake & Pandey, 1996; Palacio-Quintin, Couture, & Paquet, 1995). A more elevated mean social status and educational level have been found in abusive parents (Crittenden, 1988). Chaffin, Kelleher & Holenberg (1996) confirmed in a prospective study that low socioeconomic status is a significant risk factor for neglect and not for abuse. We also found (Palacio-Quintin & al., 1995; Palacio-Quintin, Jourdan-Ionescu, Coderre, & Desaulniers, 2001) that neglectful parents had not only low educational levels (a mean of 8 years) but also serious difficulties during schooling. More than half of all mothers and fathers had at least 1 year of school delay and several had been in special classes. Actually, many of them had serious reading difficulties. So, they suffer not only from economical poverty but also from cultural poverty.

In addition, it must be said that a lot of studies have shown that many risk factors are associated with poverty (Egeland, Carlson, & Stroufe, 1993). So, for children living in poverty, stressful life events are numerous and compounded by adverse social and economic factors. But parents and caregivers serve as mediators of the effects of poverty. That's why familial and parental risk factors are so important.

Family and parental risk factors

Family factors

Single parenthood, mostly single motherhood, is largely considered as a risk for child abuse and neglect (Kimball, Steward, Conger, & Burgess, 1980). Our research on neglectful families (Palacio-Quintin, 1995; Palacio-Quintin et al., 2001) showed that only 31 % of the families were two-parent families. Further, we observed that rather than the single parent family it was the absence of family stability that was highly related to child neglect (Palacio-Quintin, 1995). We saw that, even if a big number of families were single mothers at the moment of the intervention of the protection services (twice and more times than in the general population), these families had lived numerous changes and the mothers had several partners. We observed also a high proportion of parental divorce during the prenatal period (Palacio-Quintin et al., 2001). Svedin et al. (1996) report in a prospective study that mothers with children from more than three different fathers were much more at risk for child abuse and neglect. Very frequent house moving is also an expression of family instability associated with child neglect. Neglectful families moved frequently, that means that they had lived sometimes less than one year in the same neighborhood (Zuravin, 1989). These facts are related to their poor social network.

There is an abundance of evidence linking familial and extrafamilial limited social support and social isolation with high risk of child abuse and neglect (Garbarino & Sherman, 1980; Kotch et al., 1999). Neglectful families suffer more from isolation and show a lack of reciprocity in social exchanges (Polansky et al., 1981), while abusive families, even if they have a smaller social network than nonabusive parents, are more characterized by conflicting relationships with their extended family (Crittenden, 1985a; Palacio-Quintin, 1995). In addition and because of isolation, maltreating parents do not use community resources that are available (Corse, Schmid, & Trickett, 1990).

Being a very young mother at the birth of the first child is also a risk factor frequently quoted (Kinard & Klerman, 1980; Leventhal, Egerter, & Murphy, 1984). Few works had studied the influence of father's age. Sidebotham et al. (2001) has realized a prospective study in England with a large sample of families expecting for a baby. During the antenatal period they had collected data about both parents backgrounds and about family and social environments and during the seven following years they had screened the local Social Services Child Protection registers. Unfortunately, they did not identify different kinds of maltreatment. They found that a father aged less than 20 years as well as a mother aged less than 20 years is an important risk factor for child abuse and neglect. In addition, Stier, Leventhal, Berg, Johnson and Mezger (1993) found that the effect of parental age was greater for neglect. This is in accordance with the fact that neglect is an inability to meet the child's needs and that young parents are often immature (little independent living skills and emotional immaturity) and lack of readiness to assume the parental role. Dukewich (1996) has shown also that preparation for parenting, a construct including knowledge and attitudes about children's development, was the strongest direct predictor of adolescent mothers abuse potential. Furthermore, we must remember that adolescent motherhood is related to several risk factors: single parenthood, low educational achievement, poverty, little social support, and so forth.

Families with more dependent children at home (Kotch et al., 1999), frequent (Zuravin, 1989) or unplanned and undesired pregnancies (Marneffe, 1991) are also particularly at risk.

Finally, disturbed relationships in the family and presence of marital conflict and interspousal violence had been observed both in abusive and neglectful families (Palacio-Quintin. 1995; Rosenbaum & O'Leary, 1981; Straus & Smith, 1990). There are not only conflicting relationships but also little support from the partner (Palacio-Quintin et al., 1995). Spousal support was found to be related to better psychological well-being and more positive parenting (Coterrell, 1986; Goldberg & Easterbrooks, 1984). Furthermore, marital relations were considered by Belsky (1984) as a central factor in his process model of the determinants of parenting.

Parent factors

Research supports the proposition of intergenerational transmission of abuse and neglect (Egeland, Jacobvitz, & Papatola, 1987). Neglectful and abusive parents had themselves often been mistreated as children. For example, Kauffman and Zigler (1990) considered that 33% of parents having been victims of physical abuse as a child became abusive parents. We had found (Palacio-Quintin et al., 1995) that a very high proportion of neglectful mothers (72 %) had been neglected as a child but also physically (38 %) or sexually abused (35 %). Goodwin, McCarthy and DiVasto (1981) have also found a history of sexual abuse in mothers of abused children. Finally, Rutter, Quinton and Liddle (1983) found that many parents having been maltreated as a child, showed different kinds of parental dysfunction.

All these studies only included mothers. In their study with mothers and fathers, Sidebotham et al. (2001) have found that being reported to welfare authorities and having a violent father were significant risk factors to become a maltreating father. Our studies on neglectful parents (mothers and fathers or mother's partner) (Palacio-Quintin et al., 1995, 2001) showed that 50 to 70% neglected, half of them physically abused and 35 to 50% sexually abused children. This means that a large number of neglectful parents had a childhood history of multiple victimization.

Results about mothers and fathers showed that intergenerational transmission of child abuse and neglect was not specific. Different mediating processes can be considered as explaining this intergenerational transmission: learning of antisocial and aggressive behavior, of philosophies of discipline, of parenting models as well as emotional problems (disturbed attachment relationships, low self-esteem, aggression, lack of empathy, depression, and so forth). We think that each single mediating process cannot explain by itself all types of neglectful and abusive behavior and that several processes must be considered together.

Child abuse and neglect in parent's own child-rearing history is not the only problem. As children they lived often away from home (36 to 50% in foster care, Palacio-Quintin et al., 1995, 2001); they have been separated from their mother before the age of 14 years (Kotch et al., 1999), have witnessed severe violence at home (Kotch et al., 1999), have lived parental separation (Palacio-Quintin et al., 2001, Sidebotham et al., 2001) and have committed delinquent acts (Marneffe, 1991).

A well-known but often neglected risk factor for child maltreatment is the mental retardation of the mother. Studies among mentally retarded mothers have shown a high percentage of maltreated children (Feldman, 1986; Seagull & Scheurer, 1986; Valentine, 1990), a variety of parental difficulties (Whitman, Graves, & Accardo, 1989) and particularly a high percentage of neglected children (Accardo & Whitman, 1990; Kaminer, Jedrysek & Soles, 1981; Tymchuck & Andron, 1990). Data from studies about neglectful mothers show that mental retardation is particularly associated with child neglect (Crittenden, 1988; Sheridan, 1956). Comparison between neglectful mentally retarded mothers and neglectful mothers with normal intelligence showed that more serious neglect appeared in mentally retarded mothers (Guay, Ethier, Palacio-Quintin, & Boutet, 1997). Poor cognitive performance in general was also observed more among neglectful mothers. Svedin, Wadsby and Sdysjö (1996), making a prospective study from the pregnancy period up to 8 years old found that children of mothers with a IQ 70 or less were much more at risk for child abuse and neglect than any at risk groups (drug addiction and psychosocial circumstances). Some authors (Crittenden, 1988; Hansen, Pallotta, Thishelman, Conaway, & MacMillan, 1989) found also that many neglectful mothers had few problem-solving skills in daily life. Finally, our studies (Palacio-Quintin et al., 1995, 2001) showed that the proportion of parents having a cognitive performance (measured with Raven's scale) under the mean was twofold that of the general population. During childhood and adolescence, half of the parents of the 2001 sample had attended special classes. All results showed that low cognitive performance in both parents appeared as an important risk factor for neglect.

The hypothesis of severe parental psychopathology in the etiology of child abuse and neglect was first considered when research in child abuse and neglect began. Many years of research have failed to document any specific psychiatric disorder or distinctive psychopathological profile in abusive and neglectful parents. Nevertheless, various psychological disturbances and maladjustment in maltreating parents in a variety of areas of functioning have been documented.

A high level of depression has been found in maltreating mothers in several retrospective studies (Downey & Coyne, 1990; Kinard, 1982; Zuravin, 1989). Further, depressed mothers showed deficits in the care of their children (Billings & Moss, 1983; Tronick & Field, 1986). Both intrusive, hostile and rejecting care as well as detached and unresponsive parenting is reported (Gelfand & Teti, 1990). Nevertheless, we cannot be sure if mother's depression is an initial factor or a consequence, because in these studies only the correlation between the two facts has been observed. Also, it is not clear what types of maltreatment are particularly involved. Kotch et al.'s (1999) prospective study is particularly interesting in this regard. These authors began a study with 708 at risk mother-infant dyads at the moment of childbirth and then tracked the state central registry data every sixth month from the birth of the infants up to the fourth birthday. The results showed that 172 children were reported for child maltreatment. The incidence of maltreating reports were higher in households where mothers were depressed and complained of psychosomatic symptoms. The authors did not report results for each type of maltreatment, but, as reported in our introduction, the description of the sample showed that the majority of the reports concerned neglect only, 8% neglect with abuse and only 9 % for physical and sexual abuse alone. The results clearly confirmed that mother's depression is an important risk factor, particularly for child neglect. This can be easily understood, if we remember that typical symptoms of depression are feelings of helplessness and uselessness, difficulties to function efficiently, concentration difficulties and lack of interest for others. Mothers in this situation cannot afford the demands of child care and education and therefore are prone to neglect.

These studies about parental depression included only mothers. We have studied (Palacio-Quintin et al., 1995) both mothers and fathers/partners of neglectful families (only neglectful or neglectful and abusive), and the proportion of depressive mothers was again very high (38 % of severe depression and 47 % with depression tendencies). The proportion of fathers/partners was lower (20 % of severe depression and 20 % with depressive feelings). But we must consider that the incidence of depression in women of the general population is twice the one of men (American Psychiatric Association, 1994). In their prospective study Sidebottham et al. (2001) found a significant relationship between fathers' history of depression and children identified as maltreated. As we have already noted, no differentiation between types of maltreatment had been made in this study. The data showed that depression in neglectful and abusive fathers/partners is an important issue that needs to be studied further.

Maltreating parents live many kinds of stressful situations coming from social, familial or personal situations. This exposure to stress is prolonged rather than incidental. Maltreating mothers seem particularly stressed in relation to the parental role (Palacio-Quintin et al., 1995). Parental stress is a state of psychological uneasiness related to the specific field of the child's education (Loys & Abidin,1985). Even if parental stress seems to play a role in maltreating mothers' behavior, not every stressed mother is maltreating and mother's stress is related to other difficulties, for instance child-related problems (see for example the study by Mash & Johnson [1983] about mothers of hyperactive and aggressive children and the study by Jourdan-Ionescu, Palacio-Quintin, Désaulniers & Couture [1998] about children at developmental risk). Nevertheless, it is not yet clear which role parental stress plays as a risk factor. Prospective studies are needed in this area.

An interesting study was done by Wolfe, Fairbank, Kelly and Brandlyn (1983). They have observed parents' physiological answers to pleasant and unpleasant stimuli coming from the child. They have studied three groups: neglectful, abusive and non-maltreating parents. They found that the level of activation of non-maltreating parents varied according to stimulus types but this was much less the case in neglectful and abusive parents. When the level of physiological reaction was considered, differences appeared between neglectful and abusive parents. Neglectful parents showed little reaction while abusive parents showed strong reactions. It appeared that neglectful and abusive parents reacted with specific patterns that were independent of the actual stimulus. These patterns can constitute a specific risk factor for child abuse and neglect and more studies will be necessary.

Maternal self-esteem has been frequently considered as playing an important role in parenting (McCurdy, 1995) and several retrospective studies (Culp, Culp, Soulis & Letts, 1989; Zuravin & Greif, 1989) have reported a low self-esteem in maltreating mothers. Christensen, Brayden, Dietrich, McLaughlin and Sherrod (1994) made a prospective study with 459 pregnant low-income at risk women measuring their self-esteem and reviewing, three years later, the state protective services' records for their children. Their results show that mothers' low self-esteem appeared to be a significant risk factor for child neglect, but was not a strong predictor for physical abuse. Neglectful mothers showed not only a significant lower total score on the Tennessee Self Concept Scale than matched nonreported mothers but also on several particular scales as personal and social adequacy, perception of self-worth in family relationships, satisfaction with own behavior and perception of identity. No significant differences were found between abusive mothers and matched nonreported mothers. Low self-esteem found in studies with abusive mothers can probably be rather an effect of the perception of their own behavior, of bad interactions with the child, of social intervention and of labeling as an abusive mother. We must add that our clinical observations, while following neglectful and abusive families during a long-time intervention program (Palacio-Quintin & Calille, 1995), made clear that neglectful parents showed very little self-confidence, felt socially inadequate, rejected and particularly incompetent as a parent. They also showed a lack of social abilities and a high degree of distrust, not only towards the service agents but also towards the other parents.

High levels of alcohol and drug abuse by parents co-occurred with both child abuse and child neglect (Kelleher, Chaffin, Hollenberg, & Fisher, 1994; Kotch et al., 1999; Marneffe, 1999). This finding appeared in studies examining rates of substance abuse among identified maltreating parents as well as in studies of child maltreatment among identified substance abusers. The risk status of alcohol and drug abuse for both child abuse and neglect has been confirmed by Chaffin et al. (1996) in a prospective study. It is important to note that parent's alcohol and drug abuse was also highly related with other family dysfunctions as separation, domestic violence, mental health problems and parental imprisonment (Dubé, Anda, Felitti, Croft, Edwards, & Giles, 2001).

Little research has been conducted on the criminal involvement of a parent as a risk factor. Nevertheless, criminal involvement on the part of one or both parents has been identified in some studies as a risk factor for abuse and neglect. Svedin, Wadsby and Sdysjö (1996) have considered the fact that a woman has served a jail sentence as one of the risk factors to screen a pregnant mother's risk sample and to make a follow-up study. After eight years, they found four times more cases of abuse and neglect in their sample than in a reference group. In one of our studies on neglectful and neglectful and abusive families (Palacio-Quintin et al., 2001) we collected data about fathers and we found that 38% of the children had had in some moment a father in jail. So, it is possible to think that criminal involvement of the mother or the father is a risk factor for maltreatment.

The last, but not the least important parental factor is parental ability. Problematic parenting is a basic element in the definition of maltreatment itself. Studies have shown that maltreating mothers interacted less with their children and had more negative interactions (Twentyman & Bousha, 1984). They had also unrealistic expectations concerning their children (Marneffe,1991; Wolfe, Edwards, Manion & Koverola, 1988). These unrealistic expectations may differ between neglectful and abusive mothers. Crittenden (1988) observed that violent parents often had high educational standards not in accordance with the child's development. Neglectful mothers showed a poor knowledge of the children's needs (Herrenkohl, Herrenkohl & Egolf, 1983). During a two year-group intervention with neglectful parents (Palacio-Quintin & Calille, 1995), a systematic observation allowed us to realize that these parents needed information about the elements of child care, information that by a majority of other parents was transferred within the family. They asked questions such as: " How to use a thermometer ", " Must we speak to our baby? ", " What to do when a baby cries? ", " What to give to eat to the child?", and so forth. They do not know how to play with the child , not how to interact positively and not how to get pleasure in interacting with the child. They also lack patience and perseverance and they always expect to have results in a short time and with little effort and changes.

In order to distinguish lacking abilities in neglectful and in abusive parents, it would be useful to remember that two fundamental dimensions of parenting are control and responsiveness. We can consider that control is the amount or degree of control and influence the parent attempts to exert over the child, whereas responsiveness is the answer to the child's needs or demands. We found an imbalance between control and responsiveness in both neglectful and abusive parents, but the type of imbalance differed. Violent parents showed a higher level of control and a same quantity of responsiveness than nonmaltreating parents, but they showed more negative than positive answers and punitive discipline practices. Neglectful parents showed less responsiveness and also little direct control. Neglectful mothers tended not to initiate interaction with the child, nor to respond to the child's initiatives (Crittenden, 1985b). Limited parental abilities must be recognized as a central risk factor for child abuse and neglect and particularly for neglect. Even if it is an important factor, it cannot explain child maltreatment by itself. As Belsky (1984) described in his model on the determinants of parenting, many personal familial and contextual factors influence parental behavior.

Child factors

Some personal and behavioral characteristics of the child have been considered as risk factors for abuse and neglect. Preterm birth and low birthweight have been observed more in abused and neglected children (Klein & Stern, 1971). But observations of neglectful mothers' behavior during pregnancy showed a high level of at risk behaviors as smoking, drinking a lot of coffee and drug consuming. All these factors are associated with preterm birth and low birthweight (Palacio-Quintin et al., 2001). So, in these cases, preterm birth and low birthweight are rather a consequence of the neglectful behavior of mothers during pregnancy rather than factors provoking child abuse and neglect.

Several studies (Hawkins & Duncan, 1985; Rose & Hardman, 1981; Zirpoli, 1986) have found a greater proportion of physically and mentally handicapped children among maltreated children. A high incidence level of handicapped children has been reported among abused and neglected children. Few studies have assessed the incidence of maltreatment among handicapped children. Ammerman, Hersen, Van Hasselt, McGonigle and Lubetsky (1989) examined the presence of abuse and neglect in a sample of multiply handicapped children hospitalized in psychiatry and Diamond and Jaudes (1983) studied a sample of children with cerebral palsy. Both found a high incidence of abuse and neglect but the proportion was much higher in the sample of the multiply handicapped psychiatric children. An epidemiological study on child maltreatment carried out in the city of Buenos Aires and surroundings (Bringiotti, 2004) showed that among children attending special classes, the incidence of physical abuse was twice that of children in regular classes. Sullivan and Knutson (1996) in an epidemiological study in Nebraska found that children with disabilities were three to four times more likely to be maltreated than nondisabled children. They also found that there was a higher proportion of disabled children suffering from multiple forms of maltreatment than nondisabled children. These authors differentiated the types of maltreatment and the types of disabilities, but did not find significant associations between types of maltreatment and types of disabilities.

It is difficult to know if these child characteristics are contributors to or sequelae of maltreatment as it is well known that abuse and neglect can provoke learning disabilities and in some cases serious handicaps in the child. For example, the whiplash syndrome in babies can cause neurological lesions leading to mental retardation and neglect can be the cause of an accident causing a physical handicap. So, what is more clear is that considerable handicaps can play the role of an additional stressor for parents because of increased care requirements. This is particularly true for those parents having already some difficulties (Morgan, 1987). A handicap in the child increases the risk for child abuse or neglect.

Difficult temperament and behavioral problems in the child (Egeland & Brunnquell, 1979) have also been found to be related with child abuse and neglect. But as behavioral problems are a clear consequence of child abuse and neglect (Ammerman, Cassisi, Hersen, & Van Hasselt, 1986) it is difficult to distinguish between risk and consequence. Child difficulties become a risk factor for maltreatment only if parents lack the personal and social resources to cope with the difficulties (Engfer, 1992). In fact, the child problems will increase the already existing risks. Child characteristics may play the role of triggers for abuse. They can evoke violence or withdrawal (neglect) by the caregiver.

Young children are more at risk of abuse and neglect for different reasons. Usually, they spend more time with their parents. Young children's dependence makes them more demanding upon adults and they are more vulnerable to injuries or lack of care. Neglect appears usually in the first year of life and physical abuse increases more when the child reaches preschool age and begins to develop autonomy and becomes more "disturbing".

Two problems about child risk factors have to be mentioned. Firstly, it is particularly difficult to distinguish whether these child factors are really risk factors or only consequences of the maltreating situation in which the child lives. Secondly, risk factors have to be considered in a relational context. In the social-interactional model of child abuse and neglect the dynamic interchanges between parent and child are viewed as critical to the etiology and maintenance of maltreating behavior. This view is based on studies showing that child noncompliance and oppositional behavior can serve to maintain or increase preexisting abusive relationships and children are only contributing to the occurrence of more incidents of behavior (Reid et al., 1982). It must be noted that studies adopting this model have focused on abusive behavior and cannot be applied to neglectful behavior.

So, child characteristics can be risk factors relevant to understand child abuse and neglect, but only if they are considered in interaction with parental and contextual characteristics.

Conclusions

This review allows us to see that multiple contextual, family, parental and child risk factors are associated with child abuse and neglect and that each risk factor is frequently associated with many others. The cumulative effects of risk factors are already well-documented but we don't know yet what are the differential results from different kinds of interaction between them. More studies on the interactions between risk factors are needed. A variety of family dynamics emerge from these combinations and it is actually difficult to know whether some type of factor has a bigger influence than others. Belsky (1984) hypothesized that a hierarchy of influence must exist in determining risks of problematic parenting. He stated that parental personality and parental psychological resources are the most important factors, followed by social contextual features, with child characteristics being the least influential. Actual knowledge about child abuse and neglect risk factors seems to correspond with the direction of this hypothesis. Indeed, as we mentioned, child factors seemed to be less important contributors or rather consequences from child abuse and neglect than risk factors. It is more difficult to specify the relative importance of parental, familial and contextual factors. More studies are needed before we will be able to determine the weight of these factors.

If it is true that an increased risk of maltreatment exists in poor families, young parents, mothers and fathers who have been maltreated as children, parents with cognitive low functioning, depressed mothers, families with marital violence, why then do not all these parents maltreat their children? Probably because there are several protective factors in the lives of these parents and children. Some researchers, for instance Scott Heller, Larrieu, D'Imperio and Boris (1999) have studied resilience in maltreated children, but little is known about protective factors preventing at risk families from maltreatment. Egeland et al. (1993) found for example that mothers who were abused as children and who provided adequate care to their children, had received emotional support from a relative or a foster parent and had supportive partners. More studies in this area are needed, because it appears clearly that there is not only the interaction between risk factors but also the interaction between risk and protective factors which determines the concretization of the risk for maltreatment.

Much of the work on child abuse and neglect and on risk factors has concentrated on identifying situations from the mother's perspective. Few efforts have been undertaken to understand the role of fathers/partners. Our analyses showed that a variety of risk factors in fathers existed: low income, unemployment and low educational level, young age, a history of multiple victimization and out of home care in childhood, juvenile delinquency, instability, leaving the mother during pregnancy, violence against wife and little support to her, high levels of alcohol and drug abuse, criminal involvement, low cognitive performance and depression. More studies considering fathers' or partners' characteristics contributing to child abuse and neglect are needed and studies must also consider family dynamics.

If some factors as intergenerational transmission, alcohol and drug abuse by parents and disturbed relationships in the family and interspousal violence are related to both physical abuse and neglect, several factors seem to be more related to one or the other form of maltreatment. Even if a relationship exists between poverty, unemployment, low educational achievement, parents' young age and both forms of maltreatment, these indicators as well as familial instability, maternal depression and isolation are particularly related to neglect. Some factors as mental retardation in both parents, low cognitive performance, low self-esteem, low level of activation and lack of reciprocity with others appear as specific risk factors for neglect.

Some problems in parental abilities are observed also in both kinds of maltreatment but the type of difficulties observed are different in the two types of maltreatment. Little knowledge about children's needs, unrealistic expectations, very little responsiveness and lack of perseverance in the educational tasks are associated with neglectful parenting while abusive mothers show high educational standards, high level of control, more negative interactions with the child and high reactivity levels. At this moment, it is not possible to differentiate between child risk factors that can be more significant for abuse or for neglect. Child's age is the only one having a differential effect, very young children being more at risk of neglect. Future studies must consider risk factors in relation with each type of maltreatment separately.

Finally, we have seen that the majority of studies are retrospective and that few prospective studies exist. Or, retrospective studies cannot clearly differentiate whether a variable is a risk factor, that means pre-existing to maltreatment, or a consequence. Prospective studies enlighten the question of risk factors, but those on which we have reported, as the majority of studies in child abuse and neglect, did not differentiate cases of neglect from those of physical abuse and some used self-reported maltreatment and not substantiated maltreatment.

To summarize, we can conclude that studies with the following characteristics are needed in order to develop knowledge of risk factors for child physical abuse and child neglect that can contribute to the development of evidence-based prevention programs:

- Prospective approach,
- Integration of risk factors of different levels of the ecological model,
- Integration of protective factors,
- Consideration of interaction between risk and protective factors,
- Differentiation of neglected, physically abused and neglected and physically abused children,
- Specific maltreatment situation is substantiated,
- Characteristics of mothers and fathers (or partners) are considered,
- Family dynamics are taken into account, including information about who is the abusive or neglectful parent.

References

Accardo, P. J., & Whitman B. Y. (1990). Children of parents with mental retardation: Problems and diagnoses. In B. Y. Whitman & P. J. Accardo (Eds.), *When a parent is mentally retarded* (pp. 123-132). Baltimore: P. H. Brookes.

American Psychiatric Association (1994). *DSM-IV. Diagnostic and Statistical Manual of Mental Disorders.* Washington: American Psychiatric Association.

Ammerman, R. T., Cassisi, J. E., Hersen, M., & Van Hasselt, V. B. (1986). Consequences of physical abuse and neglect in children. *Clinical Psychology Review, 6,* 291-310.

Ammerman, R. T., Hersen, M., Van Hasselt, V. B., McGonigle, J. J., & Lubetsky, M. J. (1989). Abuse and neglect in psychiatrically hospitalized multihandicapped children. *Child Abuse and Neglect, 13,* 335-343.

Belsky, J. (1984). The determinants of parenting: A process model. *Child Development,* 55, 83-96.

Belsky, J. (1993). Etiology of child maltreatment: A developmental-ecological analysis. *Psychological Bulletin, 114,* 413-434.

Billings, A. G., & Moss, R. H. (1983). Comparison of children of depressed and non-depressed parents: A social-environmental prospective. *Journal of Abnormal Child Psychology, 11,* 463-486.

Bringiotti, M.-I. (2004). Changement de paradigme concernant l'enfance. De la maltraitance à la bientraitance: Le cas de la maltraitance physique. In E. Palacio-Quintin, J.-M. Bouchard, & B. Terrisse (Eds.), *Questions d'éducation familiale dans les années 2000* (pp.255-271). Montréal: Éditions Logiques.

Chaffin, M., Kelleher, K., & Holenberg, J. (1996). Onset of physical abuse and neglect: Psychiatric, substance abuse, and social risk factors from prospective community data. *Child Abuse and Neglect,* 20, 191-203.

Chamberland, C., Bouchard, C., & Beaudry, J. (1986). Conduites abusives et négligentes envers les enfants: réalités canadiennes et américaines. *Revue canadienne des sciences du comportement, 18,* 391-412.

Christensen, M. J., Brayden, R. M., Dietrich, M. S. McLaughlin, F. J. & Sherrod, K. B. (1994). The protective assessment of self-concept in neglectful and physically abusive low income mothers. *Child Abuse and Neglect, 18,* 225-232.

Cicchetti, D., & Carlsson, V. (Eds.) (1989). *Child maltreatment: Theory and research on the causes and consequences of child abuse and neglect.* Cambridge: Cambridge University Press.

Corbillon, M., Augain, C., Durning, P., Fablet, D., & Fablet, F. (1997). Une crèche familiale originale: Point de vue sur les apports de l'évaluation au changement social. In F. Tochon (Ed.), *Éduquer avant l'école, l'intervention préscolaire en milieux défavorisés et pluriethniques* (pp. 279-296). Paris, Bruxelles: De Boeck.

Corse, S., Schmid, K., & Trickett, P. (1990). Social network characteristics of mothers in abusing and nonabusing families and their relationships to parenting beliefs. *Journal of Community Psychology, 18,* 44-59.

Coterrell, J. L. (1986). Work and community influences on the quality of childrearing. *Child Development*, 57, 262-374.
Crittenden, P. (1985a). Social networks, quality of child rearing and child development. *Child Development*, 56, 1299-1313.
Crittenden, P. (1985b). Maltreated infants: Vulnerability and resilience. *Journal of Child Psychology and Psychiatry*, 26, 85-96.
Crittenden, P. (1988). Family and dyadic patterns of functioning in maltreating families. In K. Browne, C. Davies et P. Stratton (Eds.), *Early prediction and prevention of child abuse* (pp. 111-126). New York: John Wiley & Sons.
Culp, R. E., Culp, A. M., Soulis, J., & Letts, D. (1989). Self-esteem and depression in abusive, neglecting and non-maltreating mothers. *Infant Mental Heath Journal, 10*, 243-251.
Diamond, L. J., & Jaudes, P. K. (1983). Child abuse in a cerebral-palsied population. *Developmental Medicine and Child Neurology, 25*, 169-174.
Downey, G., & Coyne, J. (1990). Children of depressed parents: An integrative review. *Psychological Bulletin, 108*, 50-76.
Drake, B., & Pandey, S. (1996). Understanding the relationship between neighborhood, poverty and specific types of maltreatment. *Child Abuse and Neglect, 20*, 1003-1018.
Dubé, S. R., Anda, R. F., Felitti, V. J., Croft, J. B., Edwards, V. J., & Giles, W. H. (2001). Growing up with parental alcohol abuse: Exposure to childhood abuse, neglect, and household dysfunction. *Child Abuse and Neglect, 25*, 1627-1640.
Dukewich, T. L., Borkowski, J. G. & Whitman, T. L. (1996). Adolescent mothers and child abuse potential: An evaluation of risk factors. *Child Abuse and Neglect, 20*, 1031-1047.
Eckenrode, J., Laird, M., & Doris, J. (1993). School performance and disciplinary problems among abused and neglected children. *Developmental Psychology*, 29, 53-62.
Egeland, B., & Brunnquell, D. (1979). An at risk approach to the study of child abuse. *Journal of the American Academy of Child Psychiatry, 18*, 219-236.
Egeland, B., Carlson, E. & Stroufe, A (1993). Resilience as process. *Development and Psychopathology, 5*, 517-528.
Egeland, B., Jacobvitz, D., & Papatola, K. (1987). Intergenerational continuity of abuse. In R. Gelles & J. Lancaster (Eds.), *Child abuse and neglect: Biosocial dimensions* (pp. 255-276). Chicago: Aldine de Gruyter.
Engfer, A. (1992). Difficult temperament and child abuse. Notes on the validity of the child-effect model. *Analise-Psicologica, 10*, 51-61.
Erickson, M., Egeland, B., & Pianta, R. (1989). The effects of maltreatment in the development of young children. In D. Cicchetti & V. Carlson (Eds.), *Child maltreatment: Theory and research on the causes and consequences of child abuse and neglect* (pp. 647-684). New York: Cambridge University Press.
Feldman, M. A. (1986). Research on parenting by mentally retarded persons. *Psychiatric Clinics of North America, 9*, 777-796.

Garbarino, J., & Sherman, D. (1980). High-risk neighborhoods and high-risk families. The human ecology of child maltreatment. *Child Development, 51*, 188-198.

Gelfand, D., & Teti, D. (1990). The effects of maternal depression on children. *Clinical Psychology Review, 10*, 329-353.

Goldberg, W. A., & Easterbrooks, M.A. (1984). Role of marital quality in toddler development. *Developmental Psychology, 20*, 504-514.

Goodwin, J., McCarthy, T. & DiVasto, P. (1981). Prior incest in mothers of abused children. *Child Abuse and Neglect, 5*, 87-95.

Guay, F., Ethier, L. S., Palacio-Quintin, E., & Boutet, M. (1997). L'impact de la déficience intellectuelle sur la problématique de la négligence parentale. *Revue Européenne du Handicap Mental, 4*, 3-15.

Hansen, D. J., Pallotta, G. M., Thishelman, A. C., Conaway, L. P., & MacMillan, V. M. (1989). Parental problem-solving skills and child behavior problems: A comparison of physically abusive, neglectful, clinic and community families. *Journal of Family Violence, 4*, 353-368.

Hawkins, W. E., & Duncan, D. F. (1985). Children's illness as risk factors for child abuse. *Psychological Reports, 56*, 638.

Herrenkohl, R. C., Herrenkohl, E. C., & Egolf, B. P. (1983). Circumstances surrounding the occurrence of child maltreatment. *Journal of Consulting and Clinical Psychology, 51*, 424-431.

Jourdan-Ionescu, C., & Palacio-Quintin, E. (1997). Effets de la maltraitance sur les jeunes enfants et nouvelles perspectives d'intervention. *Psychologie française. N° spécial Psychopathologie et société, 42*, 217-228.

Jourdan-Ionescu, C., Palacio-Quintin, E, Désaulniers, R., & Couture, G. (1998). *Étude de l'interaction des facteurs de risque et de protection chez des jeunes enfants fréquentant un service d'intervention précoce*. Final report to the Conseil québécois de la recherche sociale, Université du Québec à Trois-Rivières, 145 p.

Kaminer, R., Jedrysek, E., & Soles, B. (1981). Intellectually limited parents. *Journal of Developmental and Behavioral Pediatrics, 2*, 39-43.

Kauffman, J. & Zigler, E. (1990). The intergenerational transmission of child abuse and the prospect of predicting future abusers. In D. Cicchetti & V. Carlson (Eds.), *Child maltreatment: Research and theory on the consequences of child abuse and neglect* (pp. 129-150). Cambridge, MA: Harvard University Press.

Kelleher, K., Chaffin, M., Hollenberg, J., & Fisher, E. (1994). Alcohol and drug disorders among physically abusive and neglectful parents in community-based sample. *American Journal of Public Health, 84*, 1586-1590.

Kimball, H., Steward, R. B., Conger, R. D. & Burgess, R. L. (1980). A comparison of family interaction in single versus two-parent abusive, neglecful and control families. In T. Fields, S. Goldberg & A. Sostek (Eds.), *High risk infants and children: Adult and peer interaction* (pp. 43-59). New York: Academic Press.

Kinard, E. M. (1982). Child abuse and depression: Cause or consequence? *Child Welfare, 7*, 403-413.

Kinard, E. M., & Klerman, L. V. (1980). Teenage parenting and child abuse: Are they related? *American Journal of Orthopsychiatry, 50,* 481-487.

Klein, M. & Stern, L. (1971). Low birth weight and the battered child syndrome. *American Journal of Diseases in Childhood, 122,* 15-18.

Kotch, J. B., Browne, D. C., Dufort, V. & Winsor, J. (1999). Predicting child maltreatment in the first years of life from characteristics assessed in the neonatal period. *Child Abuse and Neglect, 23,* 305-319.

Lafont, N. (1997). *La situation scolaire des enfants négligés.* Master thesis in Psychology, directed by E. Palacio-Quintin, Psychology Department, Université du Québec à Trois-Rivières.

Leventhal, J. M., Egerter, S. A. & Murphy, J. M. (1984). Reassessment of the relationship of perinatal risk factors and child abuse. *American Journal of Diseases of Childhood, 138,* 1034-1039.

Loys, B. H. & Abidin, R. R. (1985). Revision of the Parenting Stress Index. *Journal of Pediatric Psychology, 10,* 169-177.

Marneffe, C. (1991). Menace à la naissance: Menace prévisible? Menace évitable?. *L'enfant, 1,* 66-75.

McCurdy, K. (1995). Risk assessment in child abuse prevention programs. *Social Work Research, 19,* 77-87.

Mash, E. J. & Johnson, C. (1983). Parental perceptions of child behavior problems, parenting self-esteem and mothers' reported stress in younger and older hyperactive and normal children. *Journal of Consulting and Clinical Psychology, 5,* 86-99.

Morgan, S. R. (1987). *Abuse and neglect of handicapped children.* Boston: Little, Brown.

Palacio-Quintin, E. (1995). Les mauvais traitements envers les enfants: Les facteurs sociaux et la dynamique familiale. Actes du séminaire *Les liens entre la violence physique, psychologique et sexuelle faite aux enfants et aux femmes,* p. 5-14. CRI-VIFF, Collection Reflexions, Montréal.

Palacio-Quintin, E., & Calille, S. (1995). Une expérience de groupe pour parents négligents. *Revue Canadienne de Santé Mentale Communautaire, 14,* 181-200.

Palacio-Quintin, E., Couture, G., & Paquet, J. (1995). *Projet d'intervention auprès des familles négligentes présentant ou non des comportements violents.* Rapport soumis à à la Division de la Prévention de la Violence Familiale, Santé Canada, 256 p.

Palacio-Quintin, E., & Ethier, L. S. (1993). La négligence, un phenomène négligé. *Apprentissage et Socialisation, 16,* 153-164.

Palacio-Quintin, E., & Jourdan-Ionescu, C. (1994). Effets de la négligence et de la violence sur le développement des jeunes enfants. *PRISME, 4,* 145-156.

Palacio-Quintin, E., Jourdan-Ionescu, C., Coderre, R., & Desaulniers, R. (2001). *L'implantation du programme PAPFC dans la région Lanaudière. Processus et effets.* Rapport soumis à la Régie Régionale de la Santé et des Services Sociaux de Lanaudière, 95 p.

Polansky, N. A., Chambers, M., Buttenwieser, E. & Williams, D. P. (1981). *Damaged parents: An anatomy of child neglect.* Chicago: University of Chicago Press.

Reid, J. B., Patterson, G. R., & Loeber, R. (1982). The abused child: Victim, instigator or innocent bystander? *Nebraska Symposium on Motivation*, 29, 47-68.

Rose, E., & Hardman, M. L. (1981). The abused mentally retarded child. *Education and Training of the Mentally Retarded*, 114-118.

Rosenbaum, A., & O'Leary, D. (1981). Marital violence: Characteristics of abusive couples. *Journal of Consulting and Clinical Psychology*, 49, 63-71.

Rutter, M., Quinton, D., & Liddle, C. (1983). Parenting in two generations: Looking backward and looking forward. In N. Madge (Ed.), *Families at risk* (pp. 60-98). London: Heinemann.

Salsinger, S., Feldman, R. S., Hammer, M., & Rosario, M. (1993). The effects of physical abuse on children's social relationships. *Child Development*, 64, 169-187.

Scott Heller, S., Larrieu, J. A., D'Imperio, R., & Boris, N. W. (1999). Research on resilience to child maltreatment: Empirical considerations. *Child Abuse and Neglect*, 23, 321-338.

Seagull, E. A., & Scheurer, S. L. (1986). Neglected and abused children of mentally retarded parents. *Child Abuse and Neglect*, 10, 493-500.

Sheridan, M. D. (1956). The intelligence of 100 neglectful mothers. *British Medical Journal*, 1, 91-93.

Sidebotham, P., Golding, J. & the ALSPAC Study Team (2001). Child maltreatment in the "Children of the nineties. A longitudinal study of parental risk factors". *Child Abuse and Neglect*, 25, 1177-1200.

Stier, D. M., Leventhal, M. D., Berg, A. T, Johnson, R. N. & Mezger, J. (1993). Are children born to young mothers at increased risk of maltreatment? *Pediatrics*, 91, 643-648.

Straus, M. A., & Smith, C. (1990). Family patterns and child abuse. In M. A. Straus & R. Gelles (Eds) *Physical violence in American families*. N. J.: Transaction.

Sullivan, P. M. & Knutson, J. (1996). Maltreatment and disabilities: A population based epidemiological study. *Child Abuse and Neglect*, 24, 1257-1273.

Svedin, C. G., Wadsby, M. & Sdysjö, G. (1996). Children of mothers who are at psycho-social risk. Mental health, behavior problems and incidence of child abuse at age 8 years. *European Child & Adolescent Psychiatry*, 5, 162-171.

Tronick, E. Z., & Field, E. M. (Eds.) (1986). *Maternal depression and infant disturbance*. San Francisco: Jossey-Bass.

Twentyman, C. T., & Bousha, D. M. (1984). Abusive, neglectful and comparison mother-child interactional style: Naturalistic observations in the home setting. *Journal of Abnormal Psychology*, 93, 106-114.

Tymchuk, A. J., & Andron, L. (1990). Mothers with mental retardation who do or do not abuse or neglect their children. *Child Abuse and Neglect*, 14, 313-323.

Urquiza, A. J., Wirtz, S. J.,Peterson, M. S., & Singer, V. A. (1994). Screening and evaluating abused and neglected children entering protective custody. *Child Welfare*, 73, 155-171.

Valentine, D. P. (1990). Double jeopardy: Child maltreatment and mental retardation. *Child and Adolescent Social Work Journal, 7*, 487-499.

Whitman, B. Y., Graves, B., & Accardo, P. J. (1989). Training in parenting skills for adults with mental retardation. *Social Work* (September), 431-434.

Wolfe, D. A., Edwards, B., Manion, I. & Koverola, C. (1988). Early intervention for parents at risk of child abuse and neglect: A preliminary investigation. *Journal of Consulting and Clinical Psychology, 56*, 40-47.

Wolfe, D. A., Fairbank, J., Kelly, G. A. & Brandlyn, A. S. (1983). Child abusive parents' physiological responses to stressful and non-stressful behavior in children. *Behavioral Assessment, 5*, 363-371.

Woodward, L. J., & Fergusson, D. M. (2002). Parent, child, and contextual predictors of childhood physical punishment. *Infant and Child Development, 11*, 213-235.

Zirpoli, T.J. (1986). Child abuse and children with handicaps. *Remedial and Special Education*, 7, 39-48.

Zuravin, S. J. (1989). Severity of maternal depression and three types of mother-child-agression. *American Journal of Orthopsychiatry, 59*, 377-389.

Zuravin, S. J. & Greif, G. L. (1989). Normative and child-maltreating AFVD mothers. *Social Casework: The Journal of Contemporary Social Work, 74*, 76-84.

PART TWO

THE BEST INTERESTS PRINCIPLE IN CHILD AND YOUTH CARE PRACTICE

5

Creating 'prosthetic environments' for vulnerable children: Emergent cross-national challenges for traditional child and family services practice and research

James K. Whittaker

Introduction

This chapter addresses four key questions concerning children's mental health services in the United States:
1. What promising model interventions presently command attention in the landscape of United States child mental health services?
2. What are their similarities and differences and by what criteria should they be assessed?
3. Taken together, do these and other promising interventions constitute something greater than the sum of their parts? How should we think of them collectively?
4. What challenges lie ahead in implementing effective child mental health services in the domains of policy, practice and evaluative research?

To begin, what is the current context for children's mental health services in the United States and why do we look there for "promising interventions"? I suggest the answer to the first of these questions is an increasing concern on the part of policy makers, clinicians, school personnel and families on what I would describe as "critical unmet need".

Listen to the words of our chief mental health official on the occasion of a national conference (U.S. Public Health Service, 2000) called by the Surgeon General on the recently completed *U.S. Surgeon General's Report On Mental Health* (1999), *Section on Children and Mental Health*:

> "The burden of suffering experienced by children with mental health needs and their families has created a health crisis in this country. Growing numbers of children are suffering needlessly because their emotional, behavioral,

> and developmental needs are not being met by those very institutions which were explicitly created to take care of them. It is time that we as a Nation took seriously the task of preventing mental health problems and treating mental illnesses in youth.
>
> .....
>
> There is no mental health equivalent to the federal government's commitment to childhood immunization. Children and families are suffering because of missed opportunities for prevention and early identification, fragmented services, and low priorities for resources. Overriding these problems is the issue of stigma, which continues to surround mental illness.
>
> ......
>
> Responsibilities for children's mental healthcare is dispersed across multiple systems: schools, primary care, the juvenile justice system, child welfare and substance abuse treatment. But the first system is the family, and this agenda reflects the voices of youth and family. The vision and goals outlined in this agenda represent an unparalleled opportunity to make difference in the quality of life for America's children."
>
> (David Satcher, M.D., Assistant Secretary for Health and Surgeon General) (*U.S. Public Health Service*, 2000, Foreword)

Estimates of incidence and prevalence on the various forms of children's mental illness vary considerably. For example, our most recent Surgeon's General's Report (1999) on mental health estimates that while 20% of children & adolescents experience the signs and symptoms of a DSM-IV [a widely used diagnostic classification system] disorder during the course of a year, only about 5% of these experience what professionals term "extreme functional impairment". This *apparently* modest number (5%) grows in significance exponentially when it is extrapolated to the U.S. population of children which presently is in excess of 66 million: yielding a population of 3.3 million children with "extreme functional impairment" in need of mental health treatment, even when gauged against a conservative threshold criterion.

As Dr. Satcher's remarks indicate, children with acute mental health needs are to be found in abundance in every service system from juvenile justice, to child welfare and education and, indeed, the unmet mental health needs of children in non-mental health service systems is emerging as a major concern in its own right (Landsverk & Garland, 1999).

Besides sheer need, a second reason for turning our attention to children's mental health services is my strong belief that somewhat more critical attention has been paid to the development and testing of model interventions in this arena over the last decade or so, than in two of the other major service sectors which involve vulnerable children: child welfare and juvenile justice. Each of these, in its own way, has been occupied with other major conundrums: In the case of "child welfare", this has meant balancing "child protection" and "family preservation" and in "juvenile justice", it has meant struggling to maintain *any* treatment focus in a societal context that clamors increasingly for punishment over rehabilitation of any sort: *"Do your crime, serve your time"!*

Moreover, if our choice of focus is on those children most involved and challenging i.e. those headed for "deep-end" residential/institutional services, children's mental health offers some intriguing alternatives which command our attention both from the perspective of humaneness and cost effectiveness. In my view, a consensus exists among child mental health advocates that we continue to spend a disproportionately large percentage of service dollars on a relatively small percentage of children in restrictive residential placements, when less restrictive, community centered alternatives exist that might reach greater numbers in need in more effective and humane ways. This sentiment is strengthened by recent research which raises serious questions about the potentially harmful effects of congregating youth with behavior disorders (Dishion, McCord & Poulin, 1999; Poulin, Dishion & Burraston, 2001). For a review of the present state of residential care & treatment in the United States, see Whittaker (2004).

Thus, the three interventions I will briefly describe in a moment are specifically designed to provide alternative pathways for children who otherwise would be headed into more costly and restrictive residential provision. Dr. Barbara Burns, Professor of Psychology at Duke University in North Carolina and a principal author of the children's mental health section of the Surgeon General's Report provides a succinct rationale for why this is warranted:

> "The most critical question for the future is, what will it take to convince payers, public and private, to support the interventions that are backed up by evidence about improved outcomes? Assuming that the pool of dollars available for mental health treatment will not increase, it will be necessary to shift resources away from institutional care (which lacks evidence of effectiveness) toward community alternatives. This will require a reduction in funds allocated to institutional care, where a significant portion of the child mental health money is still being spent" (Burns & Hoagwood, 2002, p.13).

In narrowing our focus this way for the reasons stated above and also because of the limits of time, I must at least acknowledge that I omit a great deal of promising work that is presently being done on a wide range of family, school and community centered interventions that is both more *preventive* in its focus and appropriate for a much wider population of children than is our concern here (National Research Council and Institute of Medicine, 2000; Shonkoff & Meisels, 2000). Let us return now to the four questions I outlined at the beginning of this chapter.

What promising model interventions presently command attention in the landscape of U.S. child mental health services?

Stimulated in part by funding from our National Institute of Mental Health (NIMH), a variety of initiatives have stimulated research and development on several specific interventions which offer alternatives to institutional care, as well as research on the fundamental organizational, community and policy infra-structure for effective child mental health services. A foundation for all child mental health intervention planning is the path-breaking Child and Adolescent Service System Program (CASSP) launched in 1984 by our National Institute for Mental Health to provide both a framework and technology for creating an integrated system of care for children with mental health needs. Central to the CASSP initiative and several successor programs emanating both from government and private foundation resources is the concept of a "system of care" defined as:

> "A comprehensive spectrum of mental health and other necessary services which are organized into a coordinated network to meet the multiple and changing needs of children and adolescents with severe emotional disturbances and their families." (Stroul & Friedman, 1986)

The system of care thus defined is based on three main elements:

1. The mental health service system efforts are driven by the needs and preferences of the child & family and are addressed by a strengths based approach.
2. The locus and management of services occur within a multi-agency collaborative environment and are grounded in a strong community base.
3. The services offered, the agencies participating and programs generated are responsive to cultural context and characteristics. (Burns & Hoagwood, 2002, p.19)

Initial optimism for systems of care thinking is tempered by the fact that while recent evaluations have documented better service access in communities that have implemented integrated systems of care coordination, no comparable advantages can as yet be detected with respect to child mental health outcomes (Bickman, 1999). Nonetheless, within this broad context of systems of care thinking, numerous specific intervention strategies have developed. Recent reviews identify a range of potentially promising interventions and the empirical evidence that supports them (Burns & Hoagwood, 2002; Epstein, Kutash & Duchnowski, 1998; Kazdin & Weisz, 2003; Kutash & Robbins Rivera, 1996). These include: day treatment and school-based mental health programs, crisis and emergency services, intensive case management programs, mentoring programs, family support & education, psychopharmacological interventions and interventions designed for specific at-risk populations such as homeless youth and youth with co-occurring substance abuse problems.

For purposes of illustration, I would like to focus on three interventions that have received considerable attention in children's mental health services in the United States and which have been the objects of numerous community replications and research study. These include:

> *"Multisystemic Therapy"* (MST) developed principally by Dr. Scott Henggeler, a psychologist now at the Department of Psychiatry & Behavioral Sciences, Medical University of South Carolina (Henggeler & Lee, 2003; Henggeler et al., 1998; Schoenwald & Rowland, 2002).
>
> *"Treatment Foster Care"* (TFC) developed in several clinical/research teams in the United States and represented here by the model principally developed by Dr. Patricia Chamberlain and colleagues at the Oregon Social Learning Center, a highly influential applied behavior analysis developmental research center one of whose founding members is Dr. Gerald Patterson (Chamberlain, 2002 & 2003; Chamberlain & Reid, 1998).
>
> *"Wraparound Treatment"* a novel, team oriented community centered intervention developed by a variety of individuals including Dr. John Burchard, now Professor of clinical psychology at the University of Vermont), John Van Den Berg (The Alaska Youth Initiative), Carl Dennis (Kaleidoscope Project, Chicago) & others beginning in the early 1980's (Burchard, Bruns & Burchard, 2002; Burns & Goldman, 1999).

What are the similarities and differences of these interventions and by what criteria should they be assessed?

Multisystemic therapy

> Multisystemic Therapy is described by its originators as:
>
> "an intensive, time-limited, home and family focused treatment approach...that targets directly for change those factors within the youth's family, peer group, school, and neighborhood that are contributing to his or her antisocial behavior" (Schoenwald, Borduin & Henggeler, 1998: 486-487).

Consistent with many features of intensive family preservation services (low caseloads, delivery of services in home/school/community settings, time limits, 24-hour availability, comprehensive services), MST operates typically with master's level trained therapist/counselor teams with each counselor serving 4-6 families at a time for a duration of 3-5 months. The following core principles of MST inform all aspects of intervention and service delivery:

- Principle 1: The primary purpose of assessment is to understand the fit between the identified problems and their broader systemic context;
- Principle 2: Therapeutic contacts should emphasize the positive and should use systemic strengths as levers for change;
- Principle 3: Interventions should be designed to promote responsible behavior and decrease irresponsible behavior among family members;
- Principle 4: Interventions should be present-focused and action-oriented, targeting specific and well-defined problems;
- Principle 5: Interventions should target sequences of behavior within and between multiple systems that maintain identified problems;
- Principle 6: Interventions should be developmentally appropriate and fit the developmental needs of the youth;
- Principle 7: Interventions should be designed to require daily or weekly effort by family members;
- Principle 8: Intervention effectiveness is evaluated continuously from multiple perspectives, with providers assuming accountability for overcoming barriers to successful outcomes;
- Principle 9: Interventions should be designed to promote treatment generalization and long-term maintenance of therapeutic change by empowering caregivers to address family members' needs across multiple systemic contexts (Schoenwald & Rowland, 2002, p. 99).

As these principles and definition suggest, while MST has been used extensively though not exclusively in work with anti-social youth within the juvenile justice system, there has been considerable interest in the model from our National Institute of Mental Health among others as an alternative to psychiatric hospitalization for youth with serious mental health problems. MST's developers in fact see the principles and change strategies of the approach as a promising corrective to some of the disappointing results of early "systems of care" research noted earlier. They note:

"....given recent findings suggesting that systems of care initiatives may not, in and of themselves, succeed in improving clinical outcomes for youth...progress...will be enhanced by paying increased attention to the nature of treatment...and treatment outcomes. *That is, the implementation of service changes (e.g., the introduction of wrap-around services, home-based services, school-based men-*

tal health services, mentoring programs..) and service system changes (increased access, availability and array of services) are not likely to result in changes in clinical outcome unless services effectively alter those aspects of the youth's and family's natural ecology that are contributing to identified problems" (Schoenwald, Borduin & Henggeler, 1998 p. 508, emphasis added).

A recent review of child mental health interventions by Burns and Hoagwood notes that "leading child treatment researchers (such as Kazdin & Weisz, 1998) concur that MST is a well-validated treatment model" and reflects an impressive corpus of outcome research including several clinical trials (2002:113). Studies show promising results for both juvenile justice and mental health clientele and studies in process are examining the infrastructure necessary to assure treatment fidelity, an "Achilles Heel" of much earlier family preservation demonstrations. At the moment, MST is enjoying considerable attention in states and local communities across North America as a model "evidence-based" ecologically oriented treatment program.

Treatment Foster Care

Treatment Foster Care (TFC) has been broadly defined as follows:

"A service which provides treatment for troubled children within the private homes of trained families. The approach combines the normalizing influence of family-based care with specialized treatment interventions, thereby creating a therapeutic environment in the context of a nurturant family home." (Stroul, 1989, p. 13 quoted in Kutash & Robbins Rivera [1996], p. 69).

Treatment foster care has been developed in several agency sites throughout N. America such as the Pressley Ridge School in Pennsylvania and Girls and Boys Town in Nebraska. As noted earlier, one prominent model was developed at the Oregon Social Learning Center, an applied behavioral research site that has made extensive contributions to our understanding of behavioral intervention with aggressive, oppositional youth. This Oregon Social Learning Center Model of TFC is described by Chamberlain as a "family-based alternative to residential, institutional and group care for children with significant behavioral, emotional and mental health problems (2002, p. 117). TFC as developed in the Oregon Social Learning Center Model identifies three key principles of practice:

1. A proactive approach is used for dealing with antisocial behavior and teaching prosocial behavior.
2. Program staff and TFC parent's roles are stratified to create maximum flexibility and impact.

3. A consistent positive environment is created for program youth (For a detailed description of the "Multidimensional Treatment Foster Care Model", see Chamberlain, 2003)

A variety of support and clinical staff including case managers, therapists, foster parent recruiters, trainers and lay telephone helpers assist and support the primary foster parents in their work with youth and provide as well outreach to the youth's biological parents.

At this point, the evidence base for treatment foster care, while still modest, includes a range of descriptive, quasi-experimental and controlled clinical trials which report favorable outcomes in post-discharge adaptation and youth behavior, as well as treatment completion for youth who otherwise would be headed into residential treatment. Chamberlain notes a key limitation of the TFC research base as follows:

> "Results from preliminary studies on the efficacy of TFC are promising but there are clear limitations…for example, it is not known what are the necessary and sufficient components of the TFC model that lead to successful outcomes for the various populations of youngsters being served using this model".
> (Chamberlain, 2002: 137).

As with MST, there is considerable interest in many states and localities throughout the United States in replicating the TFC model within the service sectors of juvenile justice, child mental health and child welfare, in particular as an alternative to the more expensive forms of residential placement such as residential treatment.

Wraparaound Treatment

Wraparound Treatment is described as an approach to treatment that has developed over the last 15 years to help families with the most challenging children function more effectively in the community (Burchard, Bruns, & Burchard, 2002: 69). Other definitions include:

> "A definable planning process that results in a unique set of community services that are individualized for a child and family to achieve a positive set of outcomes." (Burns & Goldman, 1999 quoted in Burchard et. al.)

> "Wraparound is (an approach to child mental health treatment that is) child and family centered, focused on family strengths, community-based, culturally relevant, flexible and coordinated across agencies" (Vandenberg & Grealish 1998, Burchard, Burchard, Sewell & VanDenBerg, 1993 quoted in Burchard et. al., 2002: p.69)

Described by its originators as a "common sense" approach to child mental health treatment the core of which involves identifying the community services and supports that a family of a child with a serious mental health disorder needs and providing them as long as they are needed (Burchard, Bruns & Burchard, 2002). Services and other forms of helping are strengths based and family-centered and highly individualized. Working in a collaborative team effort with families, the wraparound treatment team first identifies and then implements a coordinated set of interventions designed to address the child's primary mental health and behavioral concerns. From its origins in a few highly visible projects – Kaleidoscope in Chicago and the Alaska Youth Initiative in Alaska – Wraparound Treatment has been the object of demonstrations in a wide variety of community settings throughout North America and several national conferences have brought together practitioners, researchers, planners and parents to share the latest knowledge on implementation. A recent leadership conference at Duke University yielded a set of "essential elements" and "requirements for practice": for a detailed description of the wraparound approach, see Burchard, Bruns & Burchard (2002, pp. 72-73).

Burchard, Bruns and Burchard (2002) identify a research corpus on the Wraparound Treatment approach that consists of 15 studies including two recently completed randomized clinical trials (RCT's). While results generally favor the children receiving Wraparound Treatment in terms of decline of behavioral symptoms and fewer placement changes post termination, study limitations include questions of treatment documentation and treatment integrity among others. The authors note a clear need to "operationally define and measure adherence to the essential elements" of the (Wraparound) process in order to ensure consistency.

What then are similarities and differences of these four promising interventions and by what criteria should they be assessed? Despite some apparent differences – MST, for example, relies most heavily on master's level trained professionals for service delivery – a recent review by Burns & Hoagwood notes several shared characteristics:

> "– All four interventions function as components in a "system of care" and adhere to "systems of care" values
> – All are delivered in a community – home, school, neighborhood – context as opposed to an office
> – All, with exception of MST as noted above, make extensive use of parents, volunteers, and other informal helpers
> – All four interventions have operated in multiple service sectors: mental health, juvenile justice, child welfare
> – All were developed and evaluated in "real world" community settings thus enhancing external validity
> – All lay claim to being less expensive to provide than institutional care."

(Burns & Hoagwood, 2002, p. 7)

As noted earlier, evaluations of virtually all of these interventions highlights the need for careful analysis and identification of the core intervention components themselves as a necessary requisite to the development of what truly may be described as "evidence-based practices" in child mental health. As our earlier reported experiences with "intensive family preservation services" suggest, there are considerable difficulties that ensue when one moves forward with increasingly rigorous outcome studies absent a clear and precise understanding of what are thought to be critical and essential intervention components. Thorough documentation, therefore, of these and other model interventions is a task of the highest priority in child mental health research. I offer the following twelve criteria as a possible template for understanding model service interventions:

- Purpose;
- Knowledge base;
- Theory of change;
- Target population;
- Indications/contraindications;
- Settings where practiced;
- Core principles;
- Essential elements of intervention;
- Roles/staffing;
- Cultural sensitivity;
- Support infrastructure;
- Empirical validation (Adapted from Whittaker & Tracy, 1989, pp. 192-193; more detailed description available from the author).

Taken together, do these and other promising interventions constitute something greater than the sum of their parts? How should we think of them collectively?

My third main question takes us from a "within" program analysis to one that focuses on this cluster of novel interventions, including others, and tries to identify an integrating concept or construct that might potentially unite them and cause us to "look" differently at them: Indeed, is the whole something greater than the sum of the parts when it comes to child mental health intervention?

As noted, all of these interventions are based on "systems of care" thinking and what might be thought of as an "ecological approach to treatment. That is, in both their assessment protocols and intervention arrays, they take careful account of the impact of both proximate and distal environments as both sources of challenge *and* support – "risk" and "opportunity". Moreover, each in its own way works to actively re-structure existing environments (family/peers/neighborhood) to meet developmental needs of children with special challenges and to reinforce parents in their parenting roles. Often, this involves creation of a specialized, albeit temporary, environment within and through which the primary help or treatment occurs. I suggest that this specialized "environment" – what I will call a "prosthetic environment" is the unifying thread that both knits these discrete interventions together and reflects in their collectivity something more than simply the sum total of their constituent parts.

In fact, the term "prosthetic environment" has some limited currency in the mental health field – in certain programs for autistic children, for example – and in the field of adult dementias where it has been defined thus: "...(an environment) which can help to compensate for loss of mental and physical disabilities while reinforcing and building upon the abilities that remain" (*Designing Facilities for People with Dementia*, 1991 p. 6 emphasis added). For our purposes, I will define "prosthetic environment" as follows:

> A "prosthetic environment" involves the planful use of a purposefully constructed multi-dimensional environment to enhance or provide treatment, education, socialization, support and protection to children with identified mental health needs and their families.

At its most fundamental level, the notion of a "prosthetic environment" is based on the idea that we need to broaden our therapeutic vision from a singular focus on individual child or even family functioning to include a deeper, more contextualized picture of *person-in-environment*. This view seeks to refine our understanding of "environment in all of its multiple levels and restore it to a position of centrality in both assessment and intervention. In many ways, this reflects a general movement in mental health and interpersonal helping away from more narrowly constructed personal therapies and toward more ecologically based forms of practice (Kemp, Whittaker, & Tracy, 1997).The theoretical and empirical underpinnings for a "prosthetic environment" are both numerous and varied. In the interests of time I will simply enumerate some of the more significant ones here:

- Bronfenbrenner's seminal contribution to understanding "the ecology of human development" and its implications for both developmental research and intervention (Bronfenbrenner, 1979; Moen, Elder, & Luscher, 1995) which drew our attention from the sterility of child development laboratories to the richly textured, lived environments of parents and children.
- The growing corpus of empirical research on "risk" and "protective" factors and the accompanying body of work on childhood "resiliency", all of which directs our attention to those factors at the individual, familial, peer, neighborhood and macro-societal levels that create or constrain opportunities for healthy development (Masten & Coatsworth, 1998; Sameroff & Gutman, 2004)
- The literature on "milieu therapy" including the singular

contributions of Fritz Redl & David Wineman (1957;1966) and later "psycho-educational" contributions by Nicholas Hobbs (1982) and others (Trieschman, Whittaker, & Brendtro, 1969/1979) which offer templates for organizing total living environments for both mastery and healing.
- Holistic models of community centered rehabilitation for adult psychiatric patients such as that developed in the pioneering "Fountain House" model in New York City and the path-breaking work of Gerald Caplan (1974) and others on the powerful role of informal support systems in psychiatric rehabilitation.
- Applied behavior analytic studies, most notably the work of psychologists Robert Wahler at the University of Tennessee which early on alerted practitioners to the negative effects of social isolation and "insularity" on parenting behavior and the critical function of social supports in the maintenance of treatment gains (Dumas & Wahler, 1983)
- Finally, the rich tradition of "orthopedagogy" in Belgium and The Netherlands, a tradition that broadens our focus and raises our vision in child treatment to a focus on use of the child's total "life-space" as both means and context for "learning through living".

Clearly, many other contributions – such as Winnicott's concept of the "holding environment" ("social provision of a safe context where an individual can elaborate his or her unique individuality") – bear relevance to the notion of a "prosthetic environment" (for a recent treatment of Winnicott, see: Rodman [2003]). What I offer here is much more a rough sketch, than a fully developed construct. My hope is that it helps us to do two things:

1. Re-frame our task in child mental health from a narrow conception of symptomatic treatment achieved through serial application of discrete interventions and towards the kind of ecologically grounded, cross-system approaches (MST, TFC and Wraparound) described earlier.

2. Offer a possible conceptual bridge between these three innovative model programs and others that allows us to see them as perhaps distinctive pathways—each creating a uniquely designed environmental space within and through which interventions are delivered—towards a common goal of improved life outcomes for troubled children and their families.

What challenges lie ahead in implementing effective child mental health services in the domains of policy, practice and evaluative research?

For this last section of my presentation, I will briefly touch on three areas of challenge in implementing the kinds of service innovations I have discussed earlier. I select these challenges as they represent three different levels from broad scale policy implementation, to the organizational level of the service program, to the individual level of the child mental health practitioner. I caution that these challenges fully derive from a U.S. context and I lay no claim to their relevance for the European child and family services scene. I do note however, that the speed with which we in the states seem both to be importing service innovations—such as "family group conferencing"—from other cultural contexts and exporting our own home grown varieties—such as "intensive family preservation"—makes even more critical the need for cross-national dialogues. In child and family services at least, we all have a contribution to make to a conversation that is increasingly international in its scope.

The "scaling-up" challenge

As with "intensive family preservation" and "permanency planning" which preceded it, child & family service innovations such as the three identified earlier all present us with a similar challenge: how to move from the often impressive small scale, "pilot phase" of an innovation to broad scale implementation. Meeting this challenge means not only being clear about the critical components of the intervention, but having the infrastructure available to train others to use these in ways that will insure fidelity to the original treatment design. This process typically includes the development of staff training protocols, treatment manuals, training personnel, supervisory structures and quality control procedures. In addition, it often means creating and maintaining adequate administrative supports to help insure the program does not "drift" from its model fidelity. For example, in the early phases of disseminating intensive family preservation, there was considerable pressure from program administrators to raise caseload sizes from the recommended two families per worker (in the original Homebuilders model) to extend the program's impact, though this would clearly have a negative impact on the intensity of service the family workers were able to provide. In my experience, this particular aspect of "bringing programs to scale" is often complicated by the fact that novel and innovative child and family programs often have charismatic "founders" associated with them who may have neither the expertise nor capacity to re-create the original model in widely dispersed locations. Of the models discussed earlier, perhaps Multisystemic Therapy (MST) has the most fully developed protocols and follow-up procedures for replication, in large measure because the lack of attention to treatment fidelity is thought to negatively affect individual child and thus program outcomes.

A related problem within the broad "systems of care" philosophy involves the integration of these three and other model interventions in a single organizational context. While the "systems of care" notion acknowledges the need for multiple services including some specialized residential provision, much work needs to be done to ascertain the relative proportions of different service strategies in a given organization: how much Wraparound? Treatment Foster Care? Or Multisystemic Treatment in a given community's "system of care"? To borrow a culinary example, it is as if we have been given the "ingredients" for a recipe for improved child mental health services, absent the correct proportions. One promising locus for conducting studies on the integration of discrete treatment innovations is the service agency itself.

The challenge of developing applied research capacity in existing service agencies

Much of child & family mental health services in the United States is delivered in the context of voluntary service agencies that typically receive funding from local and state statutory agencies, as well as a mix of private sources. Usually, these agencies operate as non-profit organizations with professional staff serving under a citizen board of directors. In many communities, voluntary child and family agencies have continuously provided valuable services for a considerable period of time. Many began as orphanages and then developed over time into multi-service centers offering a wide range of services which typically include some mix of: residential and day treatment, treatment foster care, specialized schooling, mentoring programs, family support and intensive family preservation, transitional living and substance abuse treatment programs. One such agency to which I am principal research consultant in our Pacific northwest traces its roots to the late 1860's when it was created as a residential home for children of pioneers who lost their parents in the arduous journey westward along the Oregon Trail.

While the primary mission of these child & family agencies remains service delivery, a small subset of them has made an investment in an applied research capacity. This typically includes a computerized information system which allows for tracking of program outcomes and service inputs and is achieved through the systematic analysis of routinely gathered data. In many ways, this agency centered research capacity offers a unique opportunity to answer many of the empirical questions I raised earlier: particularly those having to do with the integration of model interventions – such as Multisystemic Treatment, Treatment Foster Care and Wraparound Services- in a single agency structure. I am presently involved in one such agency – Trillium Family Services in the State of Oregon- which is in the process of transforming itself from a purely service oriented organization to one committed equally to the development of evidence-based knowledge about effective child mental health services: if you will, an "experimenting child mental health agency". We believe the pathways for achieving such a transformation involve several critical steps which we are now in the process of implementing:

- Clear and unequivocal commitment to the *systems of care philosophy* underpinning our national child mental initiative (CASSP) as outlined earlier in this presentation.
- Creation of *key partnerships* with university and institute-based researchers to help guide and shape the agency's clinical research agenda.
- *Logic Modeling* of all child & family service programs to identify key key process and outcome variables and the "theory of change" embedded within these. This activity is conducted through a staff team effort and was recently completed for all of the agency's 28 discrete programs. For further detail on logic modeling in the agency setting, see: (Savas, 1996; Savas & Ruffolo, 2001).
- *In-depth evaluation* of selected service programs: in this instance, priority was given to the evaluation of a model service effort developed in collaboration with the Oregon Department of Mental Health as an alternative to traditional residential treatment (Woodbridge & Huang, 2000).
- A final step involves *benchmarking* with evidence-based child mental health programs of national significance (e.g., MST, TFC, Wraparound). While this does not necessarily mean faithful adoption of each of these model programs, it does mean that the agency is able to clearly locate its own programs and practices in relation to what are judged to be innovative and evidence-based practices: indicating areas of congruence and, where appropriate, providing clear rationales for service variations to meet local conditions (Whittaker et al., 2004; Hoagwood, Burns, & Weisz, (2002).

I believe the potential for a national network of a small number of such agencies – a national network of experimenting child mental health agencies- will fill a critical and at present unfilled niche in our overall child mental health research capacity (Hoagwood, 2003).

Professional practitioners to "personal scientists"

In conclusion, I wish to address a personal challenge directly to individual child, youth and family workers: perhaps, in particular, those who are just beginning their careers as orthopedagogues, youth workers, specialized teachers, social workers and others. As an educator, I continue to be impressed with the energy, vitality and passionate commitment of those young persons committed to a life's work of helping vulnerable children and their families. In the United States and in Europe, we have always attracted those with an altruistic impulse: a desire to serve and to make a difference in the lives of individual children.

In addition to affirming your commitment to helping, I urge you equally to embrace the challenge of understanding the web of complex factors that predisposes some children to stand resilient in the face of overwhelming odds, while others suffer a range of adverse life outcomes. I urge you to try and tease out those critical factors in helping that seem to make a difference: to document and evaluate your own practice, to be alive to new ideas, to listen carefully to what your clients are telling you and to remain ever skeptical of "conventional wisdom".

In short, I ask to add an equal measure of *analysis* to your *altruism*. To see yourselves as what I would term "personal scientists", as well as professional helpers. You have a crucial role to play in the development of new knowledge which will aid vulnerable children and families. You are the key to discerning what is "In the best interests of the child".

References

Bickman, L. (1999). Practice makes perfect and other myths about mental health services. *American Psychologist, 54*, 965-977.

Bronfenbrenner, U. (1979) *The ecology of human development: Experiments by nature and design.* Cambridge, MA.: Harvard University Press.

Burchard, J. D., Bruns, E. J., & Burchard, M. I. (2002). The wraparound approach. In B. J. Burns & K. Hoagwood (Eds.), *Community treatment for youth: Evidence-based interventions for severe emotional and behavioral disorders* (pp. 69-91). New York, NY: Oxford University Press.

Burns, B. J., & Goldman, S. K. (1999). Promising practices in wraparound for children with serious emotional disturbance and their families. *Systems of care: Promising practices in children's mental health, 1998 series, Volume IV.* Washington, DC: Center for Effective Collaboration and Practice, American Institutes for Research.

Burns, B. J., & Hoagwood, K. (Eds.). (2002). *Community treatment for youth: Evidence-based interventions for severe emotional and behavioral disorders.* New York, NY: Oxford University Press.

Caplan, G. (1974). *Support systems in community mental health.* New York: Behavioral Publications.

Chamberlain, P. (2002). Treatment foster care. In K. Hoagwood & B. J. Burns (Eds.), *Community treatment for youth: Evidence-based interventions for severe emotional and behavioral disorders* (pp. 117-139). New York, NY: Oxford University Press.

Chamberlain, P. (2003). *Treating juvenile offenders: Advances made through the Oregon Multidimensional Treatment Foster Care model.* Washington, DC: American Psychological Association.

Chamberlain, P., & Reid, J. B. (1998). Comparison of two community alternatives to incarceration for chronic juvenile offenders. *Journal of Consulting and Clinical Psychology, 66*, 624-633.

Designing facilities for people with dementia [microform]. (1991). Pub info Ottawa: Health and Welfare Canada, Institutional and Professional Services Division, HSPB, Design for Health Unit.

Dishion, T. J., McCord, J., & Poulin, F. (1999). When interventions harm: Peer groups and problem behavior. *American Psychologist, 54*, 755-765.

Dumas, J. E., & Wahler, R. G. (1983). Predictors of treatment outcome in parent skills training: Mother insularity and socioeconomic disadvantage. *Behavioral Assessment, 5*, 301-313.

Epstein, M. H., Kutash, K., & Duchnowski, A. (Eds.). (1998). *Outcomes for children and youth with emotional and behavioral disorders and their families: Programs and evaluation best practices.* Austin, TX: Pro-Ed.

Henggeler, S. W., & Lee, T. (2003). Multisystemic treatment of serious clinical problems. In A. E. Kazdin & J. R. Weisz (Eds.), *Evidence-based psychotherapies for children and adolescents* (pp. 301-322). New York, NY: The Guilford Press.

Henggeler, S. W., Schoenwald, S. K., Borduin, C. M., Rowland, M. D., & Cunningham, P. B. (1998). *Multisystemic treatment of antisocial behavior in children and adolescents.* New York, NY: Guilford Press.

Hoagwood, K. (2003). Evidence-based practice in children's mental health services: What do we know? Why aren't we putting it to use? *Data Matter – National Technical Assistance Center for Children's Mental Health, 6,* 4-5.

Hoagwood, K, Burns, B. J., & Weisz, J. R. (2002). A profitable conjunction: from science to service in children's mental health. In B. J. Burns & K. Hoagwood (Eds.), *Community treatment for youth: Evidence-based interventions for severe emotional and behavioral disorders* (pp. 327-339). New York, NY: Oxford University Press.

Hobbs, N. (1982). *The troubled and troubling child.* San Francisco: Jossey-Bass.

Kazdin, A. E., & Weisz, J. R. (1998). Identifying and developing empirically supported child and adolescent treatments. *Journal of Consulting & Clinical Psychology, 66,* 19-36.

Kazdin, A. E., & Weisz, J. R. (2003). *Evidence-based psychotherapies for children and adolescents.* New York, NY: The Guilford Press.

Kemp, S. P, Whittaker, J. K., & Tracy, E. M. (1997). *Person-environment practice: The social ecology of interpersonal helping.* New York: Aldine de Gruyter.

Kutash, K., & Robbins Rivera, V. (1996). *What works in children's mental health services?* Baltimore, MD: Paul H. Brookes Publishing Company.

Landsverk, J., & Garland, A. F. (1999). Foster care and pathways to mental health services. In G. Dale & J. C. Kendall (Eds.), *The foster care crisis: Translating research into policy and practice.* Lincoln, NE: University of Nebraska Press.

Masten, A. S., & Coatsworth, J. D. (1998). The development of competence in favorable and unfavorable environments. *American Psychologist, 53,* 205-230.

Moen, P., Elder, G., & Luscher, K. (Eds.). (1995). *Examining lives in context: Perspectives on the ecology of human development.* Washington, D.C.: The American Psychological Association.

National Research Council and Institute of Medicine. (2000). *From neurons to neighborhoods: The science of early childhood development.* Washington, D.C.: National Academy Press.

Poulin, F., Dishion, T. J., & Burraston, B. (2001). 3-year iatrogenic effects associated with aggregating high risk adolescents in cognitive-behavioral preventive interventions. *Applied Developmental Science, 5,* 214-224.

Redl, F. (1966). *When we deal with children.* New York: Free Press

Redl, F., & Wineman, D. (1957). *The aggressive child.* New York: Free Press.

Rodman, F. R. (2003). *Winnicott: His life and work.* Cambridge, MA: Da Capo Press.

Sameroff, A. J., & Gutman, L. M. (2004). Contributions of risk research to the design of successful interventions. In P. Allen-Meares & M. W. Fraser (Eds.), *Intervention with children and adolescents: An interdisciplinary perspective* (pp. 9-27). Boston: Allyn & Bacon.

Savas, S. A. (1996). How do we propose to help children and families? In P. J. Pecora, W. R. Seelig, F. A. Zirps, & S. M. Davis (Eds.), *Quality im-*

provement and evaluation in child and family services (pp. 35-53). Washington, DC: Child Welfare League of America.
Savas, S. A., & Ruffolo, M. C. (2001). Using a three-phase decision-making model to integrate existing practices. In M. Hernandez (Ed.), *Developing outcome strategies in children's mental health* (pp. 167-183). Baltimore, MD: Paul H. Brookes Publishing Company.
Schoenwald, S. K., & Rowland, M. D. (2002). Multisystemic therapy. In B. J. Burns & K. Hoagwood (Eds.), *Community treatment for youth: Evidence-based interventions for severe emotional and behavioral disorders* (pp. 91-116). New York, NY: Oxford University Press.
Schoenwald, S. K., Borduin, C. K., & Henggeler, S. W. (1998). Multisystemic therapy: Changing the natural and service ecologies of adolescents and families. In M. H. Epstein, K. Kutash, & A. Duchnowski (Eds.), *Outcomes for children and youth with emotional and behavioral disorders and their families: Programs and evaluation best practices* (pp.485-511). Austin, TX: Pro-Ed.
Shonkoff, J. P., & Meisels, S. J. (Eds.). (2000). *Handbook of early childhood intervention, 2nd Edition.* New York, NY: Cambridge University Press.
Stroul, B. A., & Friedman, R. M. (1986). *A system of care for severely emotionally disturbed children & youth.* Washington, DC: CASSP Technical Assistance Center, Georgetown University, Child Development Center.
Trieschman, A. E., Whittaker, J. K., & Brendtro, L. K. (1969/1979). *The other 23 hours: Child care work with emotionally disturbed children in a therapeutic milieu.* New York: Aldine de Gruyter.
U.S. Department of Health and Human Services (1999). *Mental health: A report of the Surgeon General.* Rockville, MD: U.S. Department of Health and Human Services, Substance Abuse and Mental Health Services Administration, National Institutes of Health, National Institute of Mental Health.
U.S. Public Health Service (2000). *Report of the Surgeon General's Conference on Children's Mental Health: A National Action Agenda.* Washington, DC: Department of Health and Human Services.
Weisz, J. R., & Kazdin, A. E. (2003). *Evidence-based psychotherapies for children and adolescents* (pp. 439-451). New York, NY: The Guilford Press.
Whittaker, J. K. (2004). The re-invention of residential treatment: An agenda for research & practice. *Child & Adolescent Psychiatric Clinics of North America: Special Issue on Residential Treatment* (B.M. Leventhal, M.D., Editor). Elsevier Science, 13, 267-278.
Whittaker, J. K., & Tracy, E. M. (1989). *Social treatment: An introduction to interpersonal helping in social work practice. 2nd edition.* New York: Aldine de Gruyter.
Whittaker, J. K., Greene, K., Schubert, D., Blum, R., Cheng, K., Blum, K., Reed, N., Scott, K., Roy, R., & Savas, S.A. (2004). *Integrating evidence-based practice in the child mental health agency: A template for clinical and organizational change.* Unpublished manuscript.
Woodbridge, M. W., & Huang, L. N. (2000). *Systems of care: Promising practices in children's mental health. Vol. 2, Using evaluation data to*

manage, improve, market, and sustain children's services. Washington, DC: National Technical Assistance Center.

6

An American training program for parent-child communication assisted by an interactive and evaluative CD-ROM adapted for French-speaking countries

Gérard Pithon & Donald Gordon

Why has a family education therapist arrived at conceiving a training program for parent-child communication and the resolution of educational problems using an interactive CD-ROM (Gordon, 1998)? To what need is he responding? What are the public concerns? What are the underlying practices and theories of this program? What are the advantages and impediments of this type of technology over conventional therapies? What are the possible uses of this CD-ROM with parents, teachers, and therapists in family education? What are the principle results of the outcome studies in English-speaking countries? What French cultural adaptation problems would this program encounter (Gordon, Pithon, Terrisse, 2003)? What cultural validation studies must be undertaken for this adaptation (Bédard, Larose, Terrisse, Pithon, 2003)? These are the principle questions, which will be addressed in this interview between the program developer and one of the translators.

(Interviewer:) When and why have you worked in the area of parenting education?

(Gordon:) I had first taken my internship in psychology at the Oregon Health Sciences Center, and I specialized in parent-child therapy. After many years of practice of clinical psychology with children with difficulties, I realized that working with the parents was one of the most beneficial methods of improving children's appropriate behavior. It is thus that I am focused on efficient methods for improving parental competence. It was necessary first to search for programs, which could be made available to a great number of parents having difficulty with their children. Then I decided to develop a program that would respond to the most frequent problems of these parents (authority problems in step-families, associations with deviant peers, involvement with school work, conflict between siblings...), of which the majority simply need some very specific guidance, to see some brief examples of how to handle the situation. Only a minority need true therapy.

Which are the principle sources of inspiration, your theoretical and clinical orientations?

Little by little I had incorporated several standard parent-training methods into my practice (active listening of Rogers, educational contracts of Patterson, for example). One works primarily on relationship enhancement and the other on parental control of children's behavior. Thus my main inspiration came from several different approaches such as social learning theory (Bandura, 1986; Mahoney & Patterson, 1986; Patterson, 1986) which emphasizes the power of models (parents) to influence behavior through imitation (by children); cognitive-behavioral theories of Beck (1976). Also the approach of Alexander and Parsons (1973) where it is important for people to change their ineffective thought patterns and thus to change their behavior; and finally the family systems theories (Minuchin, 1974, for example) which allows a better understanding of the meaning of our behavior in the context of one's status and role relative to the other family members.

Can you give some examples of how you combined the theoretical views of these authors in your program "Parenting Wisely"?

Social learning theory (Bandura, Patterson) emphasizes how readily children learn from their parents as their primary role models, through two mechanisms. One is role modeling, where children copy the behavior, mannerisms, and attitudes of their parents. An example would be parents who frequently spank or hit their children when the children misbehave because they are frustrated and angry with them. These children will learn to hit others (children, parents) when they are frustrated and angry when they do not get their way. The other mechanism is through conditioning, where parents, wittingly or not, provide rewards and punishments that encourage or discourage certain actions by their children. An example would be parents who do not pay much attention to their children when they are playing cooperatively, but pay immediate attention when they fight. So children learn that if they want their parents to notice them, as most children do, they should fight. In "Parenting Wisely", I teach parents that they are role models and I teach them how their attention is rewarding their children's behavior, and that they need to become more aware and intentional about the power of their attention. I also teach them how to systematically (consistently) use rewards and sanctions to improve their children's behavior and their relationship with them.

Cognitive-behavioral theory emphasizes the close relationship that often exists between thoughts, feelings, and behavior. Therapy based on this theory seeks to change a person's thoughts as a method of changing their reactions to certain situations. For example, a parent usually becomes angry when their child will not keep their bedroom clean because they think this means the child either doesn't respect them or is being willfully disobedient. If the parents change their thoughts about the child's motives so that they think it is normal for children not to want to clean their bedrooms, they will become less angry about the messy bedroom. Subsequently, the parents will be able to handle the situation better, or lower their expectations. In "Parenting Wisely", I teach parents and children how the kinds of motives (negative, positive, benign) that they attribute to each other hurt or help the relationship, and to combine this cognitive approach with applying consequences in a purposeful way.

Family systems theory emphasizes that each family member's actions influence all other family members. In "Parenting Wisely" we teach parents how parental conflict has a negative effect on children's behavior, and that children may play one parent against the other when the parents do not act in unison. We also teach parents how their own parenting (and marital) relationships are hurt when they feel stressed from work, or an individual condition such as depression. For example, we recommend that when parents are feeling depressed, that they increase their contact with friends and other social support, and that this will help them react to their children's misbehavior more calmly and with more purpose.

Which are the principal intervention methods that you have used to affect parents?

I have a lot of experience observing and working with interactions between parents and children as to their system of communication in their family. To this effect I at first used discussion and direction with family members. I used other methods with parents: role-playing, modeling new educational strategies, and resolving problems that remain in the families (conflict, escalating violence). I made use of what is now called "parental coaching". Around 1988 I also used videotapes with parents which were focused on family education and which give illustrations of "good practice". The videotapes complemented well also all the methods, which I have used before developing the CD-ROM.

What are the advantages of using videotapes for training parents?

Video is especially useful in that it helps the parents understand good parenting practices and to imitate these practices. With video, both behaviors and emotions are shown, and actions can be easily retained in memory to guide a parents' future performance – much more so than words or abstract ideas, which is what most parent educators and therapists use. While each treatment approach is imperfect, each therapist tweaks the approach according to the situation. Today we can search inventories of "best practices" and the video training approach is useful for so many in the world.

What are the main disadvantages for using videocassettes to train parents?

After my personal experience and that of the graduate students working under my supervision, we have found that videos watched in a group or with a therapist don't offer sufficient privacy for optimal learning. Videos viewed at home are not always watched completely or attentively. In effect, videos present information to be received passively. Parents are often tired and sleep while watching television. Fortunately audio-visual methods and technologies have rapidly improved, such that interactive CD-ROMs overcome the disadvantages of videocassettes. Interactive CD-ROM requires you to react, to make choices and comments on your choices. But before this technology arrived, I used videos of different authors for example (Forgatch & Patterson, 1989), and then I produced videos myself (Arbuthnot & Gordon, 1994, for example). These videos have been widely used for at-risk populations and are very popular in the United States. I envision the same happening for CD-ROMs, but not quickly. With "Parenting Wisely" the conception and production was very time consuming and expensive.

Considering these costs, why promote the "new technologies" in parental education when there are already several intervention methods in this domain?

Paradoxically, because of my interest in working with disadvantaged families that easily cannot benefit from therapies or of traditional educational approaches, we need to turn to technology. These families have few economic resources, cultural norms, or access to attorneys (to protect their rights) to react quickly as soon as the first difficulties arise. It was necessary, therefore, to try to develop for them simple and useful programs they could use without assistance. The most disadvantaged families are often ashamed to seek help, which they feel is demeaning, so self-administered programs are less threatening. Economically advantaged families can more easily and promptly assist their children, or to be counseled by friends, specialists, indeed even lawyers when the children break the law. Society generally blames, labels, and stigmatizes more easily "risky behaviors" from low-income families. These stereotypes impede prevention work. Risk factors in these disadvantaged environments are very plentiful, so we should invest in secondary prevention earlier in families' lives.

But what are the principal difficulties and obstacles for disadvantaged families to access specialized interventions in parental education?

In my clinical practice, I have noticed that these parents have a great deal more difficulty in both appreciating the benefits of family therapy or parent education, and accessing them. For example, some of the real physical obstacles for these parents discourage them. They must be able to locate a competent practitioner, find childcare, get themselves to the therapist's office punctually (with unreliable transportation), and be able to arrange with their employers to miss work to make most appointments.

There are subjective barriers these families face. First, they often do not see a connection between their children's misbehavior and their parenting, so they do not even consider seeking help with their methods. These parents are more likely to feel shame or guilt for seeking help than more educated, advantaged families, and sometimes the practitioners subtly communicate negative judgment. Affluent families often are proud of seeking professional help.

The theoretical orientation of some traditional therapies is a particularly poor fit for disadvantaged families. Approaches that require parents to reflect on unconscious processes, to work on their own personal histories, and to think abstractly about these issues are more appropriate for higher functioning people with higher intelligence and a good education. Such approaches take very long periods of time and thus only reach a relatively small number of people. One reason practitioners would persist in delivering these inappropriate methods for a wide variety of families, for whom the methods were not developed, is because the practitioners were not evaluating, objectively, the outcomes, or that they do not value objective evaluations. They may also not know of effective interventions for these families.

We work with the parents with this CD-ROM approach often before the need for a family therapist, from a perspective of secondary prevention. We use an empowering approach that reinforces their strengths and entices them to both build on strengths and remediate deficiencies. Our approach therefore is supplementary to the traditional methods and does not displace their functioning.

How do you describe the parental educational competencies in order to reinforce them?

We work on the three general areas of competencies. First, basic knowledge on the psychological development of the child and adolescent for instance. It is necessary to transmit this information and verify its acquisition (declarative knowledge), which is comparatively easy to do. Another area of parental competencies is the utilization of parenting skills, such as how to resolve conflict, communicate effectively, supervising children, giving feedback, assign domestic responsibilities to all family members, and how to discipline effectively. Other competencies are how to establish educational contracts, as early as preadolescence, where the child learns to express, negotiate and defend its interests while accepting the consensus rules that arise from the process with all the other members of the family. The third area of competence is appropriate educational attitudes such as child acceptance, the interest in listening, and making benign or positive attributions for why children misbehave.

In the CD-ROM we illustrate, with video clips, each of these competencies in various situations. These "visual blueprints" act as guides to their behavior in similar situations with their own children. We also provide written descriptions and explanations of these, and a glossary of terms, which the parents can access through hypertext. Finally we provide exercises in a workbook that promote skill practice and guide parents in their daily use.

Why and when did you conceive this CD-ROM to help parents?

I began this "innovation" essentially to reply to the specific needs of the families that have difficulties with the education of their children, as mentioned above. These families are increasing in number, and they require specific service, practical and straightforward. It was necessary to find a structured approach that can reply to these needs in the first (and often, only) session.

The possible choices in terms of methods of intervention are numerous, but they divide according to two significant economical considerations. One set of methods works better while a practitioner sees in his/her office a small number of parents that can come "to consult". However, the practitioner can work only eight hours a day. This type of intervention that touches few people costs comparatively much. To be able to reach a substantially larger number of parents with the aid of technology and mass media seems worth the investment. For either approach, it is necessary to determine which produces more positive change. Given that economy of scale and consistency characterizes technological approaches, and that many therapists are not effective, it was easy for me to favor technology. These approaches are not mutually exclusive since we observed, for example, that many parents accept more easily traditional therapies after using the CD-ROM (Paull, Caldwell, & Klimm, 2001).

Which are the principal reasons to promote the new technologies, in the form of a CD-ROM, notably, in the domain of education and training?

The CD-ROM is before all an interactive tool, that parents explore according to their concerns of the moment (conflicts between a child and his step-father, dispute between siblings, etc.). When they need it, according to its availability, in privacy, and which responds to their learning style. It allows a personalized and confidential evaluation, in real time, and gives to the parent the ability to check his progress privately, a process that reinforces his attention and his motivation. The scientific literature on these applied new technologies (interactive video, CD-ROM) in training various people is generally very favorable as for their usefulness and their effectiveness (McNeil, & Nelson, 1991; Niemiec, & Walberg, 1987). More and more companies ask their employees to improve their skills with multimedia tools (CD-ROMs or online courses).

The CD-ROM favors learning by imitation (Bandura 1987). The use of videotaped examples of attitudes and skills are powerful methods for the children as well as for the parents! Webster-Stratton's (1992) research shows how videocassettes operate to change the attitudes and the behavior of the parents as well as therapy or discussion groups. For many people it is easier to remember video scenes than spoken words or text. The parents are able to recall these scenes from memory when they need them. They can use the CD-ROM privately, at an agency, their home, or their workplace. They are therefore less defensive, they often accept better guidance from the computer than from a practitioner, from whom they may feel or imagine judgment. Additionally, in the video scenes on the CD-ROM are similar parents having similar difficulties with their children, and the parent that uses the CD-ROM sees role models that change their methods. The parents are therefore very active in the construction of their own learning; they check and manage their own progress: the learning style, the timing, the type of response, which they accept, or not according to the problems that they encounter. Parents find the scenes interesting, funny, and realistic, which focuses their attention.

In our CD-ROM, we stimulate interest with the form of a game or of challenges: "what would you do if you had to deal with this situation?" On the other hand we recommend that they expand their repertoire of responses by the completion of the supplementary exercises in the parents' workbook, in order to consolidate and deepen their skills. Their first experience is to resolve concrete cases and then to go more deeply into skill development later with the workbook. Practice before theory, in a way! Thus the CD-ROM is a self-contained transparent program that is widely used and therefore frequently evaluated. These evaluations, qualitative and quantitative, permit improvement of the program.

This "transparency" renders the CD-ROM perfectible, of course, but not does it also facilitate their illegal copying?

As for all the media it is necessary to preserve the rights of the designers, manufacturers and editors, especially if one wants to have these products improved quickly, for it is necessary to be able to attract investment! If the evaluations of certain inventions in the social science domain prove useful and effective, where profit margins are difficult to achieve, it is necessary that the authorities, and the professional associations, make decisions that protect these inventions.

Are the practices of therapists who drift away from effective treatments or of popular "gurus" important?

The popular "gurus" tend to be fooled by their popularity into thinking that they, and the methods they teach, are effective. In the case of drift or slippage from effective treatment protocols, this happens without the therapist's awareness, but can result in the elimination or dilution of effective treatment components

There are a lot of young enthusiasts that want to become therapists. Their motivations are numerous. They are often altruistic, but also search for a certain prestige, and some seek a power over vulnerable persons. It is difficult to monitor practices done in private by trainees learning these methods. Effective practice means the repetition of validated treatment methods. Unfortunately it is human for therapists to tire of repetition, and they experiment, consciously or not, with new methods that may not be validated.

What are the various uses of this program?

This program is quite versatile, and can be used by parents in groups or individually, with parents in difficulty, or with concerned parents who want to better manage their families' educational and training problems. It can equally be used to complement the work of social workers and therapists, who are overloaded with families in difficulty. The program is used in groups of parents where an experienced facilitator who submits the problems to the group while projecting the video scenes with a multimedia projector connected to a computer. The group proposes solutions, examines their advantages and disadvantages, then views the solutions, and their critiques, proposed by the CD-ROM. Finally the group completes workbook exercises in class and as homework.

The parents individually can use this program with the consultation of a counselor or family therapist, or with a professional educator. The program can also be accessed directly by the parents in a library, or a resource center in the neighborhood, school, or local association. Parents can also borrow the program to use at home. Certain parents want to use this program as a couple, indeed even with their children. This becomes a family intervention (without a professional) that increases healthy family communication. This family intervention takes more time, but often illuminates parents' views of themselves when their children point out that they use ineffective methods.

The workbook is used most often individually, leaving each parent to his/her own rhythm. Training on hypothetical situations facilitates the parent's skill acquisition and generalization, and does so gently by using apparently mundane aspects of daily communication, followed by practice with more complex situations. Finally, the program can be used to resolve educational problems when it is given to teachers, and school social workers.

What are the principal effects of this program from the evaluations that have been conducted so far?

The research conducted in the United States on the effects of this program shows that the parents are satisfied, that their knowledge of the educational principles improves, and especially that they exhibit better parenting judgments and practices in problematic family situations (Gordon, 2000; Lagges & Gordon 1999). The children's behavior problems (behaviors with the peers, within the family, at school) diminish significantly, including those that already had been identified as delinquent. The relations within the family improve, such as: better communication, and organization of the family, reduction of the conflicts and domestic violence. The depressive state of the mothers improves because they participate actively to the program and because they discover that they can positively affect the behavior of their children. Most of the studies were conducted by my students (in thesis) therefore monitored by colleagues. Other studies were carried out independently with Paull, Caldwell, and Klimm (2001) in Massachusetts; Tattersoll in England, Pushak (2002) in Canada, O'Neill and Woodward (2003) in Ireland; Chetcuti in Australia (2004) and anticipate the results of the researchers with French language CD-ROM in Quebec (Terrisse, Larose, Bédard), in Belgium (Pourtois, Barras), in Switzerland (Perrez, Plancherel) and in France (Pithon, Prévôt).

But how illiterate parents, or those having serious educational difficulties are able to use this program?

The instructional design of the CD-ROM is very simple, the icons controlling navigation are easy to understand (point and click), with a tutorial in their use when users begin the program. The user can opt to have all text in the program read aloud by a narrator.

Did you find surprising results?

The CD-ROM program is being used by agencies serving very low functioning parents (i.e., the Department of Human Services in Athens, Ohio) to desensitize parents to working with computers, and also by an adult literacy program as the parent's first experience with computers. Certain parents became open to applying for jobs where they would have to use computers after they used this program. Their confidence in their social skills with other adults improved, which reciprocally reinforces use of these social skills within their families.

This program presents a certain idea of education, a certain culture or ideology. For instance, explicit discussion, elaboration of educational contracts, which is more or less a democratic ideal, but doesn't fit with other cultures. For instance how do you think traditional maghrebin parents, or gypsy families could accept this program?

The debate on this subject remains open and without clear answers. But I await the results of your research on this subject! Cross-cultural psychology warns us against the intrusions of certain dominant cultural practices that do not respect the traditions, indeed the identities, of other cultures. If one takes extreme cases, as the clitorectomies of women for example, everyone should condemn these practices whatever the cultural values they hold. Other practices seem to be in discussion in France such as the Islamic veil in the public schools. It is necessary sometimes for the experts to debate publicly certain subjects and take the time to share their conclusions with legislators, who might have to decide on this issue. Within the families there is the same debate while knowing that no culture is above the laws of the adopted country. The right of the family evolves, and our program is not in contradiction with the cultural values and laws of the countries where it is distributed. But it is necessary to know how to put into perspective the use of training programs such as ours and say clearly "here is what the researchers recommend today, take in this knowledge, and if you are certain that it will be harmful to your family, try at least to apply what you think can best help your family!"

If North African families are characterized by a top-down or autocratic approach, this program attempts to convince them that more collaborative discipline and communication strategies are more effective with adolescents. Within western cultures, not favoring autocratic methods with adolescents, there are many high-risk families who still use these methods. With these families, this program has been effective in increasing the collaborative democratic approach and reducing parent-child conflict. I would expect similar results with gypsy families. The program may have to be introduced somewhat differently, however.

What are the official recognitions that this program has received?

It is considered to be one of the most effective programs in the fight against behavior problems, school dropout, the consumption of drugs, and delinquency. The program received several designations: Exemplary Program from the Office of Juvenile Justice and Delinquency Prevention; Model Program from the Center for Substance Abuse Prevention (a division of United States Department of Health and Human Services); and Best Practices from the Centers for Disease Control. Two film documentaries of the British Broadcast Corporate on delinquency have featured this program.

References

Alexander, J. F., & Parsons, B. V. (1973) Short term behavioral intervention with delinquent families: Impact on family process and recidivism. *Journal of Abnormal Psychology, 81*, 219-226.

Arbuthnot, J. & Gordon, D. A. (1994). *Children in the Middle, Parents' Version.* Athens, OH: Center for Divorce Education.

Bandura, A. (1997). *Self efficacy.* New York: W.H. Freeman and Company.

Bandura, A. (1986). A model of causality in social learning theory. In M. J. Mahoney & Patterson G. R. (Eds.), Performance models for antisocial boys. *American Psychologist, 41,* 432-444.

Beck, A. (1976). *Cognitive therapy and the emotional disorders.* New York: International Universities Press.

Chetcuti, J. (2004). *Parent training with a CD-ROM program in Australia.* Unpublished dissertation, RMIT University, Melbourne, Australia.

Forgatch, M. & Patterson, G. R. (1989). *Parents and adolescents living together: Vol. 2, Family problem solving.* Eugene, OR: Castalia.

Freedman, E. (1985) (Eds.). *Cognition and psychotherapy.* New York: Plenum.

Gordon, D. A. (1998). *Parenting Wisely.* Athens (Ohio): Family Works, Inc.

Gordon, D. A., Pithon G., & Terrisse, B. (2003). *Être parents aujourd'hui* (manuel et cédérom). Québec, Montréal: Les Editions du Ponant. Distribué par: PAC MULTIMEDIA, 16 rue Jean Allemane 11100 Narbonne, France. E-mail: andreu.pierre2@wanadoo.fr

Harris, J. R. (1998). *The nurture assumption.* New York: The Free Press Simon and Schuster, Inc.

Hoskins, C., McFarlane, H., & Tattersall, A. (2002). *Greater Manchester Pathways Project: Parenting Wisely.* Technical report to the Youth Justice Board.

McNeil, B. J., & Nelson, K. R. (1991). Meta-analysis of interactive video instruction: A 10 year review of achievement effects. *Journal of Computer-Based Instruction, 18,* 1-6.

Minuchin, S. (1974). *Families and family therapy.* Cambridge: Harvard University Press.

Niemiec, R., & Walberg, H. J. (1987). Comparative effects of computer-assisted instruction: A synthesis of reviews. *Journal of Educational Computing Research, 3,* 19-37.

O'Neill, H., & Woodward, R. (in press) Evaluation of the Parenting Wisely CD-ROM parent-training program: An Irish replication. *Irish Journal of Psychology.*

Patterson, G.R. (1986). Performance models for antisocial boys. *American Psychologist, 41,* 432-444.

Paull, N., Caldwell, D., & Klimm, M. L. (2001). *Parental satisfaction and attitudes toward further parent training following use of Parenting Wisely.* Unpublished research report, Stanley Street Treatment and Resources, Fall River, MA.

Paull, N., Klimm, M. L., & Caldwell, D. (2001). *Use of Parenting Wisely in a community health clinic.* Technical report.

Pushak, R. (2002). *Group and individual parent training with Parenting Wisely*. Unpublished manuscript.

Webster-Stratton, C. (1992). Individually administered videotape parent training. "Who benefits?". *Cognitive Therapy and Research, 16*, 31-52.

7

The dynamics of screening and setting indications for treatment in an integrated system of child and youth care

Marc J. Noom, Erik J. Knorth & Henna J. Josias

Introduction

The system of child and youth care in The Netherlands in the last century can be characterized as a 'patchwork' of organizations. There were many different organizations for many different groups, each with their own methodology. They were mostly working independently from each other, and focusing on their own group. They were not used to exchange information about their clients, and there were only a limited number of referrals to other comparable organisations. Some of the organizations were private organizations, initiated by local groups or individuals. Others were public organizations, initiated by local or national authorities.

Tilanus (1999) described some of the problems that characterized the child and youth care in The Netherlands at that time. First, there was a diverging range of small facilities that were not adapted to each other. Second, it was often determined by chance where the children[1] went with there problems. As a result of that, children were often inaccurately referred and were sent to various organizations, even if they had similar problem behavior. This was especially the case when children (or their families) had multiple problems. Third, every organization made its own diagnosis. This was inefficient, and sometimes also inaccurate when different organizations made different diagnoses. Fourth, treatment plans from different organizations were not compatible. Finally, the responsibilities for placement and treatment were often combined, creating an entanglement of interests.

Based on the observation of these problems, some suggestions were made (Tilanus, 1999). First, more co-operation was needed between the sections of youth care, youth protection, and mental health care. Second, a central regional centre for youth was required, that was easily accessible for them. Third, an improvement of the diagnosis and the indication-for-

---

[1] In this chapter the term 'children' applies to younger as well as older children and covers the whole range of minors.

treatment statements was considered necessary. Fourth, new child and youth care programs needed to be developed, characterized by a multi-functional approach and supervised by managers (Anglin, 1999). Finally, a system of financing was needed to suit this new structure.

A new gateway: The Youth Care Office

Concretely, these recommendations were converted into the proposition to build so-called *Youth Care Offices* (abbreviated as YCO's - Van Yperen, 1997; see also Beker & Maier, 2001). For clients these YCO's function as a new gateway to care provisions. They are situated in each region, and they have combined expertise in screening, diagnostic assessment, determining indications for treatment, referral and case-management. Usually there is also expertise available in light and brief forms of ambulant care. It is expected that because of the YCO's the quality of the decision-making process in diagnostic assessment, setting indications for treatment and assignment of care will improve (Van Yperen & Pameijer, 2000; see also Petermann, 2002).

In the Youth Care Office six phases of professional exertion are distinguished as an exemplary working model: (1) entry, (2) screening, (3) diagnosis, (4) setting indications for treatment, (5) assignment, and (6) placement.[2]

Entry. The client can reach the Youth Care Office in different ways. The children (or their parents) can enrol themselves. The children can also be enrolled by other professional parties, like a school, a social worker or a medical doctor. After the initial registration the client is invited for an interview, aimed to work as a screening device.

Screening. During the screening the most important life domains are examined with regard to the problem behavior, the occurring risk and protective factors. Also the past history of the child is examined. The information of the client is recorded, together with an overview of the situation:
- behavioral and emotional functioning;
- personal and functional development;
- the primary environment (living conditions);

---

[2] The model of an YCO is a working model that shows similarities with other models in the literature, as for example the model of Petermann (2002). This German author distinguishes the phases that are depicted in the left side of the scheme below. In the right side of the scheme the corresponding phases of the YCO-model are described.

Petermann model	Youth Care Office model
First contact	Entry
Intake meeting(s) with clients	Screening and Diagnosis
Decision-making and treatment planning	Setting indications for treatment
Assignment and implementation of intervention	Assignment and Placement
Evaluation	

- the secondary environment (school and work);
- the tertiary environment (leisure time and friends).

During the screening the problem behavior is discussed and defined. Finally, a decision is made whether light ambulatory care is sufficient, or whether more intensive care and treatment is needed.

Diagnosis. If it is concluded that the problems of the child and his/her family are too complex to justify light ambulatory care, a diagnostic process is started. This process consists of a cyclical process of formulating hypotheses, gathering data, drawing conclusions and reformulating hypotheses, resulting in a clear picture of the problem.

Setting indications for treatment. After consultation of the client an indication-for-treatment statement is formulated, where problem behavior, goals of treatment, and intervention methods (including alternatives) are described. In this phase it is decided which kind of care is desirable and available. This is formulated in a care or treatment plan, where both the perspective of the client and the perspective of the social worker is incorporated.

Assignment. On the basis of the indication-for-treatment statement a specific organization is searched that should be able to respond to the articulated client needs. Ideally, in the process of searching several alternatives are considered. In this phase it is attempted to take into account characteristics of the problem behavior, requests of the client and recommendations of the social worker. Ultimately, a specific organization is selected.

Placement. When this organization is found, the client can actually be placed in the specified organization. Placement can refer to intensive ambulant care, semi-residential or day care/treatment, residential care or family foster care. In the final phase, the daily responsibility for the client is transferred to the approached care unit. An YCO staff member often stays in touch with the child, the family and the service organization as a case manager.

Various studies have confirmed the need to examine patterns and predictors in professional child and youth care (James, Landsverk & Slymen, 2004; Scholte & Van der Ploeg, 2000). If we want to answer the central question in child and youth care – the question which interventions with which kind of problem behavior create which outcome – it is first useful to work out if there is a pattern in the relationship between problem behavior and indicated interventions (Ward & Rose, 2003). The rationalization of the process of decision-making in the YCO-model suggests that such a pattern exists or should exist.

The primary aim of the present pilot-study was to examine the dynamics of screening and setting indications for treatment in the Youth Care Office model: What is the relationship between problem characteristics, client characteristics, and proposed intervention characteristics in the files of a Youth Care Office?

Method

For the present study, 270 files of a Youth Care Office in the western part of The Netherlands were examined.[3] The cases comprise a random, systematically drawn sample from the child population referred to the Youth Care Office during the period of February-December 2000 (11 months). The research on the files was carried out by using the *RED-form*, a tested inventory for mapping out personal and problem characteristics of children and their families (Van Vianen et al., 1996).

Of the 270 files 54% concerned boys, and 46% concerned girls. The files showed that 18% of the children were between 0 and 6 years old, 31% were between 7 and 11 years old, and 51% were 12 years old or older. This proportional increase of children who find their way to child and youth care services as they grow older is a pattern that comes across in other studies as well (John et al., 1995).

The cultural background of the young people was determined by the birthplace of their parents. When both parents were born in the Netherlands, their cultural background was determined as Dutch. This was the case for 59% of the children. When one of the parents was born outside the Netherlands, the cultural background was determined as ethnic. For 9% of the cases a cultural background from the Surinam was determined. In 7% of the cases there was a Turkish cultural background. Another 7% of the cases had a Moroccan cultural background. For 3% of the cases one or both of the parents were born in Indonesia. Finally, 15% of the cases had a different cultural background. In comparison with the proportion of children with an ethnic background in the Dutch youth – 21% of youth under 25 belonged to an ethnic minority group in 2001 (CBS, 2001) – there seems to be an over-representation of children from ethnic groups (41%). However, it must be noted that the ethnic groups are mostly concentrated in the western part of the Netherlands, the so-called 'Randstad'.

In the files information referring to four groups of variables was collected: (1) personal characteristics of the child; (2) characteristics of the family context; (3) characteristics of the problem behavior of the child; and (4) characteristics of the proposed intervention.

---

[3] Actually, it concerns six annexes of the Youth Care Office in the province South-Holland (3.4 million inhabitants).

Results

Child and family characteristics

The children can be characterized as follows. On the positive side personality characteristics can be found such as an attractive appearance (13%), intelligence (11%), social competence (10%), and humour (4%). On the negative side the children have characteristics such as difficult temperament (13%), difficulties with cultural adaptation (13%), lack of self-confidence (12%), low self-esteem (8%), and poor physical condition (15%).

The family of these children consists in 13% of the cases of one child, in 68% of the cases of 2-3 children, and in 13% of the cases of 4-5 children. Of the fathers 78% is employed, compared to 52% of the mothers. In 29% of the cases there are financial problems in the family, and in 25% of the cases there are problems with housing. In 7% of the families unemployment is a major problem.

As to the parental behavior, in four out of five cases (83%) various problems were observed, such as setting ambiguous rules, inconsistent parenting, insufficient stimulation of the child, or child abuse or neglect. Striking is the number of case-files (n = 102) that contained insufficient reliable information on this issue. For this reason we will focus the analysis on child characteristics.

Problem behavior

The problem behavior that was reported in the 270 files can be summarized as follows. Externalizing problem behavior, referring to oppositional behavior, aggression and criminal behavior was reported in 52% of the files. In 20% of the cases the children showed internalizing problem behavior, referring to depressive feelings, feelings of loneliness, and anxiety. In 22% of the files a combination of internalizing and externalizing problem behavior was reported. In 2% of the cases some other kind of problem behavior was reported. In 4% of the cases the child did not show behavioral problems.

In 58% of the cases the parents or primary caregivers had referred the child to the Youth Care Office. In 33% of the cases the child was referred by other agencies. In 9%, the young person had visited the Youth Care Office independently. Most of the children (73%) had previously received some kind of child and youth care. These consisted of individual psychotherapy, psychiatric therapy, general social work, family foster care or a stay in a children's home. A remarkable finding is that children from ethnic groups had less often received some kind of professional youth care in the past.

Proposed type of care

In general, four types of care are proposed. Most often an *intensive kind of ambulatory care* (43%) is indicated, including 3% of the cases where additional day treatment for the child is advised. Intensive ambulatory care refers to individual therapy for children, family therapy, and other relatively long-lasting family support services. In 24% of the cases *light ambulatory care* is indicated. Light ambulatory care refers to individual counselling or family social work for a short period of time. In 18% of the cases out-of-home placement, in particular *residential or foster care*, is indicated. These children are referred to either an institute where they stay day and night and receive treatment, or to a foster home where they are temporarily part of a family.[4] Finally, in 15% of the cases *further diagnostic examination* is requested. In these cases the YCO-worker is not able to make a judgement on the basis of the information gathered initially.

Table 7.1
Typical patterns of indicated care

	Light ambulatory (24%)	Intensive ambulatory (43%)	Out-of-home placement (18%)	Further examination (15%)
Sex	Average amount of boys (52%)	Average amount of boys (51%)	Less boys (44%)	More boys (82%)
Age	More in the age of 12-18 (65%)	More in the age of 0-11 (56%)	More in the age of 12-18 (54%)	More in the age of 0-11 (55%)
Internalizing Problems	Average amount of internalizing problems (18%)	More internalizing problems (29%)	Less internalizing problems (11%)	Less internalizing problems (11%)
Externalizing Problems	Average amount of externalizing problems (59%)	Less externalizing problems (44%)	Average amount of externalizing problems (50%)	More externalizing problems (63%)
Combined Problems	Average amount of combined problems (20%)	Average amount of combined problems (25%)	Average amount of combined problems (24%)	Average amount of combined problems (26%)

---

[4] In 12% of the cases the out-of-home placement option is unspecified, in 3% of the cases it concerns foster care, and in the remaining 3% it concerns residential care as a treatment option.

Patterns

Looking now at the four general types of indicated care, we can describe some general patterns (see Table 7.1). The light ambulatory care can be characterized as follows. This type of care is indicated mainly to adolescents (12-18 years old) with average [5] amounts of internalizing and externalizing problem behavior or combinations of these. The intensive ambulatory care is indicated more often to children in the age of 0 to 11, with relatively more internalizing and less externalizing problem behavior. Out-of-home placement is indicated more often to adolescent girls in the age of 12 to 18 with less internalizing problem behavior. The final group for whom more information was needed according to the YCO-worker consisted mainly of boys in the younger ages of 0 to 11, with less internalizing and relatively more externalizing problem behavior.

Evaluation of proposals

The proposed indications for treatment were evaluated by a team of experts in the YCO. In two-third of the cases (67%) the proposal of the YCO-worker is approved. In the other cases the team judges the information to be inadequate for appropriate decision-making (12%), the team reaches a different conclusion (11%), or the team does not give a clear judgement. The expert committee most often disagrees on the proposal 'light ambulatory care'.

Conclusion

Some indications of a typical pattern for the relationship between child characteristics, problem characteristics and characteristics of the indication-for-treatment proposals were found. They need to be examined in more detail to determine their theoretical and practical use. However, some concluding remarks can be made.

First of all we can conclude that a result of 18% out-of-home placements corresponds with national data in the Netherlands; about 20% of the children that need curative youth care entails a (temporary) out-of-home placement (Knorth, 2004).

The observation that intensive ambulant care is more often connected with internalizing problem behavior than out-of-home placement is a pattern that has also been found elsewhere (for instance, Scholte & Van der Ploeg, 1999). With externalizing problem behavior we see the opposite result: it is relatively less often combined with an indication for intensive ambulant care, and relatively more often combined with an indication for out-of-

---

[5] The 'average' qualification refers to the average in the sample, not in the population.

home placement. This difference would be even more striking if we look only at indications for residential care[6].

Intriguing is the finding that the need for 'further examination' evidently most often occurs with children presenting externalizing behavioral problems. These children tend to display a so-called external 'locus of control' (the tendency to attribute problems to others), show less evidence of introspective orientation and are more often difficult to approach in personal relations (Van der Ploeg, 1998). The result could be that YCO-workers, engaged in screening, get the feeling that they have too little 'grip' on these young clients, which might account for the need for further diagnostic assessment.

Another issue that we would like to stress is the fact that the category 'combined problem behavior' does not differentiate between different indication-for-treatment proposals, but does seem to show a relationship with ethnicity: children from families with an ethnic background most often show a mixture of internalizing and externalizing problem behavior (see also Vollebergh, 2002). This could be an indication for the vulnerability of their position. At the same time our results show that especially these children very often did not receive any professional care before. The child and youth care system seems to be less accessible for them. This deserves great attention (see also Komen, 2004).

More in general we would like to plead that a more decisive monitoring should occur in the developmental trajectories of children, also with reference to youth care interventions. More knowledge about developmental trajectories in a professional care-system can increase our understanding of the processes that guide and influence these trajectories.

From a practical perspective, collected information of clients can be an important tool to help organizations of child and youth care become 'self-learning' entities. Distinguishing several patterns may enable agencies to evaluate which clients, with specific characteristics, with specific problem behavior, with a specific (family) context, benefit the most from which intervention. There is an urgent need for this knowledge when we look at the high number of times that the quality of the 'indication-for-treatment' statements were classified as unsatisfactory (see also Metselaar et al., 2004).

From a research perspective, the systematic collection of information enables empirical examinations of typical patterns. First, collected information can provide an understanding of the frequency of several trajectories, making it possible to distinguish more and less frequent pathways.

---

[6] In several cases there isn't any problem behavior (!) in a child that is indicated for placement in *foster care*. It is the very difficult family situation at home, that makes an out-of-home placement necessary.

Second, relationships between client characteristics, problem characteristics and contextual characteristics can be examined (cf. Ward & Rose, 2003).

Finally, from a policy perspective, it can be argued that a systematic collection, evaluation and presentation of client data can elucidate societal trends in the problem behavior and the needed care for these children and families.

References

Anglin, J. P. (1999). The uniqueness of child and youth care: A personal perspective. *Child and Youth Care Forum, 28,* 143-150.

Beker, J., & Maier, H. W. (2001). Emerging issues in child and youth care education: A platform for planning. *Child and Youth Care Forum, 30,* 377-386.

CBS [Centraal Bureau voor de Statistiek] (2001). *Jeugd 2001: Cijfers en feiten [Youth 2001: Figures and Facts].* Voorburg/Heerlen: Author. (in Dutch)

James, S., Landsverk, J., & Slymen, D. J. (2004). Placement movement in out-of-home care: Patterns and predictors. *Children and Youth Services Review, 26,* 185-206.

John, L., Offord, D., Boyle, M., & Racine, Y. (1995). Factors predicting use of mental health services by children 6-16 years old: Findings from the Ontario Child Health Study. *American Journal of Orthopsychiatry, 65,* 76-86.

Knorth, E. J. (2004). Uithuisplaatsing in de jeugdzorg [Out-of-home placement in child and youth care]. In J. Hermanns, et al. (Eds.), *Handboek Jeugdzorg: Methodieken, Zorgprogramma's en Doelgroepen.* Houten: Bohn Stafleu Van Loghum (in press). (in Dutch)

Komen, M. (2004). Jeugdzorg in een multiculturele samenleving [Child and youth care in a multicultural society]. In R. Diekstra, M. Van den Berg, & J. Rigter (Eds.), *Waardevolle of waardenloze samenleving?* (pp. 307-332). Uithoorn: Karakter Publishers. (in Dutch)

Metselaar, J., Knorth, E. J., Noom, M. J., Van Yperen, T. A., & Konijn, C. (2004). Treatment planning for residential and non-residential care: A study on indication-for-treatment statements as input to the care process. In J. P. Anglin, & E. J. Knorth (Eds.), *International perspectives on rethinking residential care* (pp. 151-173) [Special Issue Child & Youth Care Forum, Vol. 33]. New York: Kluwer Academic/Human Sciences Press.

Petermann, F. (2002). Bedeutung von Diagnose und Indikationsstellung im prozess der Hilfeplanung. In K. Fröhlich-Gildhoff (Ed.), *Indikation in der Jugendhilfe: Grundlagen für die Entscheidungsfindung in Hilfeplanung und Hilfeprozess* (pp. 17-31). Weinheim/München: Juventa Verlag.

Scholte, E. M., & Van der Ploeg, J. D. (1999). Allocation of care for juveniles at risk of emotional and behavioral difficulties: Practice and opportunities. *International Journal of Child and Family Welfare, 4,* 112-129.

Scholte, E. M., & Van der Ploeg, J. D. (2000). Exploring factors governing successful residential treatment of youngsters with serious behavioral difficulties: Findings from a longitudinal study in Holland. *Childhood, 7,* 129-153.

Tilanus, C. P. G. (1999). *Jeugdzorg: Werkvelden en kwaliteitsontwikkeling [Youth care: Fields of action and the development of quality].* Utrecht: SWP Publishers. (in Dutch)

Van der Ploeg, J. D. (1998). *Gedragsproblemen: Ontwikkelingen en risico's [Behavioral problems: Developments and risks].* Rotterdam: Lemniscaat. (in Dutch)

Van Vianen, R. T., Baarda, D. B., & Ten Berge, I. J. (1996). *RED: Registratie-, Evaluatie- en Diagnostiek systeem voor de gezinsvoogdij [RED: Registration, Evaluation and Diagnostic system for family guardians]*. Utrecht: Utrecht University, Department of Education.

Van Yperen, T. A. (1997). Bureaus Jeugdzorg in wording [Youth Care Offices in the process of formation]. In J. D. Van der Ploeg, J. M. A. M. Janssens, & E. E. J. De Bruyn (Eds.), *Diagnostiek in de Jeugdzorg* (pp. 101-119). Groningen: Wolters-Noordhoff. (in Dutch)

Van Yperen, T. A., & Pameijer, N. (2000). Protocol indicatiestelling in de toegang tot de jeugdzorg [Protocol for setting the indications for treatment at the entrance to child and youth care services]. In P. Prins, & N. Pameijer (Eds.), *Protocollen in de Jeugdzorg* (pp. 39-58). Lisse: Swets & Zeitlinger. (in Dutch)

Vollebergh, W. (2002). *Gemiste kansen: Culturele diversiteit en de jeugdzorg [Missed chances: Cultural diversity and youth care]*. Professorial Inaugural Lecture Catholic University Nijmegen, Nijmegen, November 1st, 2002.

Ward, H., & Rose, W. (Eds.) (2003). *Approaches to needs assessment in children's services*. London/New York: Jessica Kingsley Publishers.

8

Selected aspects of education and contact with birth family amongst young people aged 13-14 years in long term foster care in Ireland

Robbie Gilligan & Fiona Daly

Introduction

This paper presents selected findings from a larger study on the educational and social support experiences of young people aged 13-14 years in long term foster care in Ireland. It explores certain aspects of these young people's education and schooling (including attendance, behaviour and the type of educational provision received), as well as looking at the nature of their contact with birth families (including the composition of their birth family, contact in the last six months and the frequency of this contact). The aim of the study was to gain an insight into the *daily lives* of this group of young people regarding their schooling and the social supports available to them. This is an area that has been under-researched in Ireland.

This paper considers the rationale for the study, the methods of data collection and how the study was carried out in practice before any of the results are presented. The basic characteristics of the young people and foster carers involved in the study are then identified before going on to explore some of the selected findings on this group of young people's education and contact with their birth family. The paper then draws some conclusions based on the findings reported. In order to provide some context for the results, the paper opens with a brief discussion of the nature of foster care in Ireland.

State care and foster care in ireland

A high proportion of children and young people in state care in Ireland are in foster care. Table 8.1 shows the number of children and young people in care by the type of care in the year 2000.

Table 8.1
Number of children and young people in care in Ireland by type of care (2000)*

Type of care	%	No.
Foster care	76.5	3,384
Residential care	14.4	636
Pre-adoptive placement	1.1	47
At home under supervision	3.1	139
Other	4.9	218
Total	100.0	4,424

*Source: Department of Health and Children, 2000

Table 8.1 shows that a total of 4,424 children and young people were in state care in Ireland in the year 2000. Three in four of these children and young people were in foster care, 76.5% (3,384). A further 14.4% (636) of children and young people were in residential care, with the remaining 9.1% (404) in other types of care provision, at home (under supervision) or awaiting pre-adoptive placement.

According to the Census of Population figures for 2002, there was a total of 1,013,031 young people aged 0-17 years inclusive in Ireland. This information can be used in conjunction with the total number of children in state care from Table 8.1 to estimate the number of children and young people in care in Ireland per thousand population. Based on these figures, it is estimated that 4.4 children and young people per thousand population are in the care of the Irish State.

Another trend that is apparent from the official statistics on children and young people in care in Ireland is that there is a tendency for children and young people to be in state care for a relatively long period of time. Table 8.2 shows the number of years that these children and young people have been in care.

Table 8.2
Number of years spent in care by children and young people in Ireland (2000)

Number of years in care	%	No.
Less than 1 year	22.9	1,012
1-5 years	44.0	1,949
More than 5 years	33.1	1,463
Total	100.0	4,424

Source: Department of Health and Children, 2000.

Table 8.2 shows that one third of the children and young people in care in the year 2000, 33.1% (1,463), had been in care for more than five years. A further 44.0% (1,949) of children and young people had been in care for between one to five years. If these two categories are added together, over three quarters of all children and young people in care in the year 2000, 77.1% (3,412), had been in care for more than one year. Just under one quarter of children and young people, the remaining 22.9% (1,012), had been in care for less than one year.

Based on these statistics, being in state care in Ireland has two implications for children and young people. Firstly, they are more likely to be in foster care than in any other type of care. Secondly, once placed into care, it seems that they tend to remain in care for a relatively long period of time.

Rationale for the study

There were several reasons for undertaking this study. There is a lack of information available on aspects of young people's daily lives while in care, and those in *long term foster care* in particular, both at a national and international level. Schooling plays a significant role in young people's lives, for those in the care of their families as well as in the care of the State. This needs to be reflected in any research carried out concerning young people in care. Furthermore, evidence on the educational outcomes for young people in care can be contradictory, but it often paints a negative picture. This research study was undertaken in order to explore more about the educational and other aspects of these children's daily experiences, particularly in the Irish context.

Limited research on long term foster care in Ireland and internationally

There is a limited amount of research on the area of foster care in Ireland. In general, research on children and young people in state care in Ireland has tended to look at those in residential care, despite the fact that placement in families (traditional foster care and relative care) now accounts for over three in four of all current placements (as seen earlier in the official statistics).

Most research on children and young people in care in Ireland has been historical and has often consisted of a retrospective analysis of statistical and official data at a national or regional level. Most research on foster care has been focused on the carers' own views or experience (for example, Gilligan, 1996; Meyler, 2002). In this study, the carer is the key informant but most of the data collected concerns the *young person* themselves and sheds light on aspects of their day to day lives.

Internationally, the emphasis on permanence in debates about child welfare and child placement has meant the focus has been on adoption, family re-unification or family preservation. Long term foster care was almost seen as undesirable, if not contradictory. Nevertheless, it has endured in practice as a key form of placement and is increasingly recognised as having something distinctive and important to offer (Kelly, 2000; Schofield, 2000).

Negative educational outcomes for young people in care

There is mixed evidence on the educational progress of children and young people in care. In the Anglophone world there tends to be more discouraging evidence about the educational outcomes for children in care. Several studies have found that those in care tend to fare less well in terms of academic achievement compared to young people in the general population. In particular, young people in care have been reported to make poorer academic progress (e.g., Heath, Aldgate & Colton, 1989) and to leave school early with relatively fewer educational qualifications (e.g., McMillen & Tucker, 1998). There are various possible reasons suggested for this including disrupted schooling attributed to placement moves (Altshuler, 2003; Jackson, 2001), low teacher expectations (Jackson, 2001), coming from a socially disadvantaged background (St. Claire & Osborn, 1987) and bullying (Borland et al., 1998). Given the close association between educational outcomes and life chances, this study focuses closely on the educational experiences of a particular group of young people in long term foster care in Ireland.

This study also looks at features of the young people's daily lives that could potentially be viewed as supportive influences in their overall experience of being in care, namely their educational experience, contact with birth family, friendships and participation in hobbies and leisure time activities. These factors have been seen as being associated with resilience in various vulnerable populations. The research evidence on resilient outcomes for children in adversity and more specifically, children in care, highlights the significance of factors such as positive educational experience (Jackson, 2001), family contact (Quinton & Rutter, 1988) and social support (Gilligan, 2001).

A national study

A distinctive feature of this study is its national coverage of the relevant age cohort in long term foster care. It is hoped that further funding can be secured for further rounds of data collection based on the same cases as well as the possibility of conducting a qualitative study of a subsample of young people that make up the total population of this study.

Methodology

This study aimed to explore the various aspects of the day to day education and social supports available to young people aged 13-14 years in long term foster care in Ireland. It is a national study and included the *total population* of young people aged 13-14 years in long term foster care. Information on young people's daily lives was gathered through interviews with their foster carers. These key features of the study's approach, the reasons for them and the actual steps taken in the data collection process are discussed below.

Total population of young people aged 13-14 years in long term foster care

This study involved collecting data on *all* young people aged 13-14 years who had been in foster care for more than one year all over the country. Hence there was no need for sampling. This was possible given the size of the country and the demographics of the care population. This full coverage of an age cohort is a rare research opportunity in any care system.

There were two main reasons for choosing the 13-14 year age group. First of all, young people in this age group were likely to have experienced the key transition from primary to post-primary school (or were just about to do so). Irish children normally attend eight years of primary school (usually starting at 5 years of age) and six years of post-primary school (starting at age 12 or 13). Therefore, Irish children typically attend at least two different schools in different locations over the course of their schooling. The transition from primary to post-primary school can be a difficult one. In order to capture any issues that arose in relation to this key educational experience, the 13-14 year age group was chosen for the study. Secondly, in terms of their development, young people in this age group are of an age when they would be expected to be starting to engage in social relationships and activities outside the home. Studying this age group would thus facilitate exploring young people's friendships and participation in social activities.

Criteria for the selection of young people in the study

There were three main criteria used to select young people for inclusion in the study. Firstly, young people had to be born in the two calendar years *1988* or *1989* (and therefore in the age group 13-14 years old at the time data collection was to be carried out). Secondly, young people had to be in foster care for *more than one year* (taken to define a *long term* foster care placement for the purposes of the study). Finally, young people had to be with their current foster carer for *at least six months* (so that the carer would be in a position to answer the questions in the interview). Young people were only included in the study population when they met *all* of the above three criteria.

Access to the study population was made possible through the ten regional health boards in Ireland. Following careful consideration of the legal, ethical and practical issues involved, all ten health boards in the country agreed to facilitate the study, making it possible to conduct a *national* study. Each health board compiled a list of young people in foster care that met all three criteria along with the contact details of their respective foster carers. Legal requirements concerning data protection were identified and complied with before this list was passed onto the research team. Once the list of foster carers for each health board was released, preparations began to start interviewing foster carers.

The data collection process – steps involved, consent from carers and response rate

Prior to the main set of interviews being carried out, twelve pilot interviews were conducted. The pilot interviews were set up through the Irish Foster Care Association, which has a range of functions including providing support and training to its members who are largely foster carers themselves. The information gathered through the pilot interviews helped to refine the questionnaire to be used for interviews with carers. In addition, seven of the twelve pilot interviewees were on the final list of foster carers provided by the health board, and therefore, were included in the final dataset.

After pilot interviews had been completed and the final questionnaire schedule had been drawn up, telephone interviews with foster carers were set up. There were several steps involved in doing this. Firstly, letters were sent to foster carers advising them that they would be contacted by telephone about the study by one of the members of the research team. Secondly, initial phone calls were made to carers to ask them to take part in the study and to make an appointment to carry out the interview. Finally, phone calls were then made at the agreed time to conduct the actual interview.

There were two stages involved in obtaining the consent of foster carers to take part in the study. The first involved the health boards and the second, the research team. Firstly, foster carers gave their consent to their local health board to pass on their contact details to the research team for the purpose of carrying out the study by *not* returning an opt-out slip at the bottom of the letter sent to them by the boards. Secondly, when telephoned by the research team for the first time, foster carers were informed of the study and asked to take part in it. Therefore, foster carers were interviewed where they had given both their consent to be contacted by the research team and their consent to be interviewed over the telephone.

The number of young people that met all of the study criteria across the country was 247 (based on the numbers given from each health board). Therefore, the total number of foster carers to be interviewed was 247. Interviews were completed with 205 foster carers, giving an overall response rate of 83%. However, it was impossible to contact 18 foster carers by telephone either because the relevant health board could not provide a telephone number or else the number given proved to be incorrect. So, the response rate for all *contactable cases* was 90% (205 completed interviews out of a total of 229 contactable cases). Therefore the study sample finally contacted covers 90% of all young people aged 13-14 years in long term foster care nationally in the State.

The above discussion has focused on the actual steps taken in collecting the data for the study. The rationale for the way in which information was gathered is considered below. In particular, the reasons behind the decision to interview foster carers rather than young people and for conducting interviews over the telephone are explained.

Interviews with foster carers

It is recognised that direct interviews with young people themselves would have provided first hand information on their experiences of schooling and the social supports available to them. However, for ethical, logistical, resource and pragmatic reasons, it was decided that this was not feasible.

This study is a benchmarking study of the experience of young people in the 13-14 year age group in long term foster care in Ireland. Fuller coverage of the target population was expected if foster carers were the informants rather than the young people themselves. In our experience, conducting interviews with children in care in Ireland typically involves consent from four individuals - the social worker (and possibly their managers on behalf of the placement agency), the birth parents, the foster carer, and in accordance with the policy of the Children's Research Centre (our location), the child themselves. Securing this quadruple form of consent is a cumbersome and substantially complex process. Pursuing the 'child as interviewee' route would have undoubtedly reduced the response rate from the total population, and therefore, the accuracy of the findings. It would also have required a budget larger than that available. The next best alternative source of evidence about aspects of young people's daily lives was judged to be the foster carer. Carers seemed the people best placed to talk about events in young people's daily lives and their experiences. Young people live in the carer's family household. Carers were more likely than social workers to be able to provide the information that was sought.

The questionnaire used for data collection was designed to take into account that foster carers would be the key informants and most questions were of a factual nature, such as the type of school the young person went to, feedback from the school on their behaviour and whether the young person had received remedial education. The information gathered was to provide *basic* data on aspects of young people's education and schooling as well as their social supports. So, questions were kept as simple and straight forward as possible in the interview schedule. While this was intended to make it easier for foster carers to provide answers, keeping the questions basic and based on actual events in the young people's lives was also necessary because of the lack of such information available in Ireland. Factual information on aspects of young people's lives whilst in foster care would help to establish the bigger picture through identifying the important issues prior to carrying out further and more in-depth research. Therefore, this study is of an *exploratory* nature and the data collected is mainly *quantitative*.

It should be noted here that the research team felt it was important to inform the young people concerned about the study and flyers were designed for this purpose. These could not be sent directly from the research team prior to data collection because the health boards compiled and held the list of foster carers. The flyers were sent to carers enclosed with an information leaflet for the carer themselves from each health board. Carers were encouraged to discuss the study with the young person. It should also be remembered, as mentioned above, that subject to funding it is hoped to conduct qualitative interviews with a subsample of the study population and ideally to do follow up interviews at intervals thereafter. This would give young people an opportunity to voice their own opinions on matters of their schooling and social supports. It is also hoped to repeat this study on a continuing basis with this cohort of young people to follow up their educational careers and developments in their social participation and social support networks.

Interviews with foster carers were carried out over the telephone. The next section explores some of the advantages and disadvantages of this method of data collection, and explains why it was chosen for this study.

Telephone interviewing as a method of data collection

Conducting interviews over the phone had certain advantages that were particularly relevant for this study. These included being easier in practical terms to carry out interviews (in terms of time and cost), enhancing confidentiality for the respondents and minimising interviewer effects. These considerations are discussed in turn.

As this was a national study, foster carers were widely dispersed geographically. Therefore, the research team considered that carrying out interviews over the phone would be a much quicker method of collecting data compared to carrying out interviews face to face. Face to face interviews were likely to involve considerable more time and higher cost for travel.

Conducting interviews over the telephone would mean that the interviewer did not see the respondent during the process of data collection. While the foster carer's name and address was known, they could not be identified by their physical appearance and therefore, it was anticipated that this would help to enhance their anonymity and make it easier for the interviewer to guarantee confidentiality. This was deemed an important factor in gaining foster carers' co-operation in taking part in the study but also in encouraging them to answer the questions as honestly as possible.

Interviewer effects describe the negative impact that an interviewer might have on the way that a respondent answers a question. For example, a respondent might give socially desirable answers according to what they think would please the interviewer. Such effects are less likely to occur in interviews conducted over the phone compared to those carried out face to face. The reason being that the respondent cannot see the interviewer and therefore visual clues, such as facial expressions, will not impact upon the respondent's replies (Frey and Oishi, 1995). However, it is acknowledged that there is some potential for these effects through the language used or the verbal responses of the interviewer.

It was considered that the limitations of telephone interviews could be minimised in this study in addition to benefiting from the above advantages. In particular, the questions asked in the telephone interviews with foster carers were largely closed and of a factual nature and therefore avoided the potential pitfalls of asking sensitive, complex and open ended questions over the phone. Also, the population for this study was a *specialised* and *interested* one, i.e. foster carers. It was anticipated that this would help to avoid the problem of non-response that can often be an issue for *general population* telephone surveys. Given the high response rate as stated earlier, this contention was justified.

Before the main results on aspects of young people's education and contact with their birth family are presented here, a basic profile of the young people and the foster carers and their families will be given.

Background characteristics of young people and their foster families

This section presents basic information on the young people in the study, focusing particularly on aspects of their placement histories to date. Some data on foster carers is also presented to show the type of families that foster young people on a long term basis. This information is based on the interviews conducted with the foster carers.

Basic profile of young people aged 13-14 years in long term foster care

Information on a total of 205 young people was collected in the study. A profile of these young people looks at their gender and age as well as various aspects of their placements and care histories.

Gender - There was an even split between male and female young people in the study:
- 48.3% (99) were male, and
- 51.7% (106) were female.

Age - The vast majority of young people were aged 13-14 years old, 95.1% (195) – just over one half, 51.7% (106), were aged 13 years old and the remaining 43.4% (89) were aged 14 years old. This was the target age group for the study.

Age first placed in care - Almost one quarter, 22.9% (47), of young people were first placed in care when they were less than one year old. Just over one half of young people, 53.5% (106), were placed in care when aged five years or less. Therefore, the young people in this study tended to be placed in care at a relatively young age.

Length of time with current foster carer - Young people tended to be with their current foster carer for a fairly long period of time - 42.9% (88) of young people had been in their current placement for ten years or more. On average, young people had been in the care of their current foster carer for 7.9 years.

Other care placements - Almost one half of young people, 48.8% (100), had experienced other care placements (either in residential or foster care), while 49.8% (102) had no previous placements in care apart from their current foster care placement. Of the 100 young people who had experienced other care placements, two thirds of them, 67.0% (67), had one or two other placements prior to their current foster care placement. Just over one quarter, 26.0% (26), had three or more other placements.

Related to foster carer - Almost one quarter of young people in the study, 24.4% (50), were related to their foster carer. These young people were most likely to be in the care of an aunt or uncle.

Placed with a sibling - Just under one half of young people, 48.3% (99), were living with one or more of their birth siblings in the same foster family.

Basic profile of foster carers and their families

Background characteristics of foster carers (including gender and age), along with some information on the foster family (including geographical breakdown and length of time involved in fostering) are presented below.

Gender - The vast majority of respondents were female carers, 89.8% (184).
Age - The age of foster carers ranged widely from 21 to 80 years. The majority were aged between 40 and 59 years, 73.0% (150). On average, respondent carers were 49 years of age.

Geographical location - There was a fairly even split between families living in urban and rural locations – 32.7% (67) were from urban areas (large city or town), 28.3% (58) lived in a small town or village and 38.5% (79) were living in the 'open countryside'.

Educational attainment - Carers were most likely to have finished their schooling at primary level - 28.3% (58) of female carers and 30.7% (63) of male carers. Female carers were slightly more likely to have taken the national school leaving exam (Leaving Certificate) compared to male carers – 19.5% (40) and 16.6% (34) respectively. A slightly higher percentage of male carers had a third level qualification (e.g. diploma, degree) compared to female carers – 19.0% (39) and 15.6% (32) respectively.

Other foster children in the family - Almost two thirds of carers, 61.0% (125), were caring for another foster child in the family in addition to the young person that was the focus of this study.

Duration of time spent fostering - On average, respondents had been fostering for a fairly long period of time - 11.4 years. The number of years ranged greatly from one to thirty-seven across all carers.

Two adult carer families - The majority of foster families consisted of two adult carers - 81.0% (166). A further 10.2% (21) – 1 out of 10 families – consisted of one adult carer.

Selected results on education and schooling

The first set of results presented here focus on aspects of the young people's education and schooling. These results will largely look at four issues:
- school attendance
- behaviour at school
- specialist educational provision, and
- the beneficial nature of education and schooling for the young people.

In addition, some relationships between variables will be explored with the aim of identifying potentially important factors that appear to have an impact on aspects of the young people's education and schooling, in particular gender and features of their care placements (e.g. length of time in care and being in relative/non relative care).

The results presented here are based on events that took place in the young people's schooling in the school year prior to the start of data collection. Again, it should be pointed out here that the information on the young people's education and schooling was given by their foster carers. School attendance is the first issue to be considered.

Young people's school attendance

The findings presented here look at the *type* of school attended by the group of young people in this study, in particular whether they went to a mainstream or special school and the number that attended primary or post-primary school. In addition, the *regularity* of school attendance will be explored.

Young people were most likely to attend mainstream schools, 93.7% (192), while the remaining 6.3% (13) went to a special school that catered for a specific special need. Based on the total number of young people who attended mainstream schools - 192 - there was a fairly even breakdown between those in primary and post-primary schools. Just under one half of young people went to primary school, 47.9% (92) and the remaining 52.1% (100) attended post-primary school. Most of the young people in primary school were in their final year (sixth class) and the majority of those in post-primary school were in their first year. Therefore, the information on young people's education and schooling gathered in the study largely refers to events that occurred in these two school years.

The vast majority of the young people, 98.0% (201), were said to attend school on a regular basis. Reasons for irregular school attendance were given for two of the four remaining young people. However, all four young people had gone to school during the school year 2001-2, and therefore they were included in the results.

'Mitching' from school is the colloquial term used to refer to young people being absent from school without the permission or knowledge of their parent or guardian, in this case the foster carer. This was not found to be a major issue for the majority of these young people. Just 6.3% (13) of the young people were reported to have 'mitched' from school in the school year. In most cases, mitching from school was of a short term nature.

School behaviour

One indicator of the young people's behaviour at school involved asking the foster carer to answer a question based on feedback from teachers at parent teacher evenings, school reports or through other means of contact.

Table 8.3
Young people's behaviour at school in the school year as reported by foster carers

Young people's behaviour at school	%	No.
Very good	51.2	105
Good	31.7	65
Not good	12.7	26
Other	3.9	8
Don't know	0.5	1
Total	100.0	205

Table 8.3 shows that the behaviour of just over half of the young people in the study, 51.2% (105), was reported as being 'very good' by foster carers. In addition, the behaviour of just under one third of the young people, 31.7% (65), was said to be 'good'. Combining these two results, carers reported that the behaviour of 8 out of 10 of the young people was either 'very good' or 'good' – a total of 82.9% (170). The behaviour of 12.7% (26) of young people was rated as 'not good', just over 1 out of 10 young people. Therefore, this result gives a largely positive picture of young people's behaviour at school. Further indicators of young people's school behaviour were also obtained through additional questions in the interview schedule, including whether the carer had been contacted by the school about the young person's behaviour.

Contact from school about young people's behaviour
Foster carers for 3 out of 10 young people, 30.2% (62), said they had been contacted by the school at some point during the school year about the young person's behaviour. This additional indicator of behaviour shows a slightly less rosy picture than that shown above but nonetheless, it still points to the majority of young people being seen as behaving well at school. This indicator of young people's behaviour at school is less susceptible to foster carer's opinions because contact from the school has either happened or not. However, it does depend on the ability of foster carers to remember such events that have occurred during the previous school year.

Contact from school about young people's behaviour by gender
It was found that carers of boys were *twice* as likely to have been contacted by the school than the carers of girls during the school year – 40.4% (40) of carers of boys compared to 20.8% (22) for those of girls. This result was found to be statistically significant (based on the chi-square test). Therefore, this relationship is unlikely to be due to chance factors. The young people's behaviour at school, measured by the indicator for school contact with foster carers, was found to be significantly different for males

and females. School contact is only one indicator of the young people's behaviour at school but this finding does point to a possible trend where school behaviour varies by gender for the young people in long term foster care in this study.

Specialist educational provision

Young people's educational needs were explored by looking at the nature of the educational provision they had received during the school year. This was based on the carer's responses to three questions:

- type of school attended (mainstream/special school),
- whether the young person had received remedial help in the school year, and
- whether the young person had been placed in a special class in the school year.

The aim of compiling this single variable of educational provision was to distinguish between young people who had experienced mainstream schooling only and those who had received specialist educational provision, either in the form of remedial help in a mainstream setting or by being placed in a special class (within mainstream school) or attending a special school. Young people who had received such educational supports in the school year obviously had been judged to have additional educational needs compared to those who had experienced mainstream schooling only.

Table 8.4 shows that just over one half of young people, 52.2% (107), experienced mainstream schooling exclusively in the last year. One third of young people, 33.7% (69), had received remedial help within mainstream schooling, and the remaining 14.1% (29) had received the highest degree of specialist educational provision, either being placed in a special class (within mainstream schooling) or attending a special school. The results show that although 5 out of 10 young people had attended mainstream schooling only in the school year, there was a relatively high percentage who had received remedial help and a sizeable minority that had particular educational needs that were met through specialist educational provision, either by being in a special class or attending a special school. In total, 47.8% (98) of young people received some form of educational assistance above and beyond mainstream schooling. Unlike contact from school about behaviour, the likelihood of receiving specialist educational provision did not vary for males and females.

Table 8.4
Nature of educational provision received by young people as reported by foster carers

Type of educational provision	%	No.
Mainstream schooling only	52.2	107
Mainstream with remedial help	33.7	69
Special class or special school	14.1	29
Total	100.0	205

Further analysis was carried out to establish if specialist educational provision varied according to two factors – firstly, the length of time young people had been in care, and secondly, whether they were in relative or non-relative care.

Specialist educational provision by length of time in care
Young people first placed in care (either foster or residential care) at a relatively older age (9-13 years) were *significantly* more likely to have received some form of specialist educational provision compared to young people who were first placed in care when they were younger. Over one half of young people who were first placed in care when aged between 9-13 years, 59.6% (28), received specialist educational provision compared to 50.0% (30) of those aged 3-8 years and 36.8% (28) of those aged 0-2 years when first placed in care. This result was statistically significant. Therefore, it would appear that young people who were placed in care at an earlier age, and as a result had been in care for a longer period of time, were more likely to follow a pattern of 'normal' mainstream schooling. Those young people who were first placed in care at a relatively older age, and therefore had been in care for a relatively short period of time, were more likely to receive specialist educational provision. It would seem that this group of young people who had been first placed in care at a relatively late stage were more likely to have educational needs that required increased educational inputs.

Specialist educational provision by relative/non-relative care placement
Young people in relative foster care were less likely to have received specialist educational provision than those in non-relative care – 39.2% (20) and 51.3% (78) respectively. While there is a relatively large difference in these two percentages, this difference was not large enough to be statistically significant. However, it could be indicative of a potential trend where young people who were placed with relatives tended to follow a pattern of mainstream schooling. In contrast, young people who were placed in non-relative care, and possibly within a different social environment, were more likely to have received specialist educational provision.

Beneficial experience of education and schooling

Table 8.5 shows that school was reported to be a positive experience for the vast majority of young people in the study, 85.4% (175). Foster carers of 7.3% (15) of the young people stated that their schooling had not been a positive experience for them. For these young people, there were wide ranging reasons cited for having a poor educational experience including having concentration difficulties, lack of friends and bullying.

Table 8.5
Beneficial experience of school for young people as reported by foster carers

Beneficial experience of schooling	%	No.
Yes	85.4	175
No	7.3	15
Don't know	3.4	7
Missing	3.9	8
Total	100.0	205

Bullying in school

Despite the positive results on the young people's experience of schooling overall, almost half of the carers, 45.4% (93), reported that the young people had experienced some form of bullying at school, whether it be teasing/name calling, being excluded or physically hit by other young people. The likelihood of being bullied was similar for those attending primary and post-primary schools – 44.6% (41) of those at primary school had reportedly experienced some form of bullying and 46.0% (46) of those who went to post-primary school. These results are relatively higher than the national rate for bullying, estimated to be 31.3% for children in primary school and 15.6% for young people in post-primary schools (O'Moore et al, 1997).

Although being bullied at school appeared to be fairly prevalent amongst the young people in the study, it was clear that the majority of foster carers felt that school had been a largely positive experience for the young people in their care.

Young people's contact with their birth family

The aim of this section is to explore the nature and extent of contact between the young people and their birth family. This information helps to build up a picture of young people's social supports, as birth family members are one potential source of social support available to them while in long term foster care. Although it is acknowledged that contact with birth family members could have potentially negative consequences. Four main categories of birth family members were identified in the interviews with foster carers. These were birth mother, birth father, siblings (including step siblings) and extended family. The results discussed here look at three particular aspects of young people's contact with each of the four categories of birth family members identified above: the level of contact with birth family members in the last six months, the frequency of such contact and the perceived impact of this contact. Before presenting any of the results on these issues, three particular clarifications need to be made in relation to these results.

Firstly, contact with birth family members is only one indicator of social support available to the young person beyond the foster family. One of the aims of the study is to examine the range of social supports that these young people have available to them and make use of. More of these findings will be available in the final report on the research findings. Secondly, for the purpose of this paper, 'contact' is defined as being face-to-face contact only. Therefore, the results measure the level and frequency of times that young people actually see members of their birth families, for example, during arranged visits etc. Finally, the source of information on young people's contact with birth family members is the foster carer. It is acknowledged that the foster carer may not have full information on the level of such contact but they are the people most likely to be able to provide the most accurate information possible.

To place the results on the level and frequency of contact between the young people and their birth families into context, the composition of their birth families will be examined first.

Composition of young people's birth families

Table 8.6 shows that the vast majority of young people had siblings, 95.6% (196), and also extended family, 91.7% (188), who were known about by the foster carer. The birth mother of 83.4% (171) of young people in the study was alive and known about by the foster carer, with the remaining being deceased. The birth father of just over two thirds of young people, 68.8% (141), were alive and known about by the foster carer. The remaining cases were evenly split between those young people whose birth father was deceased or 'not known' (just over 15% in each category). So, compared to other birth family members, birth fathers were more likely to be 'unknown' to the foster carer, and ultimately to the young person.

Table 8.6
Composition of young people's birth families as reported by foster carers

Birth family member 'present' by category*	%	No.
Birth mother	83.4	171
Birth father	68.8	141
Siblings	95.6	196
Extended family	91.7	188

* 'Present' here is used to mean that a birth family member is currently alive or known about by the foster carer.

After establishing the members of the young people's birth families, questions were then asked of the foster carers about the level of face to face contact between the young people and birth family members in the six months prior to interviews.

Level of contact in the previous six months

Chart 8.1 shows the results for the proportion of young people who had actually seen birth family members in each relevant category in the last six months.

The dark bar for each of the four birth family member categories in Chart 8.1 represents the proportion of young people that had seen members from each birth family member category in the last six months. It is clear that the young people were more likely to have seen their birth mother and siblings in the last six months – 71.9% (123) and 75.0% (147) respectively. A relatively high proportion of young people with extended birth family members had seen one or more of them in the last six months, 61.7% (116). Of all four birth family categories, young people were *least likely* to have seen their birth father in the last six months. The proportion of young people that had seen their birth father in the last six months, 49.6% (70), was almost equal to those that had not, 48.9% (69) (light bar). This result is based on those young people whose birth father was alive or known about by the carer. Therefore, either of these two factors cannot be used to explain the lower tendency for young people to have seen their birth father compared to other birth family members.

Long term foster care

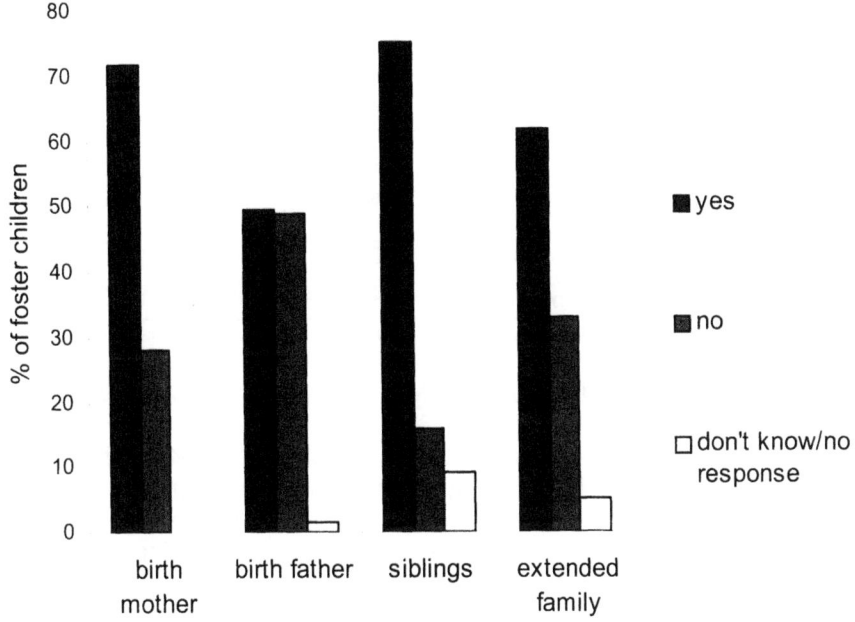

Chart 8.1
Level of contact between young people and birth family member categories in the last six months

Frequency of contact in the last six months

Where the young people had seen birth family members in the last six months, foster carers were asked to state how often face to face contact occurred over this time. There were various categories for different frequencies in the original questionnaire. These were collapsed into two main categories which represented 'regular contact' - weekly, fortnightly, monthly and every 2/3 months - and 'irregular contact', which referred to young people that had seen birth family members in the last six months but not on a regular basis, that is less often than every 2/3 months.

Table 8.7 shows that of the young people that had seen birth family members in the last six months, the majority had fairly regular contact with them, especially with their birth mother and siblings – 80.4% (99) of young people whose birth mother was alive and known about by the foster carer saw her on a regular basis and similarly, 80.3% (118) of young people saw their siblings regularly. However, there were a significant minority of young people that had *irregular contact* with birth family members, especially with their birth father and extended family. Out of those young people that had seen their birth father in the last six months, 28.6% had irregular contact with him (i.e. they saw him less often than every 2/3 months).

Table 8.7
Proportion and number of young people that had regular contact and irregular contact with each birth family member category in the last six months

Regular contact	Irregular contact
80.4% (99) mother	19.5% (24) mother
80.3% (118) siblings	19.0% (28) siblings
67.1% (47) father	28.6% (20) father
55.2% (64) extended family	34.5% (40) extended family

Note. Where percentages do not add up to 100%, data was missing for the remaining cases.

Further analysis on young people's contact with birth family members

Further analysis was undertaken to establish whether the young people's contact with birth family members varied under particular conditions. To make this analysis possible, a single variable was created for the level of this contact which measured the *number* of birth family member categories each young person had seen in the last six months. The aim of this single variable was to distinguish between young people who had no contact with birth family members in the last six months and those who had a medium or high level of contact.

Table 8.8 shows that 10.2% (21) of all young people had seen no members of their birth family in the last six months - that is 1 out of 10 young people. Young people were most likely to have seen 2 or 3 birth family member categories in the last six months – 32.2% (66) and 31.2% (64) respectively. The results from Table 8 were used to divide young people into three groups representing the differing extent of contact with birth family members in the last six months. These were: low (young people had seen no birth family member category) – 10.2%; medium (young people had seen relatives from one to two birth family member categories) – 45.9%; and high (young people had seen relatives from three to four birth family member categories) – 43.9%. This classification was used to analyse whether contact varied according to two particular factors. Firstly, the length of time that young people had been in their current foster care placement. Secondly, whether young people were in relative or non-relative care.

Table 8.8
Number of birth family member categories that young people have had face to face contact with in the last six months as reported by foster carers

No. of birth family member categories	%	No.
None (i.e. no family contact)	10.2	21
1 family member category	13.7	28
2 family member categories	32.2	66
3 family member categories	31.2	64
All 4 family member categories	12.7	26
Total	100.0	205

Contact with birth family by length of time in current foster care placement

It was shown earlier that the young people in this study tended to be in their current foster care placement for a relatively long period of time – on average for 7.9 years – and 42.9% (88) had been with the same foster carer for ten years or more. When the results for the newly created variable on level of contact were analysed by the length of time young people had been in their current placement, the following results emerged.

Young people who were in their current foster care placement for a relatively short period of time (one to three years) were more likely to have had a fairly high level of contact in the last six months (i.e. had seen relatives from three to four birth family member categories). However, this high level of contact was not sustained over time. The likelihood of having such a high level of contact fell the longer young people had been in their current foster care placement. For those young people in their current placement for one to three years, 61.7% (29) had seen relatives from three to four birth family member categories in the last six months, this fell to 48.6% (34) of those in their current placement for four to nine years and, further still, to 30.7% (27) of those in their placement for ten years or more. Furthermore, young people who had been in their current placement for ten years or more were most likely to have had no contact with any birth family members in the last six months. Out of the 21 young people that had not seen any birth family members in the last six months, 20 of them had been in their current placement for ten years or more. The relationship between young people's contact with birth family members in the last six months and length of time in their current foster care placement was found to be statistically significant.

Level of contact by relative/non-relative care placement

The profile of young people in long term foster care in this study presented earlier on in this paper showed that one quarter of young people were in relative foster care, 24.9% (51). When the level of contact was explored separately for those in relative and non-relative care, it was found that young people in relative care were more likely to have had a high level of contact (i.e. seen relatives from three to four birth family member categories) in the last six months compared to those in non-relative care – 52.9% (27) of those in relative care had seen relatives from three to four family member categories compared to 40.8% (62) of those in non-relative care. In addition, out of the 21 young people who had no contact with any birth family members in the last six months, 20 were in non-relative care. While these results are interesting, they were not statistically significant (borderline significance). Nonetheless, this finding could be indicative of a potential relationship where the level of young people's contact with birth family members differs for those in relative and non-relative care.

Impact of contact with birth family

The impact of contact with birth family was explored for the young people that had seen at least one birth family member in the last six months, that is a total of 184 young people.

Table 8.9 shows how foster carers viewed the young people's contact with their birth family overall in terms of being beneficial for them or not. The results show contact with birth family was seen to be beneficial for over half of young people, 54.3% (100). Contact was deemed as *not* beneficial for 14.1% (26) of young people. Some uncertainty was expressed by 15.2% (28) of carers who replied 'yes and no' or else that the answer depended on the family member in question. In general, the overall results show that contact between the young people in long term foster care and their birth family was more likely to be seen as positive than not by their foster carers.

Table 8.9
Foster carer's assessment of the impact of contact with birth family members in the last six months for young people

Beneficial	%	No.
Yes	54.3	100
No	14.1	26
Both yes and no / depends on family member	15.2	28
Not applicable (very little contact)	2.7	5
Don't know / no response	13.6	25
Total	100.0	184

Summary of main results

Characteristics of young people and their foster carers

The young people in the study were found to have the following characteristics.
- They were evenly divided by gender - 48.3% of young people were male and 51.7% were female – and they were mostly aged 13-14 years old - 95.1%.
- Young people were likely to have been placed in care at a very young age – 53.3% were placed in care at age five years or younger.
- They had been in their current care placement for a relatively long period of time – 42.9% of young people had been with their current carer for ten years or more.
- 48.8% of young people had other placements in care. Just over one quarter of these young people, 26.0%, had experienced three or more previous placements in care.
- Finally, 24.4% were related to their current foster carer, whom was most likely to be an aunt or uncle.
-

The foster carers interviewed in the study had the following characteristics.
- Respondent carers were largely female – 89.8%. Across all foster carers, ages ranged widely from 21 to 80 years old.
- Foster carers were just as likely to live in rural areas as in urban locations.
- Foster carers were most likely to have finished their schooling at primary level.
- 6 out of 10 foster carers and their families were fostering another child or young people in addition to the young person that was the focus of this study – 61.0%.
- On average, foster carers had been fostering for 11.4 years. Across all foster carers, the number of years fostering ranged from 1 to 37 years.

Education and schooling

School attendance – Most young people attended mainstream schools, 93.7%. There was a fairly even breakdown between those in primary and post-primary schools – 47.9% and 52.1% respectively. The overwhelming majority of young people, 98.0%, attended school regularly. Being absent from school without the carer's permission or knowledge was not an issue for most of the young people.

Behaviour at school – The majority of the young people, 82.9%, were reported to be well-behaved at school during the school year. On the other hand, 3 out of 10 carers had been contacted by the school about the young person's behaviour in the school year. Carers of boys were twice as likely as those of girls to have been contacted by the school during the year. However, in general young people's behaviour at school was not an issue of concern for the majority of foster carers interviewed.

Specialist educational provision – Almost 5 out of 10 young people had received some form of specialist educational provision during the school year, either in the form of remedial education or placement in a special class or school. Young people who had been in care for a relatively short period of time (and were older when first placed in care) were significantly more likely to have received specialist educational provision. While young people in non-relative care were also more likely to have received such specialist educational provision compared to those in relative care, this result was not statistically significant.

Beneficial experience of schooling – School broadly seems to have been a positive experience for the majority of young people in the study, as reported by their carers. However, this group of young people were more likely to have experienced bullying at school compared to young people in the general school going population.

Young people's contact with birth family

Composition of young people's birth families – The majority of young people, 83.4%, had a birth mother who was currently alive or known about by the foster carer. The birth fathers of just over two thirds of young people, 68.8%, were alive and known about by the carer. Most young people had siblings and extended family members that were known about by the carer also. So, out of all birth family member categories, birth fathers were most likely to be 'unknown' to the carer, and therefore, to the young person.

Level of contact in the previous six months – Young people with birth family members alive or known about by the foster carer were more likely to have seen their birth mother and siblings out of all the birth family member categories – 71.9% and 75.0% respectively. Young people were least likely to have seen their birth father in the last six months.

Frequency of contact in the last six months – This contact was largely of a regular nature, especially with birth mothers and siblings. However, a significant minority of young people had irregular contact (that is, less often than every 2/3 months over this period) with their birth father and extended family – 28.6% and 34.5% respectively.

Further analysis on the level of contact – A single variable was created which measured the number of birth family member categories (out of the four), members of whom young people had seen in the last six months. Based on this classification, 10.2% of young people had not seen any birth family members in this time, while 45.9% had a medium level of contact (had seen relatives from one to two birth family member categories) and 43.9% had a high level of contact (had seen relatives from three to four birth family member categories). Some interesting results to emerge from this further analysis were the following:

- As the length of time that young people had been in their current care placement increased, the chances of them having a high level of contact with birth family members progressively decreased. (significant).
- Young people in relative care were more likely to have had a high level of contact with birth family members than those in non-relative care. (not significant).
- *Impact of contact with birth family* – Contact with birth family members was deemed as beneficial for 54.3% of young people. Overall, it was considered to be more positive than not by foster carers.

Conclusions

This study has focused on a particular group of young people in long term foster care in Ireland, that is those aged 13-14 years. The findings presented in this paper can be used to support three main conclusions.

Favourable educational progress overall despite two areas of some concern – educational need and bullying

The results on the educational progress of the young people in long term foster care are comparatively favourable. The majority of young people were found to have regularly attended school and there tends to be few problems regarding their behaviour. However, almost half of the young people in the study, 47.8%, had some degree of educational need, which was being responded to through remedial classes or being in a special class or school. In addition, bullying was found to be more prevalent for the young people in the study compared to those in the general school going population. Therefore, the two areas of educational need and bullying amongst young people in long term foster care would appear to require further research and particular attention from social work practitioners and schools.

Importance of birth family ties for placement decisions and maintaining contact

The importance of family ties in the lives of the young people that were the focus of this study is clearly shown here. Almost one half of the young people, 48.3%, had been placed with a sibling in the same foster family. Placing siblings together in the same foster family would appear to be one of the major considerations when placement decisions are made. Also, one out of every four young people in the study were in the care of relatives. Therefore, the role of relative foster care in the care system in Ireland seems significant. The results on the level of contact between young people and their birth family members reflect the efforts that are made by all concerned to maintain these links. Where the passage of time is associated with reducing contact, it is important to ensure that this is due to considered choice, rather than neglect.

Long term foster care is a reality

Finally, it can be argued that long term foster care in Ireland is a reality. While half of the young people were found to have experienced other care placements before their current foster care placement, it is the case that the other half have remained in the same foster care placement since first entering care. Further support for this conclusion is provided by the finding that 42.9% of young people had been in their current foster care placement for ten years or more. Therefore, one of the key features of the Irish foster care system is that it has provided stable and continuous care to many young people on a long term basis. This would not be possible without the dedication and commitment of Irish foster carers and their families.

References

Altshuler, S. J. (2003). From barriers to successful collaboration: Public schools and child welfare working together. *Social Work, 48*, 52-63.

Borland, M., et al. (1998). *Education and care – Away from home.* Edinburgh: The Scottish Council for Research in Education.

Department of Health & Children (Ireland) (2000). *Child care interim minimum dataset* (unpublished).

Frey, J. H., & Oishi, S.M. (1995). *How to conduct interviews by telephone and in person.* Thousand Oaks, London and New Delhi: Sage.

Gilligan, R. (1996). The foster carer experience in Ireland – findings from a postal survey. *Child Care, Health and Development, 22*, 85-98.

Gilligan, R. (2001). *Promoting resilience – A resource guide on working with children in the care system.* London: British Agencies for Adoption and Fostering.

Heath, A., Aldgate, M., & Colton, M. (1989). The Educational progress of children in and out of care. *British Journal of Social Work, 19*, 447-460.

Jackson, S. (Ed.) (2001). The education of children in care. In *Nobody ever told us school mattered: Raising the educational attainments of children in care* (pp. 11-53). London: British Agencies for Adoption and Fostering.

Kelly, G. (2000). The survival of long term foster care. In G. Kelly & R. Gilligan (Eds.), *Issues in foster care – Policy, practice and research* (pp. 12-39). London and Philadelphia: Jessica Kingsley.

McMillen, J. C., & Tucker, J. (1998). The status of older adolescents at exit from out of home care. *Child Welfare, 78*, 339-360.

Meyler, M. (2002). *Counting on foster care.* Dublin: Northern Area Health Board.

O'Moore, A. M., Kirkham, C., & Smith, M. (1997). Bullying behaviour in Irish schools: A nationwide study. *Irish Journal of Psychology, 18*, 141-169.

Quinton, D., & Rutter, M. (1988). *Parenting breakdown: The making and breaking of intergenerational links.* Aldershot: Avebury

Schofield, G. (2000). *Growing up in foster care.* London: British Association for Adoption and Fostering.

St.Claire, L., & Osborn, A. F. (1987). The ability and behaviour of children who have been "in-care" or separated from their parents. *Early Child Development and Care, 28*, 187-354.

The Central Statistics Office (2003). *Census 2002 – Principal demographic results.* Dublin: The Stationery Office.

Appendix of supporting tables

Table A1
Contact from school about young people's behaviour by gender

Contact from school about young person's behaviour	Male % (n)	Female % (n)	Total % (n)
Yes	40.4 (40)	20.2 (21)	30.0 (61)
No	59.6 (59)	79.8 (83)	70.0 (142)
Total	100.0 (99)	100.0 (104)	100.0 (203)

Note. $x^2 = 9.857$, df =1, $p<.01$.

Table A2
Specialist educational provision by age of young person when first placed in care

Type of educational provision	0-2 years % (n)	3-8 years % (n)	9-13 years % (n)	Total
Mainstream only	63.2 (48)	50.0 (30)	40.4 (19)	53.0 (97)
Specialist educational provision	36.8 (28)	50.0 (30)	59.6 (28)	47.0 (86)
Total	100.0 (76)	100.0 (60)	100.0 (47)	100.0 (183)

Note. $x^2 = 6.348$, df =2, $p<.05$.

Table A3
Specialist educational provision by relative/non-relative care placement

Type of educational provision	Relative % (n)	Non-relative % (n)	Total % (n)
Mainstream only	60.8 (31)	48.7 (74)	51.7 (105)
Specialist educational provision	39.2 (20)	51.3 (78)	48.3 (98)
Total	100.0 (51)	100.0 (152)	100.0 (203)

Note. $x^2 = 2.239$, df = 1, p>.05.

Table A4
Level of contact between young people and birth family member categories in the last six months

Did young person see birth family member?	Birth mother % (n)	Birth father % (n)	Siblings % (n)	Extended family % (n)
Yes	71.9 (123)	49.6 (70)	75.0 (147)	61.7 (116)
No	28.1 (48)	48.9 (69)	15.8 (31)	33.0 (62)
Don't know/ no response	-	1.4 (2)	9.2 (18)	5.3 (10)
Total	100.0 (171)	100.0 (141)	100.0 (196)	100.0 (188)

Table A5
Frequency of face to face contact between young people and birth family member categories in the last six months – regular versus irregular contact – as reported by foster carers

Frequency of contact	Birth mother % (n)	Birth father % (n)	Siblings % (n)	Extended family % (n)
Regular contact	80.4 (99)	67.1 (47)	80.3 (118)	55.2 (64)
No regular or ongoing contact	19.5 (24)	28.6 (20)	19.0 (28)	34.5 (40)
Other or no response	-	4.3 (3)	0.7 (1)	10.3 (12)
Total	100.0 (123)	100.0 (70)	100.0 (147)	100.0 (116)

Note. Where percentages do not add up to 100%, 'other' responses were given or data was missing.

Table A6
Level of contact with relatives from birth family member categories over the last six months by length of time in current foster care placement

Duration in current placement / Level of contact	1-3 years % (n)	4-9 years % (n)	10 years or more % (n)	Total % (n)
Low (none)	-	1.4 (1)	22.7 (20)	10.2 (21)
Medium (1-2 birth family member categories)	38.3 (18)	50.0 (35)	46.6 (41)	45.9 (94)
High (3-4 birth family member categories)	61.7 (29)	48.6 (34)	30.7 (27)	43.9 (90)
Total	100.0 (47)	100.0 (70)	100.0 (88)	100.0 (205)

Note. $x^2 = 31.613$, $df = 4$, $p < .001$.

Table A7
Level of contact with relatives from birth family member categories over the last six months by relative/non-relative care placement

Level of contact	Relative % (n)	Non-relative % (n)	Total % (n)
Low (none)	2.0 (1)	13.2 (20)	10.3 (21)
Medium (1-2 birth family member categories)	45.1 (23)	46.1 (70)	45.8 (93)
High (3-4 birth family member categories)	52.9 (27)	40.8 (62)	43.8 (89)
Total	100.0 (51)	100.0 (152)	100.0 (203)

Note. $x^2 = 5.922$, $df = 2$, $p > .05$.

9

User participation and child protection: A structural framework for collaboration in core groups

Marit Skivenes & Elisabeth Willumsen

Introduction

In Norway and other welfare states the authorities are promoting participation and collaboration between professionals and service users (The Norwegian Government White Papers; 35/1994-1995, 34/1996-1997, 40/2001-2002). The debate regarding user participation as an individual right might be regarded as an important aspect of a democratic order (Eriksen, 1999). However, we see that many people experience their rights being violated and that the welfare state might be regarded as a remote system. Often service users and professionals express their concerns about public services themselves creating problems that lead to marginalisation and powerlessness (Bergwitz, 2001, Eriksen, 2001, Underlid 2003). By applying a participatory oriented approach the intention behind welfare policy is to prepare for better decisions and provide more adequate welfare services in collaboration with the parties involved.

Although there is continuing interest in user participation, knowledge is scarce with regard to how to make participation function, its goals, and the types of structural criteria needed. In general user participation raises several challenges, such as the asymmetrical balance of power and knowledge between officials and service users, as well as a possible disagreement regarding the types of values and norms to be applied (Eriksen & Skivenes, 1998). Some of the beneficiaries of welfare services might be "socially deprived" in relation to education, resources, and political influence. This is also the case in connection with child protection. Children's rights and participation raises further challenges. In child care, decisions must be justified according to "the child's best interest", which is a normative question. When public authorities take responsibility for "a child's best interest" decisions have to be legitimate, this means that they in principle may withstand public scrutiny. When working in child protection the goal is to ensure reasonable user participation in order to be able to make legitimate decisions in accordance with "the child's best interest". The question we will elaborate here is how to organize collaboration to ensure user involvement and legitimate decisions in child protection service. Our point of departure is a deliberative model of collaboration where user involvement is central and which establishes four structural criteria for organising collaboration. Using these criteria, we will analyze the formal and structural framework of core groups in child protection. Secondly, we will analyze the actual interaction in core groups. Thirdly, we will make recommendations for establishing and organizing core groups in order to increase user participation and legitimate decision-making.

Theoretical and methodological framework

User participation may be defined in various ways, but usually it has to do with "the people who are involved in a decision, or users of services, having influence on decision making processes and the framing of the service" (The Government White Paper; 34/1996-97:9). The concept of 'user participation' is present at different levels; individual as well as collective. Moreover, there are different degrees of participation, from a passive form of participation to be fully in control of the service (Rønning & Solheim, 1998). The focus of this study is on the individual level, addressing user participation in child protection of young people having psychosocial problems, living in residential care. In order to properly analyse and evaluate the potential user involvement, it is necessary to have a theory that can capture the relevance of participation for the parties involved. Our theoretical approach builds on normative political theory, where procedural criteria to handle difficult value-based questions, such as defining "the child's best interest" in a just manner are developed.

A structural framework for collaboration

Our starting point is that the notion of "the child's best interest" is a normative category, implying that it is a matter of values and norms applied in connection with children's rearing and upbringing. "The child's best interest" is a multi-faceted concept, which makes it a challenge to both professionals and legislators. It implies that different norms may stand against each other, and that we do not know exactly what is in the "the child's best interest". Central perspectives in normative political theory state that when normative questions are at stake and the standards for determining the reasonableness of outcomes are disputed, one should address the process itself. The criteria underpinning reasonable procedures differ according to theoretical perspectives. In this study, a deliberative framework is applied, because it focuses on the procedural rules of communication between affected parties as an imperative to reach legitimate decisions (Eriksen, 1993, Habermas, 1992/1996). This conceptual framework has also previously been used in analyses of Norwegian child protection at different levels, and should be subject to further elaboration (Backe-Hansen, 2001, Eriksen & Skivenes, 1998).

In the deliberative perspective, standards have been developed for differentiating and evaluating different types of deliberative processes in relation to the handling of normative questions. One might distinguish between four general criteria that must be satisfied (Eriksen 1993, Eriksen & Skivenes

1998, Skivenes & Eriksen 2000, Skivenes 2002). Firstly, the affected parties must be involved in the decision-making process. Secondly, there must be meeting places at hand where deliberation can take place. Thirdly, differences in capabilities to present one's views and ability to deliberate must be compensated, and fourthly, there must be public accessibility.

The *involvement of the affected parties* is required to make sure that information is complete, and that relevant interests and needs are included. Parents and children have knowledge and opinions about personal relations and important issues in the family, and as such they must be heard in order to make reasonable decisions. But, the opinions and arguments of the affected parties might be unwise, incomplete and limited, and, thus, must therefore be tested and balanced against other arguments and types of knowledge. Hence one must establish *meeting-places* where affected parties and child care personnel may discuss and exchange information. When the actors meet to deliberate what to do, it provides an opportunity to make sure that relevant arguments are included, that the information collected is correct, and that arguments can be tested and opinions changed.

Differences in dispositions might hinder authentic deliberation, and thus for instance children may need support to express their views. There is a need to *reduce the effects of the imbalances that exist* in the power, knowledge, and capabilities to present arguments and views. If arguments are going to be genuine, arrangements must be made so that understandable information is given to all. For example, it is important to specify the nature of participation, its normative implications and preconditions, and the formal and informal means by which it is best realised. Education and social background may affect the capacity to argue one's case. Parents and children, depending on age, may need help to clarify their opinions. There are different ways in which children may participate (Arnstein, 1969). Furthermore, there should be arrangements providing legal aid and support, such as the opportunity to be supported or represented by a lawyer or a trustee, rules for the allocation of speaking time and how to discuss topics, and finally, arrangements supporting constructive group processes.

The final criterion is *public accessibility*. In order to make sure decisions are 'correct' and in "the child's best interest", it must be possible to control the decisions and their content. For example, to what extent are decision-makers emphasizing relevant arguments, and are they able to provide sound justifications for applying the values and norms imbedded in the measures recommended? Another reason why public accessibility is important is that it enables citizens to learn about child protection and to make up their minds about what one ought to do, and the types of norms applied in public child protection. In short, decisions must stand up to public scrutiny (in accordance with the necessary confidentiality) to be regarded as legitimate.

In this article, we will focus on structural criteria for collaboration and legitimate decisions in child protection. Deliberative theory emphasizes that it is only through actual discussions between the relevant parties that one may know what is just. This dimension is not subject to discussion in this article. General structural criteria are considered necessary conditions, but not sufficient to achieve legitimate decisions unless attuned to specific contexts. The current context is user participation in core groups in connection with child protection with regard to young people in residential care.

Norwegian Child Protection and core groups

According to the Norwegian Child Welfare Act (1992), municipal child care services work under a general duty to safeguard and promote the welfare of children in need. The Act acknowledges the individual needs of children and families and stipulates that actions should be taken in "the best interest of the child". Professionals, usually social workers, in the childcare service at the municipal level assess the situation of a given child and initiate relevant action. If the child or the family have serious and complex problems and these are seen to require comprehensive services, and possibly entailing the child being moved away from home, the child might be referred to a residential institution, which is run by the county child care service. Such cases are based on formal decisions made by the County Social Welfare Board either voluntarily or through care orders. According to the Child Care Act (1992), childcare services, both at municipal and county levels, are obliged to collaborate with other relevant services and actions shall be taken in accordance with the Acts normative foundation, this means the child's best interests (§4-1).

Accordingly, the County Social Welfare Board makes the formal decision, and an individual child protection plan is formulated by the local child care services, at the municipal level. These documents form the formal framework for further collaboration and participation. Most residential child care institutions organize core groups as a compulsory part of their provision of care to residential children. Particularly in complex and serious cases, such as young people with psychosocial problems in residential care, the goal of the core group is predominantly to ensure coordination and participation over time (Godeseth, 1995; Hallett, 1995; Havnen & Iversen, 1996). This implies regular meetings, about every six weeks, between the people involved in the case; professionals and the young people themselves (depending on age) and their families. Together they formulate action plans which are then jointly implemented. In the work of the core groups, openness to other parts of the network is emphasized as a means to empower the service users to participate actively in meetings as well as for coping with day-to-day living. This corresponds with Payne's (2000, p. 5) understanding of "open teamwork", which is characterized as *"the professional and multiprofessional teams and the network of people we link with in the community and team working and networking together as an integrated form of practice"*. In consequence we consider the core group as part of an implementation process where members try out different actions to find fruitful solutions (Willumsen & Hallberg, 2003).

The core group meetings can be characterized as milestones to assess the progress made in a child care case, to discuss the participation and collaboration, as well as decide on further development. As illustrated in this study, the core group involves additional networking and team working to be able to include the complex relations between the professionals, young people, their families and *a wider* network. The focus is on the core group's meetings where they deal with different issues relating to both practical and value-based questions. As mentioned, it is primarily normative questions that must meet the requirements of legitimacy, and thus must be subject to a strictly deliberative procedure.

At first glance, we might assume that core groups are roughly based on the criteria of the deliberative model. However, there is a need, both theoretically and empirically, to specify the strengths and weaknesses of these criteria when applied to a practical child protection context. Thus both the organisational framework and the actual interaction in core groups are being analyzed according to the procedural standards outlined above. We are emphasizing the criteria for participation and the balancing of power. Based on this analysis we will make suggestions about possible structural means to improve user involvement and decision-making in core groups. Thus, the empirical material described below will be used to illustrate and to find strengths and weaknesses with some of the assumptions the deliberative theory states.

Method and ethics

This study is based on an examination of relevant legal documents as well as material from five core groups regarding young people, aged 12-18. The youngsters appear to have psychosocial problems and as such are placed in a residential unit. Professionals describe these cases as complex and difficult to approach. Over the period of a year, the researcher (Elisabeth Willumsen) undertook a series of observations of core group meetings held in relation to five children, 13 meetings in total. A licence from the Data Inspectorate in Norway was obtained and written consent was provided. All data has been anonymized. Notes and tapes will be erased when the study has been concluded. This present study is part of a larger project which includes open interviews with parents and professionals involved in each case. There has therefore been access to information concerning the background, experiences and perceptions of participation and collaboration, of a range of different participants, to supplement our observations.

Observation is particularly suitable as a research method when studying processes and interaction. When undertaking observations the researcher has to define his own role and degree of participation. This will also depend on the research question (Fossåskaret et al., 1997). The purpose was to observe how participants interacted in core group meetings when discussing various issues, particularly looking for collaboration strategies. The researcher was not supposed to interfere with the ongoing discussions, but nevertheless be intimate enough to be able to observe all participants, listen to what they were saying and observe their non-verbal language. In other words the researcher was undertaking "selective observations" and had a "peripheral-membership role": primarily observation and passive participation (Angrosino & Mays de Perez, 2000). The researchers' role and positioning at the meeting were discussed with the professionals, and they suggested that the researcher sat down at the same table as the other participants, at the end of the table. The researcher was concerned that she influenced the participants, particularly in the first couple of meetings. When inquiring about this the participants (professionals as well as parents) stated that after a few minutes of the meeting they got so involved in what was going on that they completely forgot that the researcher was present. This may also be the result of the fact that the researcher had interviewed most of the group members previously and as such they were already familiar with her. During the core group meetings the researcher took notes to describe as detailed as possible the interaction between the participants. Immediately after the meeting the researcher went through the notes, making supplementary comments trying to complete the observations from the meeting.

Core groups in practice

Core group meetings are usually led by the managers of the residential care institution according to a pre-fixed agenda consisting of three points: a summary from each participant regarding what has happened since the last meeting, plans for the next period, and matters of special concern like holiday plans, particular incidents which need further discussion, and so on. At the beginning of the meeting all members have the opportunity to raise issues requiring particular attention. After each meeting a report is formulated by one of the professionals and distributed to the participants, which also included date and time for the next meeting. The cases of Andy and John are highlighted in this article. In short their stories are as follows:

> *Andy is 14-year-old. He used to live with his mother, stepfather and two half-brothers. Andy had numerous problems in school; with teachers and the other pupils, and with bullying. The school reported his case to the childcare services about a year before he came to stay in the residential institution. Andy was also having problems at home; he was aggressive, and depressed. His mother said she could not take responsibility for him, and Andy was placed in an emergency care institution before he went into residential care for a long-term stay. There are great conflicts in the family, especially between Andy's mother and his grandparents regarding their roles and responsibility vis-à-vis Andy. The boy has been offered treatment at the local psychiatric youth clinic where he receives individual therapy. He attends the residential school.*

John is a 14-year-old boy, the middle of three brothers. John and his younger brother are both residents in child care institutions. There have been major conflicts between his parents for several years including acts of violence in their home. John's parents are now separated. There is much disagreement between the parents over contact arrangements and planning for John's future. The boy is quiet and introverted and has gone through many painful experiences in his family. He has also had problems at school, conflicts with other pupils, and bullying. John moved to the residential care institution a year ago. He attends a special school for a small group of pupils situated outside the institution. A therapist at the local psychiatric clinic is responsible for his treatment. There are plans to move John so he can go and live with his father, who has moved to another town.

The following analysis is structured according to the theoretical criteria; "inclusion of all relevant parties", "balancing power", "meeting-places" and "public accessibility". For analytical purposes we distinguish between the criteria, but in practice they overlap to some degree.

Analysis and reflections

Inclusion of relevant parties

According to the critical standard outlined above there should be structural arrangements to ensure that all affected parties are able to participate in a childcare case. In the Norwegian system there are no formal procedures to determine who shall participate in core groups, with exception of guidelines relating to the rehabilitation of children (Norwegian Board of Health, 1998).

Despite the lack of formal arrangements, our material shows that the professionals tried to include all parties directly affected, usually representatives of the institution, schools, the child protection services, the child's parents, and the child. In Andy and John's core groups different participants were involved, who raised different challenges to be discussed.

In Andy's core group eight people participated. In addition to Andy and his mother, it was one child care worker from the child protection services (responsible for Andy), one teacher from the residential school, four staff members from the residential institution (manager, two residential care workers responsible for Andy, and occasionally the psychologist). In John's case both parents and professionals involved participated, including professionals representing the psychiatric youth service. John never participated. One might question the extent of his capacity to choose or to be able to be present by referring to his difficulties with expressing himself. The professionals involved consisted of two staff members from psychiatric youth service, one person from the local child protection agency, three staff members of the residential institution (manager, two residential care workers responsible for John), and occasionally two staff members from John's school (principal and teacher). In sum, there were ten people: two private parties and eight professionals.

To make legitimate decisions the children's extended network must participate

The size and representation of the group has a bearing on what information is available, and whose needs and interests are heard. The challenge is to find out who should participate in the core group meeting, and on the basis of this, what type of information is needed to establish a nuanced picture of the child and the family. In both Andy and John's core groups there was an overweight of professionals participating, and very few private parties. According to the deliberative model a reasonable point of departure, when discussing the question of who should be included, is to identify who are the people important to Andy and John in their extended network. In Andy's case, one might ask why his grandparents, weekend parents and his stepfather were not participating. His grandparents were central in his life and had taken a lot of responsibility for Andy and his problems. They have given him in many respects a second home, and in some ways acted as his parents. Andy's stepfather came into his life when he was approximately 8 years old and has been living with the family. Andy also had a weekend home. He spent every fourth weekend on a farm. His weekend parents were not considered relevant partners in the core group, although this had been subject to some discussion. It was however decided to include them in a separate meeting. Andy's siblings were to young to be involved in the case.

John's absence raises serious challenges to child protection work, because it is his interest that is at stake at the same time as it is his legal right not to participate. Perhaps John would have participated if he could have brought a friend, or if his eighteen-year-old brother had participated. He lives on his own, but has been supporting John during their adolescence. The challenge is to establish what is in John's future interests ("the child's best interest"). According to both Norwegian welfare policy and our theoretical standard it is regarded as an imperative that those affected should participate. Thus John could have been encouraged to attend, by discussing why he does not want to attend, and by providing measures that would make John more comfortable in the situation. If it would not be possible for John to participate after all, there should have been appointed a trustee to represent John's views, for instance the residential care worker in charge of John.

Meeting places

Collaboration requires some form of meeting place so that information can be exchanged and discussions take place. It may take the form of a physical place, but it may also be a virtual meeting place. The important thing is that the participants' needs and the purpose of the meetings are taken into account. Neither the law nor regulations provide any guidelines as where meetings shall take place.

Our cases (case studies) show that meetings where held at the residential care institutions. The main reasons were said to be that the professionals were on standby. Because of lack of resources it was not possible to hire additional staff so that the professionals involved in the case could attend the meeting somewhere else. Another reason was the number of participants that had to travel. Parents and external collaborating partners usually represented a smaller number of people, which made it more practicable to meet at the residential institution. Thus, the institutions were the place at which the participants met. Time of meetings differed according to the participants' needs and wishes. Although the institutions for practical reasons were the best places to hold meetings, the disadvantages were that persons from the children's network had to travel a long distance. This was both time consuming, costly and, avowedly, exhausting. In one of the cases the parent had to use parts of her holidays to be able to attend the meetings.

The empirical material shows that practical considerations determined choice of meeting place. There were no explicit evaluations of what would be the best place to meet. Core group meeting places is not an issue in legal regulations and procedures. It is however important to consider type of meeting place most convenient to carry out deliberations. Considerations about alternative meeting places might also be regarded as a way of balancing power and including relevant parties. One question to be asked in this regard is whether or not children and their family felt comfortable about meeting at the institution.

The advantage of using the institution as meeting place is that this is the place in which the youth live while in care. It might make him/her more comfortable in the collaboration process and more positive towards participation. Additionally it would have been more flexible if the young people participated parts of the meeting. It might also be beneficial to the youth to see that her/his network is physically present just for them. However, in some cases the best meeting place may be considered to be at the family home. It would be particularly helpful in the phase when the child is planning to move back home. Another means by which to carry out meetings are through videoconferences or other interactive media aids. It became apparent that parents and other family members used a lot of time and money to attend meetings, and maybe some travelling could have been avoided by some of the participants if such aids had been used. The importance is, as for criterion one, that the purpose of the meeting determines how and where to meet. If it is primarily an exchange of information, then virtual meeting places should at least be considered. When the purpose is to make decisions about important matters and learning, face-to-face interaction seems to be the best alternative.

Balancing power

In this section the focus is on the expected imbalance of power between the adults and children, as well as between professionals and non-professionals. No formal procedures or arrangements for the balancing of power are established for core groups in general. Neither was there made any explicit arrangement in our material and thus nor for John and Andy's groups.

Observations indicate that collaboration was organized in accordance with ordinary meeting rules that created a routine for how the meetings proceeded. There were three main items on the agenda; summary of developments since last meeting, future plans, and particular events that needed discussion. One agreed on the need for flexibility; partly to give the participants opportunity to present issues at the meeting, and partly to be able to handle what was occurring during the meeting. For example, if a youth was in a bad mood when he/she entered the meeting, shouting and swearing, and he/she needed instant handling. Such incidents disturbed the overall agenda.

The participants in the core group had various skills and competencies, which raised challenges on different levels. For example Andy was occasionally aggressive, John was not present and John's father appeared to be very determined. Andy's mother seemed to function quite well, but John's mother apparently had a hard time to adapt to rules and ordinary meeting behaviour. The following section identifies three strategies we saw used to facilitate authentic communication, focusing on how to make parents and the young people comfortable and how to include them and support them in core group meetings.

Informal meeting rules

There were no explicit meeting rules established in the core groups. A chair was appointed, usually one of the managers of the institution. General meeting procedures were adopted, such as to providing everyone with an opportunity to express their opinion(s), wait for their turn to speak, no interruption, and so forth. For instance, John's mother was not accustomed to ordinary meeting rules, making interruptions and commenting when others were speaking. Staff told her to wait for her turn, and when she got the opportunity she often could not manage to present her views in an understandable way. Conflicts between the parents seemed to explain some of her problems in the situation. Observations show that the other members of the core group seemed to adjust to the meeting rules except for Andy when he was aggressive or in a bad mood.

Facilitate communication

The observations show that several measures were taken in the core group to facilitate user involvement, such as the professionals asking parents and young people questions to hear their opinions. The interaction proceeded in a positive manner; for example, the residential workers asked Andy's mother what she wanted them to say to Andy on the issue of civil versus church confirmation. It was also observed that they regarded parents and young people as equals and treated them with respect; they explicitly asked Andy's mother if they could be of any help when Andy visited the family and how she suggested they could go about providing such help. The observations showed that the professionals listened very carefully, made follow-up questions, and signalled non-verbally that they were interested and showed empathy.

Another observation showed that the residential staff acknowledged Andy's mother's actions and supported her when she felt defeated. When the professionals shared information and experiences with Andy's mother they used the opportunity to discuss and reflect on different solutions. They asked what she did to handle a given situation and if she had other solutions and suggestions, in an attempt to create alternative strategies. They compared their experiences or referred to incidents from previous meetings, and exchanged views on the best ways to handle Andy. This interaction showed how dependent they were on each other, the challenges they were facing, and their own vulnerability. At the same time, they were establishing alliances and supporting each other. The professionals, and the mother in particular, were creating and learning new ways of coping with Andy. One might call this "a therapeutic attitude" that apparently also had a great potential for learning, which had the additional effect of acknowledging Andy's mother and reinforcing her parenting role.

Andy was often capable in participating and presenting his views, being polite and arguing sensibly. In these situations it seemed sufficient to ask him questions and give him time to express his views. These observations correspond with the parties' own opinions. In interviews John and Andy's parents confirmed that they were being listened to and were happy with the way they were treated.

However, Andy could be aggressive. The observations showed that when Andy was aggressive or things did not turn out the way he wanted, the meeting changed from a discussion to a matter of dealing with his behaviour. In these situations the professionals took different roles and responsibilities; at least one person supported Andy by trying to help him clarify his thoughts. Although the adults did not necessarily agree with him they supported him expressing himself. By doing this they used the opportunity to show him alternative strategies, which served as a way of empowering Andy, and additionally represented a way he could change behaviour and learn new strategies. Handling Andy's aggression during the meeting also provided insight into how Andy was functioning at the time and knowledge of relevant strategies. In spite of the very demanding situations that could occur, Andy's presence gave the staff an important opportunity to demonstrate strategies and skills. Andy's mother and the other professionals observed a live demonstration that gave them an insight into the challenges and possible ways of handling him. At the same time they developed trust in the institution; they were "confident that Andy was very well taken care of", Andy's mother and the social worker said in the interviews. Additionally the incident served as a means of learning for Andy's mother about alternative strategies and skills. The adults also had the opportunity to raise these mutual experiences in later meetings, in which they reflected on what had happened, alternative solutions, and so forth.

Spokesperson and trustee

Referring to the critical standard, no formal arrangements were established to compensate for John's absence or other participants' need for support. John appeared to be introvert, spoke very little, and had a limited vocabulary. His father said he had a good relationship with his son and could represent his views. The residential workers reported that it took time and energy to get to know John, and to find out about his thoughts and needs. The psychologist stated that John probably found it difficult to know what he wanted. The residential worker in charge of John was responsible for explaining matters to him, but found this to be a challenging task. Observations showed that during the meeting the members of the group usually asked if John had expressed any views on the topic discussed. People reported if they had talked to John. Generally staff tried to obtain information about his views. However no person was appointed to the role as John's trustee.

Regarding John's mother the observations showed she needed some help during the meetings. Perhaps there should have been appointed a trustee to support her. Another solution could be separate meetings with John's mother. These arrangements could also have been a way to balance the fathers' dominance. John's father was usually very well-prepared for the meetings, stating clearly his objective; he wanted John to live with him. He had made plans for how to accomplish this in relation to schooling, family life, friends, and leisure activities. John's father asked for advice about how to handle John's challenges and he was very receptive to proposals regarding arrangements to meet John's needs, stating that he would like to learn about these issues, and suggested a meeting to discuss it. The psychologist had separate meetings with him at his request. The father apparently behaved very appropriately in the meetings. He did not criticize John's mother, nor did he pay much attention to her. Instead, he opposed *her arguments when he thought necessary*. The researcher got the impression that although the child care worker seemed to believe that the father was the most capable parent, it was not made into an explicit topic. Instead, they were captured in the conflict between the parents. As a consequence, they lost sight of John's interest and progress stopped because the core group seemed unable to deliberate and make a decision.

Usually, the meetings in the core group took a natural course. But sometimes conflicts arose, in particular when the members became more concerned about their own point of view and quarrelled. John's parents would also argue, which led to some difficulty with regard to carrying out the meeting. John's father was very articulate which made his mother feel inadequate. The professionals found it difficult to negotiate between the parents, and also got involved in the disagreements. For example, in relation to the issue of time to be spent with John there was a major conflict between the parents. This also included the childcare services, which had the formal authority. The subject of contact was also relevant to John's future custody, and therefore also concerned "John's best interest", and as such all parties in the core group got involved in the discussion. They all had different opinions, which they put forward. In these debates power struggles developed undermining reflections on and deliberations about the best interest of John. There was little effort made to understand each other, and they stated that "John more or less disappeared in the discussions". Nobody seemed to cater for John's interests in this situation. This illustrates the need for a trustee or someone to take responsibility for presenting John's views and interests.

In spite of the lack of formal procedures, our observations indicate that measures were invoked by the professionals to remedy imbalances in influence and to support the views expressed. This seemed to empower the private parties and led to learning situations, in which trust and alliances developed between them. The key issue here seems to be the opportunity for reflection; through reflection the participants could give acknowledgement and support and create new strategies. These reflective processes seemed to fulfil the ideals of authentic deliberation. This happened irrespective of the young people's presence in the core group meeting. However when Andy was present the opportunity to demonstrate how to handle his aggression occurred. If John had been present an opportunity to demonstrate how to handle his shyness may possibly have arisen. In other words, it seemed like the young people's behaviour (psychosocial problems) might represent an additional dimension to the learning potential.

Public accessibility

Theoretically public accessibility has three purposes. First, it makes deliberations more qualified in that one must give reasons acceptable to other discussants. Second, it provides an opportunity to control the outcome of decision-making according to its legal and normative content. Third, it creates a channel into the public sphere and as such the political system. Thus politicians and citizens can get input about the nature of child protection and if existing practice, normative content, and laws are adequate. In child protection one must consider confidentiality regarding personal information, and therefore public accessibility must be limited to some extent. So the question is how to address both questions at the same time.

In core group meetings participants are subject to confidentiality regulations. However, personal information about the young people and family can be revealed to all members in the meeting when the parents give their consent. In the core groups studied, a written report of what had happened at the core group meetings was distributed to all parties. In addition, the young people got oral information from the residential worker in charge of the case and other staff at the institution. In the reports information was given about whom participated at the meeting, what issues were discussed and which decisions were made. Apparently no information was withheld. However, there were some preparatory meetings for the professionals at the residential institution for the purpose of co-ordination, exchange information and views, and supervision.

The empirical material shows that information was made available for the participants before the meeting. Particular efforts were made to make sure the young people were kept informed. One might question the practice of "secret", preparatory meetings before core group meetings, in which plans and strategies were discussed. The content of these meetings was not made known to the other participants of the core group. On the one hand, preparatory meetings are necessary to make sure that the core group meetings are properly carried out, in particular who and how one shall support Andy in the core group meeting. On the other hand it might easily be misused for other purposes, and that might alter the discussion in the core group meetings as well as establish distrust. Thus, it is important that 'secret' meetings are kept to a minimum, and information is given to the other core group members about the necessity and purpose of such meetings.

Turning to the other dimension of the concept of public accessibility, there were not to our knowledge any enquiries from politicians or media about the child protection cases examined in this study. However, if this had been the case it would have been possible to produce publicly available documents in which personal information would have been erased or made unidentifiable. Perhaps child care workers need to be more offensive in this respect. Nevertheless it is always possible to give general information about child protection and core group practice without disclosing personal information. Both strategies are important to consider when handling mass media. One could also consider so-called active publicity. The child protection system suffers from an inability to legitimize its activities. One way to improve legitimacy is to inform the general public so that they get more insight into successes, failures and the day-to-day work of the child protection service. Support from citizens is a central criterion for legitimacy.

Conclusions and recommendations

Core groups have several functions. The intention is to enable rational decisions to be made in an instrumental way. As a practical decision-making system those affected will contribute relevant information and arrangements to balance inequalities, which serves the function of ensuring participation, and that the case is sufficiently illuminated. The purpose of the core groups is co-ordination of efforts and effective use of resources, which, strictly speaking, do not require extensive deliberation. The situation changes when more important issues are at stake, for instance where John shall live in the future. Then it is essential that all affected parties are involved in the making of legitimate decisions about "the child's best interest". Core groups as a deliberative forum use communication as a way of relating to people when handling normative questions. This perspective emphasizes understanding through communication. Participation and deliberation are in themselves important because they help clarify and justify opinions. This is the most adequate way to make legitimate decisions. Deliberation brings about a potential for learning, and requires one or more of the participants involved to change their positions, and learn something new when making legitimate decisions. The analysis also reveals another learning potential in core group collaboration, which is closely connected to the reflective processes of deliberations: on the one hand, one is learning to be a 'deliberative actor' in the collaboration processes, on the other hand, learning to be a more 'autonomous' person outside the core group, for instance when a parent is learning to handle a young person's problems.

Learning potential in core groups is rarely made explicit and is perhaps underestimated as a means to change both strategies and behaviour in dysfunctional families. In other words, when trying to obtain authentic deliberation about what is in the young person's "best interest", one creates a climate for learning. Ideally speaking, the outcome will be both legitimate decisions and service-users coping with daily life in a more confident way.

The analysis shows that the criteria for establishing meeting places and public accessibility were almost met. However, we found weak points concerning the criteria for participation and formal arrangements for compensating inequalities. Our starting point is that core groups' formal framework is based on deliberative criteria. Although there are good reasons to include all those concerned we have seen that this is neither always possible nor convenient.

There are several arguments for including all those who are relevant to the young people in the core group; a wide range of 'information' gives a coherent picture and can be the basis for legitimate decision processes. Collaboration in core groups can additionally imply learning potential for participants' ability to take part in discussions and handling challenges concerning the youth. Learning from each other's experiences enables co-ordinated approaches to be taken. In organizing core groups when important value questions are at stake it is imperative to include all relevant persons in the children's network. However, core groups also deal with less principal tasks, where the purpose is to handle day-to-day activities. In addition, there are also considerations of efficiency and the young person's special needs.

There are good reasons for keeping the size of the core group as small as possible. Working with young people with psychosocial problems requires structure, consistency and predictability. Particularly, when working directly with young people, it is important that they relate to as few people as possible to obtain familiarity, develop trust, and maintain continuity (Ogden, 1997). This is harder when the number of core group members is increasing. Other reasons for keeping core groups small are that they are time-consuming and that it may often be harder to assemble larger groups at any given time. Moreover, progress is usually easier to obtain in small groups. In addition, small groups provide better overview and place responsibility in the right actors, which is important in complex cases. Finally, the need to share experiences and learn from each other, which means revealing defeats, but also supporting each other, apparently works better in relatively small groups (Heap, 1998).

Therefore, there has to be *explicit discussion about the purpose* of the meeting and where the meeting shall take place. Thus one has to establish a procedure or guidelines for making core groups flexible, so that it is possible to make deliberate decisions to change the size and structure of the group according to its purpose. It is important to include people for different purposes, but not necessarily at the same meetings. In other words in these efforts networking and team working has to be combined. Establishing links between the different groups and systems is necessary, in order to get a general overview of the situation.

There is also a need to establish formal structures to make sure that those participating are heard and can take part in the collaboration process in a reasonable way. In this study we found no explicit formal framework for such activities in core groups. However different "informal" collaboration strategies were used, corresponding to the deliberative standard to compensate weak structural arrangements.

Thus, there is a need to strengthen the structural arrangements for a well-functioning core group. It is helpful to have an explicit framework for collaboration in the core group, where the ideals for authentic deliberation as a basis for legitimate decisions are elucidated and agreed upon. Moreover, it is important to meta-communicate about the ideals of deliberation and subsequently establish strategies to obtain authentic deliberations. The intention is that an explicit "deliberation framework" will moderate conflicts because the members may feel obliged to communicate adequately focusing on 'the best interests of the child'.

For example, when conflicts arose in the core group meetings, either because of the young people's behavior or because of power struggles between parents, these would disturb the opportunities for reflection and ambitions to achieve authentic deliberation. However, conflicts regarding behavior might lead to learning situations that could contribute to reflection and deliberation later on. Nevertheless, conflicts leading to power struggles apparently destroyed reflection and deliberation processes and led to difficulties making decisions and progress.

Public accessibility should be a matter of concern in core groups and in the child protection system. It is the key to establish public legitimacy and trust among participants, which is necessary to achieve authentic deliberations. The formal framework surrounding core groups seems adequate, although with the exception of the potential pitfalls of 'secret meetings'. What remains, then, is to secure that the general public and the political system gets information about childcare practises. This is an issue often ignored in Norwegian child protection, and contributes to reduce the system's legitimacy.

Based on this analysis, we are now able to provide five recommendations regarding the establishment and organisation of core groups. At first, decisions about whom to include in the core group should relate explicitly to the group's purpose. There should be opportunities to vary the size of groups in a flexible way. It is important to include the child as far as possible and note the balance between lay people and professionals. Secondly, there is a need for discussions about relevant meeting places. Practical necessities and the participants' needs for a 'safe' and comfortable place to take part in the collaboration, as well as the purpose of the meeting, have to be taken into consideration. Thirdly, in the meeting one should establish distinct roles and tasks; appoint a chair who is responsible for conducting the meeting in accordance with the deliberative procedures as well as keeping track of the overall concerns in the case. The chair is particularly responsible for undertaking explicit assessment of which questions to be subject to legitimate versus pragmatic decision-making, and assesses the need to invoke trustees who can support or represent parties if necessary. Fourthly, there is a need to clarify the legal basis of the authority of the core group. The deliberation cannot exceed the law. Finally, one should consider public accessibility both in core groups and especially towards the general public and the political system.

Acknowledgements

This study was supported by a grant from the Norwegian Research Council. We are grateful to the young people, families and professionals who participated at the core group meetings. Thanks to Elisabeth Severinsson, who has been very helpful with reviewing the manuscript. Thanks also to Jill Manthorpe and Håvard Lismoen who have been helpful with reviewing the English.

References

Angrosino, M. V., & Mays de Perez, K. A. (2000). Rethinking observation. In N. K. Denzin &, Y. S. Lincoln (Eds.), *Handbook of qualitative research* (pp. 673-702). Thousand Oaks: Sage Publications, Inc.

Arnstein, S. (1969). The ladder of citizen participation. *Journal of the American Institute of Planners, 35*, 216-224.

Backe-Hansen, E. (2001). *Rettferdiggjøring av omsorgs-overtakelse.* NOVA Rapport 2/2001 Oslo. (in Norwegian)

Calder, M. C., Barratt, M. (1997). Inter-agency perspectives on core group practice. *Children & Society, 11*, 209-221.

Child Welfare Act Services (1992). Oslo: Norway.

Eriksen, E. O. (1993). *Den offentlige dimensjon.* Oslo: Tano. (in Norwegian)

Eriksen, E. O., & Skivenes, M. (1998). Om å fatte riktige beslutninger i barnevernet. *Tidsskrift for samfunnsforskning, 3*, 352-380. (in Norwegian)

Eriksen, E. O. (1999). *Kommunikativ ledelse.* Bergen: Fagbokforlaget. (in Norwegian)

Eriksen, E. O. (2001). *Demokratiets sorte hull.* Bergen: Abstrakt Forlag. (in Norwegian)

Fosså skaret, E., Fuglestad, O., & Aase, T.H. (1997). *Metodisk feltarbeid.* Oslo: Universitetsforlaget. (in Norwegian)

Fraas, E. (2000). *Ansvarsgrupper. Et samarbeidsforum hvor foreldre har muligheter til å delta?* Hovedfagsoppgave, spesialpedagogikk, UiO. (in Norwegian)

Godeseth, M. (1995). Arbeid med og i ansvarsgrupper – noen metodiske erfaringer og refleksjoner. In V. Bunkholdt & E. Larsen (Eds.), *Metodisk barnevernsarbeid* (pp. 207-231). Oslo: Tano. (in Norwegian)

Habermas, J. (1981/96). *Teorien om den kommunikative handlen.* Aalborg: Aalborg Universitetsforlag. (in Norwegian)

Habermas, J. (1992/1996). *Between facts and norms.* Massachussets: The MIT Press Cambridge, Massachusetts.

Hallett, C. (1995). *Interagency coordination in child protection.* London: HMSO.

Havnen, K., & Iversen, O. (1996). *Ansvarsgrupper: Ein metode for å tryggja tverretatleg samarbeid og langsiktig planlegging?* Bergen: Barnevernets Utviklingssenter på Vestlandet. (in Norwegian)

Heap, K. (1998). *Gruppemetode for sosial- og helsearbeidere.* Oslo: Universitetsforlaget. (in Norwegian)

Loxley, A. (1997). *Collaboration in health and welfare.* London: Jessica Kingsley Publishers.

Mittler, H. (1997). Core groups: A key focus for child protection training. *Social Work Education, 16,* 77-91.

Nilsen, B. E. (2002). *De som er med i ansvarsgruppen må ha lyst til å gjøre noe for barnet ditt.* Oslo: HiO-hoved-fagsrapport, nr. 16. (in Norwegian)

Norwegian Board of Health (1998). *Guide for rehabilitation of children and young people.* No 1.

Ogden, T. (1997). Risiko, sosial kompetanse og forebyggende arbeid i skolen. In K. I. Klepp & L. E. Aarø (Eds.), *Ungdom, livsstil og* helsefremmende arbeid (pp. 205-214). Universitetsforlaget, Oslo. (in Norwegian)

Ovretveit, J. et al. (1997). *Interprofessional working for health and social care.* Houndmills: Macmillan.

Payne, M. (2000). *Teamwork in multiprofessional care.* New York: Palgrave.

Repstad, P. et al. (1993). *Dugnadsånd og forsvarsverker.* Oslo: Tano. (in Norwegian)

Rawls, J. (1971/1995). *A theory of justice.* Massachussets: The Belknap Press of Harvard University Press.

Shier, H. (2001). Pathways to participation: Openings, opportunities and obligations. *Children & Society, 15,* 107-117.

Skivenes, M. (2002). *Lovgivning og legitimitet – En evaluering av lov om barneverntjenester av 1992 i et deliberativt perspektiv.* Bergen: UiB, Institutt for administrasjon og organisasjonsvitenskap, Rapport nr. 79. (in Norwegian)

Skivenes, M.I., & Eriksen, E. O. (2000). *Nye deltagelsesformer og demokratisk medvirkning.* Bergen: UiB, LOS-Senter rapport R0010. (in Norwegian)

The Norwegian Government White Paper No 72:1984-1985. *Om barne- og ungdomsvernet.* (in Norwegian)

The Norwegian Government White Paper No 4:1992-1993. *Langtidsprogrammet 1994-97.* (in Norwegian)

The Norwegian Government White Paper No 35:1994-1995. *Velferdsmeldingen.* (in Norwegian)

The Norwegian Government White Paper No 40:2001-2002. *Om barne- og ungdomsvernet.* (in Norwegian)

Underlid, K. (2001). Fattigdommens psykologi. *Tidskrift for Norsk Psykologforening, 38,* 917-991. (in Norwegian)

Willumsen, E., Hallberg, L. (2003). Interprofessional collaboration with young people in residential care: some professional perspectives. *Journal of Interprofessional Care* (in press).

PART THREE

ORGANIZING CHILD AND YOUTH CARE ACCORDING TO THE BEST INTERESTS PRINCIPLE

10

Respect for diversity in early childhood education

Michel Vandenbroeck

Introduction

The Resource and Training Centre for Childcare, based at the Department for Social Welfare Studies of the Ghent University has a long tradition of cooperation with the governmental organisation in charge of Flemish child care, Kind en Gezin (Child and Family). The Centre worked in connection with Kind en Gezin on topics of quality and on diversity issues, through pilot projects and research. This long lasting collaboration has recently lead to a partnership agreement. In this paper, I will discuss an evolution in the thinking about the concepts of "Quality" and "Diversity" in early childhood education in Flanders, as it occurred through this collaboration over the last decade. I will discuss how the traditional use of quality standards occured and how this meant an important step forward in the reflection on early childhood. At the same time however, the unintended effect of the quality concept used, was affecting and excluding specific groups in the Flemish society. The perspective of "diversity" challenges some assumptions that are made in the quality discourse and raises new questions. Recent changes in the quality legislation are an attempt to overcome part of the tension between qualtity and diversity and to formulate some preliminary answers to the questions on monitoring, quality, diversity and parental involvement.

In my analysis, I will mainly draw on the following sources. The first is social constructionism and Foucault's ideas about power (Deleuze, 1986; Foucault, 1975; 1990; 2002) and how the concepts of the knowledge-power paradigm, of discourse and of governmentality are applied to the educational field (Dahlberg et al., 1999; Mc Gurck et al, 1993; Moss et al., 2000; Popkewitz, 2000: Popkewitz & Bloch, in press; Popkewitz & Brennan, 1998) and to the field of science (Bourdieu, 2001). In this vein "quality" is often perceived as a "regime of truth" (Popkewitz & Brennan, 1998) or a "desire for truth" producing a separation between who belongs to the order of discourse and who is excluded from it (Foucault, 2002).

The second source is my own ongoing "history of the present" research on the genealogy of inclusion/exclusion in Flemish infant care (Vandenbroeck, 2003). Historical research in this sense can function as "a form of critique for ourselves" and reveal the hidden assumptions and social constructions (Hendrick, 1997) that underpin exclusion. A closer examination of this history of inclusion/exclusion helps to understand present-day discourses on childcare and its place in the West-European welfare society. It also shows how policy and research are influenced by dominant discourses and are in turn influencing daily practice (McGurck et al., 1993). This research shows that what - from a "quality" perspective - can be seen as a progress in the thinking about early childhood education, can and should be problematized from a "diversity" perspective. Indeed, one century ago, the Belgian childcare system with its "crèches" was mainly addressing female blue collar workers, the lower socio-economical groups in our society. Today precisely those groups are to a large extent excluded from this public welfare system (Vandenbroeck, 2003). I will also show that actual societal changes are counterproductive for a social policy on diversity. In this vein, I will look at globalization/regionalization as a world-wide societal change occurring over last few decades, influencing the relation between individuals and the state and producing a changing discourses on childhood and early childhood education. This is not only the case in Belgium, but also in other countries that have a long tradition in state funded services for child care, in Eastern Europe (Bloch & Blessing, 2000) as well as in Northern Europe (Dahlberg, 2000; Hultqvist, 1998).

Finally, I will give an example of a small-scale qualitative research showing the complexity of the paradigm of quality monitoring taking into account a diversity of parental perspectives.

Who is childcare for?

In the late 19th and early 20th centuries the first infant care centres were established in Belgium at the initiative of bourgeois philanthropic groups and inspired by the French model. They were located in the cities and in the vicinity of the new emerging factories that employed women. The infant care was designed as a "machine" (Foucault, 1975) to combat infant mortality as well as to facilitate (cheap) female labour. It was therefore regarded as a "necessary evil" for the labour class. The emergence of this form of infant care took place in a period of industrialisation that enhanced the (economic) value of the physical health (Foucault, 1975). It was marked by the rising popularity of eugenetic and Darwinist sciences, which received scientific status from the emerging statistical science. Together with the abolition of child labour, this constructed the image of the "fragile child" as an investment for a later future and an image of the mother with a dual responsibility. In the eugenetic framework the "fragile child" was a metaphor for the "fragile race" that had to be safeguarded for the sake of the nations' future. *"[La crèche] est nécessaire dans le présent et elle s'impose dans l'avenir, pour assurer au pays une race belle et forte" (Plasky, 1910)*. Hence, the mother was responsible both for the physical survival of her (decontextualized) child and the future of society (the nation state). In that sense, child mortality became a public offence of the (decontextualized) mother towards society and this discourse legitimated far-reaching intrusions of bourgeois private philanthropic organizations into family affairs. There was a tension between the bourgeois need for female labour and their desire to "educate" the women of lower socio-economical groups on the one hand, and the dominant idea of the mother as the sole educator on the other hand. This tension is clearly expressed in official texts of that time. Most infant care centres aimed at controlling the poverty as well as the morality of their clients: *"On n'y admet que les enfants âgés de moins de 3 ans dont les mères sont pauvres et se conduisent bien »* (Lecointe et al, 1899). It was common practice that the philanthropic organization responsible for infant care did home visits to check on the "morality" of the mother and to make sure she was not using day care for her own benefit (whatever this may mean). Furthermore, private day care in the home of the carer (one would say family day care providers nowadays) became an "illégalisme" (Foucault, 1975) and all legislative texts were profoundly sceptical towards the educational capacities of people from the labour class.

The social function of child care as normalisation of the lower classes, remained prominent until the seventies and was even reinforced in that time by prevention programmes such as Head Start and High Scope, that contributed to focus on the mothers role as the sole educator, on her incompetence and thus on the state's role to intervene. But since the mid-1960s female labour changed dramatically. Before World War II, female workers had very little formal education and worked in factories. By the late sixties they had secondary school or higher diplomas and worked in the rapidly growing tertiary sector (administration, trade, education, tourism and other services). It is striking to notice that in official documents regarding child care, such as governmental reports, in this period the rise of the socio-economic class of the users of day care goes hand in hand with a more positive discourse on child care. The "necessary evil" of child care was since then regarded as an accepted necessity, much less because of the influence of psychologists, than by the mere socio-economical status of its users. As a result, the feminist movements won their case and important new budgets were invested in childcare. The number of children in publicly funded day care in Belgium multiplied by six in one decade (Vandenbroeck, 2003). In the early eighties, Belgium had a leading place in Europe as far as publicly funded preschool was concerned (Moss, 1988). Until now, Belgium is one of Europe's countries with the largest public investment in this sector (Moss, 1996; OECD, 2001).

However, at the same time the social function of child care was increasingly being hided while the economical function becomes prevalent. The "target public" dramatically changed from the lower social classes to the higher educated middle class female workers, the blue collar workers (men as well as women) being the main victims of the dramatic increase in unemployment in the seventies and eighties and the new female white collar workers, being higher educated and arriving in force on the labour market. Child care in research of the eighties and nineties mainly becomes an instrument of female employment in a discourse on equal opportunities for men and women (Moss, 1988, 1996), hiding the inequalities of social class and the social function of this public service. Moreover the focus on childcare as an instrument of employment reinforced the feminization of it.

My own research shows how in this period it becomes increasingly difficult for lower income groups, such as unemployed people, people from ethnic minorities and people in training to get access to these public services. Research from the Antwerp University also clearly shows how in the nineties a new form of social discrimination has taken shape in Flemish early childhood education, privileging higher income groups and systematically excluding marginalized groups. The study on nearly 4000 families indicated that no less than 60 % of families with children younger than 3 years old from high income groups use child care, while they comprise only 36% of the population. Conversely, only 20% of the families with the lowest incomes, comprising 41% of the population, request child care (Storms, 1995).

Exclusion in Brussels

The consequences of these evolutions can be seen in a recent research I conducted on inclusion/exclusion in 83 day care centres in Brussels (Vandenbroeck et al, 2003). In a first phase, all 83 centres of the Dutch community were interviewed on their accessibility policy. In a second phase a subgroup consisting of 14 centres were asked to gather data on parents that were refused access during a time period of two months. They gathered data on 138 "refused" parents. The research shows that the access policy is to a very large extent the individual responsibility of the director. In 80% of the centres the director designs the criteria for acceptance quite independently. In the other 20% of the cases a board of directors has a major say in this policy. This is the case in all three "types" of centres:
- municipal centres organized by one of the 19 local municipalities of Brussels,
- community centres, organized by the Education Department of the Flemish community (i.e. state schools),
- free centres, organized by an independent board of directors, but also publicly funded.

All centres have clear accessibility criteria. There is a large consensus for example that siblings of children who attend the centre have a strong priority. The two main criteria next to this are a priority for parents who are at work and a priority according to the place on the waiting list (who subscribes first, gets in first). These criteria are in the top-three for the three types of day care centres, with scores varying from 3.94 to 3.31. This means that in practice the economic function of child care is – as we have seen – very dominant, as compared to the other possible (social) functions. Indeed, the place on the waiting list is a criterion that favours parents who can plan their economic life longer in advance and that need a regularity of care, excluding unemployed or marginalized parents, who have to find solutions "at the last minute" or need more irregular forms of care, according to their changing employment or training situation.

Some centres (with not very much consensus) however accept exceptions on these criteria and favour "crisis care" for people "in social need". The score of this criterion ranges from 4.6 for some municipal centres to an unsignificant 2.09 for the community centres. Then follows a series of criteria that have very few consensus and/or very few impact such as the regularity of care, the fact that parents follow a training course, or live in the neighbourhood. Finally it is interesting to note that there is again a large consensus among all 83 centres on two criteria that are considered generally to be absolutely *not* important: parental income and family composition (ranging from 1.86 to 1.26). This is quite amazing in the sense that Flemish legislation calls for 4 priorities:
- parents at work
- parents in crisis (we have seen that these two criteria are more or less applied)
- single parents
- parents with the lowest income (we see that these two criteria are completely ignored).

The conclusion is therefore that the first two criteria in legislation are (more or less) implemented, while the last two are completely ignored.

When we look at the data on the 138 refused parents, we can clearly see the social consequences of these choices made by the directors of the centres. It is clear for instance that ethnic minority people are largely over-represented in the group of refused parents, compared to their prevalence in Brussels society as well as compared to the population of parents who use the day care centres. Also not less than 17% of the refused parents appear to be single parents, although the Flemish legislation considers them to be a priority target group. Further, a large proportion are parents who follow trainings in order to facilitate their chances on the labour market and also 17% is unemployed, but looking for an employment. The reason for refusal is in almost all cases (85%) that there is no place anymore. But this very general reason hides of course the socio-economic exclusion that affects certain groups of parents more than others. Although the accessibility is perceived as the individual responsibility of the individual director, we can clearly see a link with the more general tendency to individualize and decentralize and with the growing focus on the economic function child care, hiding the social function of it.

Evolutions in the quality discourse

Parallel with the historic evolution, regarding the accessibility of early years services, there is an evolution in the view on quality. Since the child care sector gained legitimacy and therefore public funding in the seventies, the state has felt a growing need to monitor the quality of the funded services. In the seventies child care was constructed as a place for the physical well-being of children, embedded in the historical concern on neonatal and infant mortality. The quality legislation of 1994 was a significant step away from the paramedical discourse and a first strong outcome of a long and slow evolution where psychology (and especially developmental psychology) became dominant.

In 1994, Child & Family, the governmental organization for child care in Flanders developed an instrument for assessing the quality in all Flemish day care centres (Verhegge, 1994). As it was the case in many countries worldwide, where the need was felt to quantify and assess quality, this instrument was based on American research, namely on the ECERS and ITERS scales developed by Harms and Clifford. The Flemish rating scales focused on the adult-child interactions as the core element of quality and defined a series of criteria for defining what "pedagogical quality" was. The author claims that these criteria are universal and "based on scientific literature" (Verhegge, 1994).

The universalistic (and therefore highly modernistic) claim was legitimized by what Bourdieu (2001) called "la mathématisation". The reliability and the validity of the instrument were tested. The instrument was welcomed by practitioners working with families with young children, because it valued the educational aspirations and therefore was perceived as a relief from the former strictly hygienical quality criteria. Moreover, training centres experienced that many staff members of day care centres who had never attended any training at all, subscribed to staff development projects in order to meet the new standards. In this sense, the instrument added to the debate on "what is good for children" during the mid-nineties.

However, recently there is a growing concern about unintended counterproductive effects of this concept of quality, especially from a diversity point of view. The critique is growing under the influence of post-structural scholars who have criticized the developmental concepts underpinning the construction of quality (such as Singer, 1993 and Burmann, 1994) for their gender or cultural bias. Building on this, postmodern thinkers have advocated to leave the quality discussion for what it is worth. Dahlberg et al (1999) have argued that globalization produced a need for standardization and decontextualization of quality standards, when local production evolved towards a worldwide market. This tendency, together with a tendency to decentralize, produced a growing need for quality standards in public service. Quality standards ensure a productive cost-benefit of these services and protect the citizen/consumer. Indeed, quality standards with universalistic claims, would be a "scientific" insurance for the individual parents, choosing an individual type of child care. A scientific approach of quality makes that the focus shifts from the quality discussion to the measurement issue. Quality, in other words, is reduced to what is measured by the quality assessment scale. In this vein, after a period where the quality discussion was enhanced, we face now a new period, where the discussion is rather limited by the rating scale, because of this reduction.

One of the most striking consequences of this reduction is that accessibility disappears from the agenda, since it is not included in the instrument. However, a large group of European experts had produced a few years earlier an interesting discussion document on quality criteria, defining accessibility as the first criterion (Balaguer et al., 1991). Secondly, reduction makes that the way parents are involved in the daily practice becomes a peripheral condition. A more fundamental critique is that since quality is now defined by experts and monitored by the state, the individual is protected and can fully play the role of "client", as opposed to the role of a critically and actively participating citizen. In this vein, we can look at quality assessment as depriving citizens from their own judgement and therefore as a counterforce against sub-politics. Moreover, since it is feasible to decontextualize and universalize quality, as done by science, the discussion on cultural diversity, complexity and heterogeneity disappears from sight, as it devalues parental ethnotheories or family cultures.

Evolutions in the diversity discourse

The well-documented critique of the prevailing quality concepts is in part produced by the growing awareness of the diversity paradigm. In the seventies and eighties diversity was primarily seen in a context of "multiculturality". This concept focused on different ethnic or cultural minorities, often in a way that was "othering the Other" (Moss & Brannan, 2003), in particular stereotyping and with a strong "us" versus "them" focus. In the later years the diversity discourse shifted from this "multicultural" approach towards an "intercultural" approach, giving more attention to the interaction between cultural groups and the dynamic of culture as a concept. In a transnational research, Vedder et al. (1996) showed that in the ninetees day care centres in Europe appeared to have very few consensus on what a "multicultural" or "intercultural" approach could be. The discourse on diversity however faced a growing critique from minority groups: feminist critique, critique from ethnic minorities, from the majority world or from the gay and lesbian movements. The critique challenges the normalizing aspects of the discourse. Indeed in many multicultural as well as intercultural work, the white, male, middle class majority still remains the norm (however one advocates for 'tolerance' towards 'deviations' from that norm). For instance, "queer theory" is not so much a theory about the queer, but rather a queering up of theory, challenging the concept of normality.

In Flanders, the awareness on diversity grew considerably due to a project that the Resource and Training Centre for Child Care and Child & Family undertook from 1995 to 1998, as well as to some follow-up projects from 1999 on. In the first project 24 day care centres hired co-workers from ethnic minorities and a staff development project on diversity was set up in all these teams. The project was the start of a reflection on diversity and on how the concept of diversity challenges the concept of quality (Peeters, 1998). In a first phase this reflection was largely influenced by the work of Louise Derman-Sparks in the United States. Later, following an intense and fruitful collaboration in a European network, DECET, the reflection was adapted to what is now called an approach of "equity and respect for diversity". In this approach the concept of diversity is enlarged from the former cultural diversity to gender, family composition, sexual preferences, class, disability and other aspects. Also more attention is given to unequal power relations that affect or are affected by these elements of diversity. In this vein accessibility of services for marginalized groups became an issue as well as parental participation of minority parents and as a consequence the universality of the quality rating scales was challenged.

The recent quality act in a globalizing context

The evolutions in the quality disocurse as well as in the diversity discourse, have influenced legislation. A new legislation on the publicly funded day care (centres as well as family day care providers) has been in place since 23 February 2001. It is worthwhile to mention that one of the first articles is a clear statement on accessibility and equity:

"The services cannot discriminate on the grounds of culture, social background, nationality, gender, religion or philosophy. The centres are open for all children, but give priority to children
- whose parents cannot take care of them because of their labour conditions;
- for whom it is advisable that they are taken care of outside of their family for social or educational reasons;
- of low-income parents;
- of single parent families.

The centres respect the International Convention on the Rights of the Child".

Although this legal framework does not change reality like a magic spell, it expresses a clear statement on the accessibility paradigm I described earlier, including some necessary ethical choices.

The legislation of July 12th 2001 implemented also a new vision on quality control. This is labeled as "the quality act". This act gives a large responsibility to the local organizers of day care. The local municipality or private board of directors is responsible to develop a (written) philosophy and quality management document on issues such as accessibility as well as on the educational service and the parental involvement. This means that the state does not impose an educational philosophy, but that it does impose the necessity of each service to develop a philosophy, to write it down and to act in accordance with the vision. The quality act also imposes each service to involve staff, parents and children in the development of the quality management.

In this sense, the new quality act signifies a major change from the expert discourse that disqualified parents to take part in the quality discussions. It is the expression of a postmodern view of quality as a social and cultural construction and provides new opportunities for overcoming the quality problem. The act illustrates that "the problem with quality is not really a problem once we recognize that it is not a neutral concept, but that it is a concept which we can choose to take or leave" (Dahlberg et al., 1999). Dahlberg et al. (1999) suggest to leave the quality concept for what it is "because it is situated within the project of modernity, the discourse of quality is inadequate for understanding a world of multiple cause and effects, interacting in complex and non-linear ways all of which are rooted in a limitless array of historical and cultural specificities". Cross-cultural studies such as the famous research of Tobin et al. (1989) have indeed shown very clearly that there is no such thing as universal quality and that what parents want for their children, or how they understand what "the good life" is about, varies significantly from one culture to the other.

Although the new quality legislation undoubtly means a significant step to resolve some of the tensions between the "quality" and the "diversity" approach, we have to be aware that it occurs in a period of societal change that is counterproductive to the social function of early years services.

Historically, demands that are placed upon national educational systems are best understood within a complex set of relations with international systems. This relation is best expressed linguistically as globalization/regionalization in which the two terms are viewed as mutually tied to each other and thus conceptually as one (Popkewitz, 2000). Globalisation and regionalisation are in this sense major societal changes since the seventies, which affect global, worldwide issues (such as economy and ecology) as well as intimate and private family affairs, such as the education of young children. Globalization has clearly produced weaker nation-states. As well as economy and economical themes such as employment and unemployment gain importance on the political agendas since the "crisis" of the late seventies, it is obvious that the tools to conduct an economic policy are less and less in the hands of governments. As much as nation states attach importance in convincing investors to invest in their countries rather than in their neighbours, nation states have only very limited influence on these decisions (Dahlberg et al., 1999). This is what Giddens (1994) called "the penetration of modern institutions into the tissue of day-to-day life".

Most Western European countries react to these evolutions by the production of what we came to call a neo-liberal discourse. The shape this discourse takes, will of course vary considerably according to differences in political constellations, specific local histories and social and cultural contexts. But the neo-liberal discourse is recurrent beyond national borders (Popkewitz, 2000: Popkewitz & Bloch, in press; Popkewitz & Brennan, 1998). The emergence of this neo-liberal discourse goes hand in hand with the upcoming of a managerial discourse that penetrates all aspects of the welfare society.

In a society with a neo-liberal discourse, welfare organizations (whether they were private or public) tend to take over the managerial discourse in an attempt to legitimize their existence and escape from the prevailing threats of budget cut down. This tendency, together with a tendency to decentralize, produces a growing need for quality standards in public service, that ensure a productive cost-benefit of these services as well as they would protect the citizen/consumer. In this vein, parents are seen as clients, rather than as partners. Hence, there is a stronger focus on parental satisfaction (as consumer satisfaction) and satisfaction measures, rather than on parental cooperation. In addition, there is a growing focus on autonomy of parents and children as important outcomes, rather than on interdependency and solidarity.

In Flanders, one of the key constitutive aspects of the neo-liberalization of day care is the rise of small-scale private care organizations that are run by self-employed persons, without substantial public funding. As previously stated, Flanders had a leading role in Europe in the eighties and the nineties with regard to the proportion of publicly funded day care centres. In the nineties, this was in large part due to the investment in family day care providers. However, since then, the most spectacular change in day care is the rise of "private day care centres". The number of these centres has been increasing steadily (see Figure 10.1).

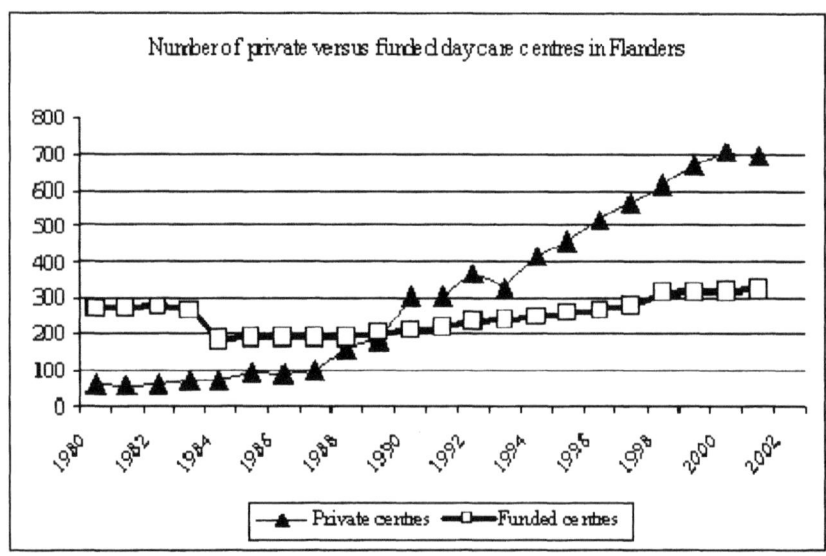

Source: Child & Family annual reports 1980-2001.

Figure 10.1   Number of private versus day care centres in Flanders.

A trend towards the commercialization of day care can be found in many countries, including Poland, Hungary and Bulgaria (Bloch & Blessing, 2000), Sweden (Hultqvist, 1998) and the United Kingdom (Moss & Brennan, 2003). It goes hand in hand with a growing pressure to deregulate and to narrow down child care services as merely economic "tools" for female employment. It will therefore be extremely important in the near future to have an ongoing reflection on how the new quality act is monitored and to see wether it serves a neo-liberal deregulation, avoiding the ethical dimension or on the contrary enhancing the ethical debate on the local level.

It is clear that this is not an easy task. As a recent small-scale qualitative study shows, a quality discussion that takes diversity and parental opinions into account is a very complex matter (Bloch et al., 2003).

Deconstruction, reconstruction and co-construction

The new quality act gives some opportunities for services to make a significant step towards the concept of "making sense", such as Dahlberg et al. (1999) suggest. This means a critical dialogue and reflection on daily experiences. It is based on the concept of the co-construction of knowledge and culture. This dialogue, leaving the modernistic project behind, gives more possibilities to take the complexity and (cultural) diversity of today's cities and countries into account. It can be seen as a way of giving a voice to those parents who are traditionally excluded from the quality discourse. This is what we have tried to do in a local, small-scale research at the Department of Social Welfare Studies of the University of Ghent (Van Nuffel, in press). It was inspired by the ethnographical methodology of Tobin et al. (1989) and Hoshi-Watanabe et al (2001) and made use of a polyvocal analysis (Hatch, 2002). The research was conducted in the toddler group (children aged 18 to 36 months) of a day care centre in the inner city of Antwerp. After a participatory observation period, a specific scene of the life in the day care centre was identified together with the staff of the centre. The scene was – in the view of the staff – seen as illustrative for their practice and considered as a "good practice". The scene (total nine minutes) was videotaped avoiding (as much as possible) editing or cutting, to preserve all details and prevent any form of interpretation by the researcher. The videotape served as a trigger to collect narratives of different possible "stakeholders" on what good practice in a given context might mean. In a first phase, the narratives of the staff were collected. In a second phase, narratives of 19 parents were collected. The sample was not representative. Nevertheless, there was sufficient heterogeneity with regard to use of daycare, parental age (varying from 21 to 46 years), cultural, religious and ethnic background (Belgian, Dutch, Algerian, Turkish, Catholic, Muslim and not religious), family composition ("traditional", recomposed or single, with 1 to 7 children), degree of formal education and professional status (unemployed, civil servant, agriculture, lawyer). In addition, the narratives of an official (governmental) inspector were collected. All the narratives were collected during individual interviews of approximately one hour. Finally, the narratives of all participants were given to the staff of the centre and discussed. The research is still in progress, so we will present here only some preliminary results.

It is very clear that the videotape was "read" quite differently by its subsequent viewers. The scene consisted of a toilet situation in the bathroom of the day care centre. The video showed 18 children, either sitting down on a removable pottie or a small toilet waiting to get dressed, or waiting at the side until the others were 'fixed'. While the children were taken by one of the three co-workers to get dressed, one child, D., was moving around with his potty. By running it from one side of the bathroom to the other, he uses it as a sort of vehicle. None of the co-workers seems to pay attention to his 'different' behavior. He keeps on playing for several minutes untill one child grabs her pottie, so they both start to amuse themselves by splashing in her piss. On this occasion, the co-worker reacts verbally and takes D. firmly by the hand. Somehow, he escapes from her grip and starts all over again. The co-workers command him several times to put the pottie back where it belongs. After a while they grab him by the arm and take the pottie away from him. D. is protesting and takes it back to 'drive' around. After this 7 minutes period of ignorance towards D., a co-worker distracts him by dressing and talking to him.

In the view of the staff, D. is seen as noncompliant, "causing trouble" and "seeking attention in a negative way". D. has always conducted such behavior in the day care centre, they claim. At first they tried to put D. consequently back on his pottie, accompanied with a firm "No, you have to sit". Due to the perceived failure of this approach for this child, the staff had a series of discussions about the education of D. They decided to try to ignore his behaviour and only intervene when he 'disturbs' other children. They view their behavior on the videotape as consistent with the rules they discussed before and thus as a "good practice".

Some parents spontaneously share this view and depict D. as a "naughty" child, "noncompliant", "lacking structure" and other "negative" labels, often interpreted as a result of unsuccessful parenting (spoiled or not enough attention). Other parents label D. on the contrary as "adventurous" or "jolly", "funny" and "normal for his age". Still others focus less on the boy and more strongly on the situation and condemn it as too harsh, disciplining the body (in the sense as described by Leavitt & Power, 1997 as bodily civilization). They deplore the setting in which such a large number of children are forced to sit still such a long period of time. They condemn the "lack of privacy" or the lack of "respect for the child's own rhythm". They view D. as the only "normal" child and label the behaviour of the other children who sit quietly as "problematic". We could say that they interpret D.'s behaviour as a normal and carnivalesque reaction (in the Bakhtinian sense, see Bakhtin, 1968) and thus as an important contribution to the social dynamics and power relations in the group. Some parents say that due to the carnivalesque behaviour of this one boy the rest of the group adapts so passively to the situation in which they are compelled to sit still for such a long period. Others focus primarily on practical aspects, giving advice such as "they should give D. a fixed potty and not a mobile one" or "one co-worker should stay with some children in another room".

It is striking that, however contradictory parents' narratives may be, they are (with very little exception) all very sound, thought of and well-argumented with reference to their theories and values on what is good for children. The inspiration for parental theories comes from transgenerational influence (especially through a maternal line) as well as from popular literature and doctors.

A majority of the parents interviewed at first spontaneously condemned the educators' behaviour as being "too strict" or "too harsh" and "inconsequent" due to the amount of time between the beginning of the behaviour and the actual reaction of the co-workers. However, some parents immediately softened their judgement by referring to the context of the daycare, which is seen as difficult and stressful. When confronted with the co-workers' narratives, the majority of parents appeared to be very empathic. They focussed on the context and the position of the co-workers and estimated their work as "very difficult and stressful under these conditions". Even when they did not "agree" with the co-workers, they "understood" their point of view and their actions. Possibly, although disputable, the parents were influenced by the power dimension. When the co-workers were depicted as professionals, their expertise was not questioned, even if their behaviour was contradictory to the parents' beliefs.

Further analysis of the data is necessary and the feedback of the co-workers on the parents' narratives is still to be collected. Previous research in France and Japan (Hoshi-Watanabe et al., 2001) shows that this can have an important effect on staff development. But so far a first analysis of the data conveys the idea that what is good for children is a social and cultural construction, full of antinomies (Bruner, 1996 in Vandenbroeck, 2001). There is no expert science that can, as an ultimate judge, devise parental ethnotheories in rights and wrongs, as the black sheep will be divided from the white at Judgement Day. It is also very clear that – providing a concrete starting point of daily practice – all parents have a lot to say in the quality debate. It also shows that co-constructing quality, taking into account a multivocal point of view and embracing paradoxes rather than compromise, is feasible, but very difficult and most urgent.

The research is consistent with experiences we had in different previous action research projects on cultural diversity in early childhood education centres in Ghent, Brussels and Antwerp (Vandenbroeck, 2001). Taking respect for diversity and equity into account in the educational philosophy asks for a shift in the profession of the educator. The educator becomes less the "expert" in knowing what the (decontextualized) children's needs are. The expertise of the educator cannot be generalized and has not the status of scientific knowledge. Rather it is in deconstructing existing discourse on quality, and in reconstructing with the parents and the local community an educational practice that is a local co-construction. This asks for a professionalism in decentring and mediation and a turn to radical reciprocity (Grieshaber & Canella, 2001; Smith, 2001; Vandenbroeck, 2001). In this sense, a post-structuralist approach is quite different from a permissive approach that states that since there is no universal definition of quality anymore, "anything goes". On the contrary, it is an approach favouring explicit and contextualized ethical choices and a strong social commitment.

A final comment

We are confident that the new Flemish quality act can contribute to this ethical and political dimension of early childhood education. It can be seen as a further step towards liberalization, where the discourse on local responsibility serves as "newspeak" for a further withdrawal from central authority. But it also gives new chances for real co-construction, taking into account diversity and equity in the sense of how these are defined by the European DECET network. This would mean that in assessing the impact of the new quality act, standards are discussed on *how* stakeholders are involved in the process and *how* traditionally excluded groups who often fail to have access to either the services or the quality discussion are being taken on board. A historical perspective has shown that there is no such thing as an inclusive policy that has no (often unintended) exclusive effects. The questions about quality monitoring and diversity (and, hence, the questions on the role of the state versus the service and the parents) will probably remain a matter of debate and reflection.

References

Bakhtin, M. (1968). *Rabelais and his world.* Bloomington: Indiana University Press.
Balaguer, I. Mestress, J., & Penn, H. (1991). *Kwalitatieve dienstverlening aan jonge kinderen, een discussiedocument.* Brussel: Netwerk Kinderopvang van de Europese Commissie. (in Dutch)
Bloch, M., & Blessing, B. (2000). Restructuring the state in Eastern Europe: Women, childcare and early education. In T. Popkewitz (Ed.), *Educational knowledge. Changing relationships between the state, civil society, and the educational community* (pp. 59-81). Albany: State University of New York.
Bloch, M., Holmlund, K., Moqvist, I., & Popkewitz, T. (2003). Global and local patterns of governing the child, family, their care, and education. In M. Bloch, K. Holmlund, I. Moqvist, & T. Popkewitz (Eds.), *Governing children, families and education. Restructuring the welfare state* (pp. 3-31). New York: Palgrave.
Bourdieu, P. (2001) *Science de la science et réflexivité. Cours du Collège de France 2000-2001.* Paris: Raisons d'Agir Editions.
Burman, E. (1994). *Deconstructing developmental psychology.* London: Routledge.
Dahlberg, G. (2000). From the "People's Home" – Folkhemmet – to the enterprise. Reflections on the constitution and reconstitution of the field of early childhood pedagogy in Sweden. In T. Popkewitz (Ed.), *Educational knowledge. Changing relationships between the state, civil society, and the educational community* (pp. 201-220). Albany: State University of New York.
Dahlberg, G., Moss, P., & Pence, A. (1999). *Beyond quality in early childhood education and care.* London: Falmer Press.
Deleuze, G. (1986). *Foucault.* Paris: Les Editions de Minuit.
Foucault, M. (1975). *Surveiller et punir.* Paris : Gallimard.
Foucault, M. (1990). *Politics, philosophy, culture. Interviews and other writings 1977-1984.* London: Routledge.
Foucault, M. (2002). *L'ordre du discours. Leçon inaugurale au Collège de France prononcée le 2 décembre 1970.* Paris : Gallimard.
Giddens, A. (1994). Living in a post-traditional society. In U. Beck, A. Giddens, & S. Lash (Eds.), *Reflexive modernization. Politics, tradition and aesthetics in the modern social order* (pp. 56-109). Cambridge: Policy Press.
Grieshaber, S., & Canella, G. (2001). *Embracing identities in early childhood education.* London-New York: Teachers College Press, Columbia University.
Hatch, J. A. (2002). *Doing qualitative research in education settings.* Albany: State University of New York Press.
Hendrick, H. (1997). Constructions and reconstructions of British childhood: An interpretative survey, 1800 to the present. In A. James & A. Prout, A. (Eds.), *Constructing and reconstructing childhood* (pp. 34-62). London: Falmer Press.

Hoshi-Watanabe, M., Rayna, S. & Takahasi, H. (2001). *The daily life of babies in French and Japanese daycare centres: Realities and narratives.* Paper presented at the 11th EECERA Conference, Alkmaar, 2001.

Hultqvist, K. (1998). A history of the present on children's welfare in Sweden: From Fröbel to present-day decentralization projects. In T. Popkewitz & M. Brennan (Eds.), *Foucault's challenge. Discourse, knowledge, and power in education* (pp. 91-116). New York and London: Teachers CollegePress – Columbia University.

Leavitt, R., & Power, M. (1997). Civilising bodies. Children in day care. In J. Tobin (Ed.), *Making place for pleasure in early childhood education* (pp. 39-75). New Haven and London: Yale University Press.

McGurck, H., Caplan, M., Hennessy, E., & Moss, P. (1993). Controversy, theory and social context in contemporary day care research. *Journal of Child Psychology and Psychiatry, 34,* 3-23.

Moss, P. (1988). *Childcare and equality of opportunity. Consolidated report to the European Commission.* Brussels: European Commission Network on Childcare and Other Measures to Reconcile Employment and Family Responsibilities.

Moss, P. (Ed.) (1996). *A review of services for young children in the European Union 1990-1995.* Brussels: European Commission Network on Childcare and Other Measures to Reconcile Employment and Family Responsibilities.

Moss, P., & Brannan, J. (2003). *Rethinking children's care.* London: Open University Press.

Moss, P., Dillon, J., & Statham, J. (2000). The 'child in need' and 'the rich child': Discourse, constructions and practice. *Critical Social Policy. A journal of Theory and Practice in Social Welfare, 20,* 233-254.

O.E.C.D. (2001). *Starting strong. Early childhood education and care. Education and skills.* Paris: OECD Publications.

Peeters, J. (1998). Ervaringen van het MEQ-project. In A. Somers (Ed.), *Diversiteit in de kinderopvang* (pp. 99-106). Gent: VBJK. (in Dutch)

Popkewitz, T. (2000). *Educational knowledge. Changing relationships between the state, civil society, and the educational community.* Albany: State University of New York.

Popkewitz, T., & Bloch, M. (in press). Administring freedom: A history of present rescuing the parent to rescue the child for society. In K. Hultqvist & G. Dahlberg (Eds.), *The changing child in a changing world.* London: Routledge Press.

Singer, E. (1993). Shared care for children. *Theory and Psychology, 3,* 429-449.

Smith, L. (2001). *Decolonizing methodologies. Research and indigenous people.* London-New York: Zed books.

Storms, B. (1995). *Het mattheüs-effect in de kinderopvang.* Antwerpen: Centrum voor Sociaal Beleid – Universiteit Antwerpen. (in Dutch)

Tobin, J., Wu, D., & Davidson, D. (1989). *Preschool in three cultures. Japan, China and the United States.* New haven – London: Yale University Press.

Vandenbroeck, M. (2001). *The view of the Yeti. Bringing up children in the spirit of self-awareness and kindredship.* The Hague: Van Leer Foundation.

Vandenbroeck, M. (2003). Exclusion in the history of Belgian (Flemish) infant care. *Contemporary Issues in Early Childhood Education, 4,* 137-148.

Vandenbroeck, M., D'Hoore, K., & Van Nuffel, K. (2003). *Onderzoek naar inclusie/exclusie in de Brusselse kinderdagverblijven.* Gent: VBJK - Vakgroep Sociale Agogiek, Universiteit Gent. (in Dutch)

Van Nuffel, K. (in press). *Een "goede" opvoeding van het jonge kind als socio-cultureel bepaalde constructie.* Gent: Department of Social Welfare Studies, University of Ghent. (in Dutch)

Vedder, P., Bouwer, E., & Pels, T. (1996). *Multicultural child care.* Clevedon: Multilingual Matter Ltd.

Verhegge, K. (1994). *Ratingscale for the pedagogical environment in creches.* Brussels: Child & Family.

11

Networking in youth care: Towards a common engagement

Rudi Roose

Introduction

The Flemish government is currently engaged in a reform of youth care within the context of the Strategic Youth Care Plan. Youth care needs to be better attuned to the demands of clients if it is going to improve its results. One of the ways of achieving this is for the various institutions and sectors to work together at improving coordination, by creating new networks and by reinforcing existing ones.

The Strategic Youth Care Plan is given an initial trial period in three experimental regions: new concepts are tested for practical relevance and feasibility and, if successful, should then be implemented in the whole of Flanders (from the end of 2004).

When it became known that the Flemish government would work on a reform of youth care, a number of non-experimental regions also took action. The Waasland region initiated a youth care network consultation. At the end of 2000, this consultation service requested that the Ghent University Department of Social Welfare Studies conducted research into the forming of a regional youth care network. This led eventually to the launch of the 'Waasland Youth Care Networking' action research project.

This paper discusses the intentions and results of this action research. The project – which ran from April 2001 to June 2003 – suggested that a participative care service requires a change in the concept of 'expertise', with an acknowledgment of the powerlessness of care services being central to the issue rather than the 'organizing' of networks. However, there doesn't seem to be evidence that such a vision will evolve, since a participative approach can be seen as diametrically opposed to the formulated social and policy expectations (explicit or not) related to care. We will discuss in depth the tense environment in which care providers conduct their work and offer a basis for a reflective approach to this area of care.

Waasland Youth Care Networking Action Research

The frame of reference

'The criteria that networking needed to fulfil in order to increase the quality of care *in the mind of the client*' was a central question posed at the start of the research project. 'Better cooperation' does not always mean better value for the care receiver: networking can take such a form that there is a one-sided collaboration between care providers and insufficient consideration for the viewpoint of the 'care receivers'. The care provider – care receiver relationship suffers as a result with a contraction of space for individual handling of cases and for dialogue between the care provider and the care receiver. So networking can make a major contribution to the actualization of a qualitative care supply, but this is not the case purely by definition.

The researchers introduced the concept of '*the right to social service in order to lead an existence worthy of human dignity*' as the frame of reference for this study. Through this frame of reference we aligned ourselves with the policy text of the Flemish government, for which the Convention on the Rights of the Child (CRC) was advanced as the cornerstone of an integrated youth care service. This reference to the CRC implies that integrated youth care services are seen basically as a function of the equal rights of children to human dignity.

The development of a care proposal aimed at the realization of 'the right to a dignified human existence' recognizes that 'well-being' is an intersubjective concept: human dignity includes the right to one's own opinion and the right of potentiality to bring this opinion into the debate. This participative starting point entails that the possible diversity of opinion on what 'well-being' means becomes acknowledged and that the added value of this diversity is recognized. The premise is a positive approach to well-being: not only a concession to *lack* of well-being but the promotion of well-being as a primary concern. The characteristics of a 'right to social service' – availability, accessibility, affordability, usefulness and comprehensibility (Parmentier, 1998) – are translated to a differentiated care offer that connects to a concrete situation in which the care is offered, and within the environment of the people who as 'care receivers' are directly concerned.

Availability refers to the existence of a supply and to the fact that social services can be called upon for matters that are not directly related to the assessed problem. Accessibility refers to the (lack of) thresholds when care is needed, for instance, an inadequate knowledge of the supply. Affordability refers to financial and other costs that the client may encounter, such as losing one's privacy and other negative social and psychological consequences of an intervention. Usefulness refers to the extent to which the client experiences the care as supportive: is the help attuned to the needs, the skills and the language of the clients? Comprehensibility refers to the extent to which clients are aware of the reasons for intervention and of the methods of approach to the problem.

If there is to be an evolution in participative care, it is important to be aware of the enduring difficulty of the participative approach. Our care tradition, in which a putative consensus on what is in the interests of the people dominates even when the 'care receivers' concerned have admitted to their own doubts, is a remnant of history and exists in uneasy opposition to the acknowledgment that there are many relevant definitions of well-being.

The 'right to social services' implies that care must be of such a nature that people who seek help receive 'the full advantage' of services. This means that care should not only be seen in terms of the minimum necessary to 'social functioning', rather it should offer support in enabling skills that can ease possible tensions between individual aspirations and social expectations. Seen in this light, a good care offer is not only oriented to the individual but also to society, in the sense that it encourages the debate pertaining to conditions considered acceptable for a dignified existence.

From the perspective of the right to social services the research set out to examine the criteria that networking needed to fulfil in order to contribute to a more qualitative care service. Two questions were posed:
1. Firstly, how can networking contribute to minimum conditions required of care services, from the perspective of the right to social services? These minimum requirements are: availability, accessibility, affordability, usefulness and comprehensibility.
2. In connection with this, the question was posed as to whether clients would receive 'the full advantage' of services within this network. The presence of minimum conditions are not in themselves a guarantee of quality care services but offer a framework in which it should be possible to receive care that contributes to the implementation of the right to a dignified human existence.

Moving towards the problem area

In the first phase of research we noticed great unanimity of opinion with regard to the reference frame discussed. The organizations concerned could see, in this context, the possibility of a reorganization of the youth care service from the perspective of the care receivers and thus of arriving at a more participative care offer. The first step towards concretization consisted of interviews with 34 of the institutions involved, in which they were given the opportunity to tell their views on youth care and their experience of problems. An analysis of the interviews informed our understanding of (the problems of) the care provided but gave little understanding of the client perspective. It also seemed from this initial analysis that the unanimity alleged earlier with regard to the reference frame was not in fact that apparent. Thus, for example, the concepts of availability, accessibility, affordability, usefulness and comprehensibility were employed in different, sometimes even opposite, ways by the various institutions and care workers. 'Demand-oriented' working was, for example, approached very passively by some care workers, with no action taken so long as there was no demand for it, while other care workers pointed to the importance of an outreach approach in cases where people cannot, do not wish to or do not dare, see themselves as care receivers. Analyses showed that the common goal of the project appeared to be only present in the abstract sense.

The client perspective was only indirectly introduced in this first phase, in the form of a written report on 'the client view on formal care' (Roose, 2001). From this, rather limited, written study it appeared that clients – both children and adults – desired a respectful care service in which they would be taken seriously. So, clients were referring more to the attitude of the care worker than to the method used by the care organization. Service providers were asked to discuss this report within their organizations and to propose improvements on the basis of these discussions. However, in general, these proposals remained rather abstract and noncommittal and did not lead to any concrete action.

The second step towards concretization consisted of setting up thematic working groups. These working groups discussed the interview findings from the perspective of concrete cases. The idea was to concretize the abstract problem definitions that arose from the interviews and eventually to arrive at proposals for changes in the organization of care provision: the development of criteria for referral being one example. The themes for the thematic working groups were chosen by the institutions concerned in response to data from the interviews.

It emerged through discussion of the cases presented by caseload workers that the initial problem formulation – with the emphasis primarily on the organization of care provision – needed to be redirected: it seemed that many problems concerned the practices of individual care providers, the vision of institutions and the engagement with clients from both perspectives rather than a poor organization of care services.

The conclusions reached by the thematic working groups indicated that a redefinition was called for: the youth care problem should no longer be seen as *an organizational problem* but really as *an operational problem*. The focus changed from external to internal factors. We assessed that improvement was needed primarily in the area of the care provider – care receiver interaction.

There was also unclarity about whether the clients shared the problem formulation that care providers had formulated. To what extent problems were perceived by the client? At this stage it was difficult to get a clear picture of the client perspective, of the impact of intervention on a client's concrete situation or to be able to reflect on the significance to a client of an intervention.

This assessment led to the decision to move even closer to the problem area and to involve clients more directly with the research. This was implemented by means of case studies. Service providers were asked to introduce current cases into the discussion. Clients were also addressed, through interviews conducted by the researcher. There was a poor response to this request for cases: only four institutions provided one. Although interviews with clients resulted in interesting material, the choice of cases created questions in itself. In direct contrast to the first round of interviews, where innumerable problems were mentioned – including those related to collaboration with other institutions – it appeared that the cases now being presented were only those of satisfied clients. These cases provided little leverage for a more engaging debate. The selection of cases was nevertheless food for thought. For example, one of the institutions declared that they had a good case for discussion, but that it would be too difficult to speak with the clients due to their poor verbal skills. This raises the question of how care workers are supposed to handle or communicate with these 'difficult clients' on a daily basis.

The call for more, as well as more substantial, cases did not engender an immediate response. The researchers wondered if this non-response was indicative of a lack of engagement with the premise of the research: was the problem formulation – that the focus must shift from the organization to the handling of cases – still shared by all the institutions? After sustained consultations with the organizations involved in the study, it appeared that the nonresponse should not be understood so much as a lack of commitment, but rather as a fundamental problem, that is, a question of how much space for manoeuvre exists within current rules and structures for care workers to operate reflectively. Care workers may be employing this discretionary space defensively. Lipsky (1980) stated that in fact care workers (street–level bureaucrats) mainly do employ this space defensively, in order to manage their own workload. This was confirmed Ellis, Davis and Rummery (1999). However, other research found that care providers could in fact operate reflectively within existing rules and environmental influences (Baldwin, 2001).

In order to expand the space for reflective operating a number of (half-day) training sessions were organized within the framework of the research, on subjects such as confidentiality and open reporting. The object of these training sessions was to set in motion a discourse on a number of (alleged) participative operating thresholds - for example, the idea that confidentiality makes good cooperation impossible.

The various stages of this research can be collectively defined as 'moving towards the problem area': from 'discussing' participative care provision (interviews/thematic working parties) to the expectation of actual participative operating (case studies). This type of movement is necessary in order to penetrate the complexity of concrete care service practices (Proctor, 2002) and clarify the possible gap between 'discussing' participative care provision and 'participative operating' (Van Nijnatten, Hoogsteder & Suurmond, 2001).

By testing each stage of the research against the aforementioned frame of reference, it became clear that the initial problem formulation needed to be redirected. Where the emphasis of the research lay in the poor organization of care services it became apparent during the process that a lot of problems were derived from the vision and concrete operating of the care providers. Therefore, the focus for change was moved from reorganizing to rethinking care services, with particular attention on individual commitment and the vision behind it.

The 'rethinking' of the care service and consequent concrete action, however, did not happen. From research it emerged that this was primarily connected with a tension that may exist between various discourses used in (youth) care: on the one hand a management discourse, on the other an involvement discourse.

Diverse frames of reference in youth care

The Flemish government's Strategic Youth Care Plan emphasizes participation on the one hand and bureaucratic demands and standardization (modulation, case management...) on the other. These bureaucratic demands are a reversion to the scientific management principles – developed by Taylor circa 1911 – in which the production process is dissected into the smallest possible entities. One deduces from this that the care provision process is linear and that one can cut the whole into pieces: application, preliminary interview, placement, care assignment, implementation and evaluation. These stages, which need to be glued back together again, are mostly assigned to different officials. This type of model leads to a revival of the socio-technological thinking in which the outcome of an intervention must be predictable and the client is only the object of the intervention (Bisschops, 2001, p. 126). The basis for such an approach is the utopian idea that for every unique problem there is a unique solution (Degheldere & Notredame, 1987). In the care sector this is translated as 'the right client in the right place'. This idea is primarily responsible for bureaucratic demands and solutions: problems are defined in terms of organizational problems. This was the case in the Waasland Youth Care Networking action research, where the finger was pointed at inadequate organization of care: an unclear profile of the service, a lack of front line services, a poor coordination of diagnostic instruments, unworkable legislations, and so forth. The solutions proposed should then have led to a simpler and more manageable care service.

This tendency is reinforced by the emphasis on the efficiency and effectiveness of the care service, for example in the context of quality management, whereby the care worker is only considered an expert if s/he keeps him/herself as busy as possible with rational, objective and measurable matters (Van Tilt, 2002).

However, the Strategic Youth Care Plan also focuses on a participative approach. Thus, the Convention on the Rights of the Child is advanced as the cornerstone of youth care, a parent's statute and a minor's statute are being elaborated within youth care (De Wilde, 2003) and the emphasis is put on participative diagnosis.

However, participation can receive both broad and narrow definitions. Participation can be given an instrumental interpretation where it is seen as a 'means' to realizing an efficacious care provision. A comprehensive interpretation of participation really means a shift from the 'client implication' to a consideration of the care provision itself and its significance for care receivers (Roose, 2003).

Tensions between management and involvement

The two approaches to care provision – management and involvement (Bisschops, 2001) - are interconnected. Demand-oriented working refers to more respect being shown for the client's needs but also to an image of the client as an autonomous and rational being who must be capable of competing on the care service 'market' (Van der Steege, 2003). However, a comprehensive view of participation suffers strained relations with the idea of management, as became apparent from the Waasland Youth Care Networking action research project.

A unique solution to a unique problem versus respect to diverse possible trajectories

The practice of care provision shows that there may be several possible trajectories for clients to follow within care services. The issue is then not so much what the best route may be for them but really what defines adequate care within each route. This refers to *ethical handling* (Tronto, 1993) of each demand (e.g., is each demand listened to? has a response been formulated?) and the commitment given to the care receiver in every situation.

Modulation as a management strategy versus 'being there'

Modulating can be seen as a strategy for a more transparent care service. However, it can also refer to 'specialization of the care provision': in this way, institutions are demarcated according to 'what they're best at'. In the light of an emphasis on efficient care provision this can lead to organizations narrowing their services to situations or problems where they can be certain of 'success'. Specialization then becomes a strategy for managing powerlessness in the face of situations that they can't, or don't want to, deal with (Hasenfeld, 1987). The idea that for each unique problem there is a unique solution may reinforce this dynamic and lead on the one hand to a referral carousel – problems that don't match with an organization's profile are passed on to the 'right service' – and on the other hand to an oversimplified demand for specialized services, heavier methodologies, and resources that would be better employed for work with 'difficult' groups or problems.

Participative care assumes that the client perspective is taken into account. Various research data highlight a discrepancy that may exist between the definition of quality care from the client perspective and from the care worker perspective. Clients – both adults and children – are not so concerned with the problem-solving capability or technical expertise of care services as the 'quality of being there' (Warmenhoven, 1973): is the service accessible, is it respectful, is it taking the care receiver seriously? There can also be a perception gap as to the need for intervention. For example, young people do demand support in terms of personal attention and engagement with them but not always in terms of an active (proactive) mediation, preferring space to explore their own problem-solving capacities (Verschelden & Bouverne-De Bie, 2000). This can mean that care provision that seems pointless in the eyes of the care worker – for example, a preliminary interview that does not lead to intake – can be very meaningful to the care receiver, perhaps simply because s/he is being taken seriously at that moment. So 'problem-solving' and 'meaningfulness of care' are not the same thing.

Quality in relation to 'clients' versus quality in relation to 'people who need care'

The quality of care provision is defined usually by 'clients', that is, by care receivers whose demand was recognized as legitimate by a particular institution. Thus participation is principally defined by the way care receivers who use the service are handled. However, it appeared from research that, in general, there was little commitment to people who need care. Quality is considered as a property of its own functioning rather than of the overall care service in the region. What happens to people on the waiting list? What happens to those who are referred? How do people experience this referral? These and similar questions are seldom considered. The commitment usually begins only when the person is 'officially' registered (and becomes known as the 'client') and stops at the moment that the person is officially dismissed and stops being a client. Such an approach to quality takes little account of the selection procedure of organizations or the likely creation of 'left-over groups', namely groups that institutions can not, or do not wish to work with.

Emphasis on organization versus emphasis on vision

Research suggested that a lot of youth care problems were not a question of organization but of vision. Thus, one of the core problems of youth care is a too large and too quick referral of children and their families to child protection services. The proposed solution concerns an expansion of front line services. In practice, referral to child protection services is not only due to a shortage of other services. One possible reason could be a narrow interpretation of the demand-oriented care concept: if there is only a commitment when someone 'asks' then situations where more commitment is required can be referred to child protection services, considering that these interventions are more compelling. From this perspective, an expansion of the front line service could at times lead to an increase in the child protection services intake instead of a decrease. Another reason could be a particular perception of free choice in the care service: care providers assume that 'free choice' is diametrically opposed to 'setting limits' – for example, stating that as a care worker you find something unacceptable - because it will cause the trust relationship with the client to suffer. Apart from the experience that clients tend to appreciate clarity from the care worker, this perception can also lead to a diminished commitment to 'unruly' clients and an accelerated referral to 'more compelling care'. Paradoxically, this referral leads to a breakdown of trust and of the relationship with the client.

Standardizing versus differentiating

The discussion on efficient care provision refers to standardization of care. For example, in the Strategic Youth Care Plan this manifests as working with care programmes: a combination of modules tailored to the client. Again, the idea is that similar problems require similar approaches. However, quality care cannot be a predetermined, standardized package: every individual case needs thoughtful consideration in order to be pertinent. Thus, Arendt (1994: 102) states with regard to crisis situations, that a crisis only becomes a disaster if we respond to it with preconceived judgements. This attitude not only compounds the problem but also represents a lost opportunity to grow and arrive at understanding through practical experience.

Towards a different legitimization of care

Our study showed that participative care demands a change of focus from 'organizing' to 'operating': from the 'correct route' to 'correctly operating within each route'. Therefore, the care service needs 'rethinking' instead of simply 'reorganizing'. This concerns the question of engagement with each individual situation and the vision that gives that commitment form. This also implies a different legitimization of care service: from a powerful to a powerless care service.

A powerful care service

An emphasis on the ability to find solutions is central to the efficiency mentality: care provision is set in motion in order to manage problems or keep them manageable. This approach has a considerable impact on the dialogue between clients and care workers as well as between care workers themselves. The pressure to manage a situation can mean not enough, or no account, being taken of the client perspective if, for example, the situation is too chaotic, changeable, slow, irrational, ... in view of the care worker. Thus joint responsibility – of client and care worker – is narrowed down to that of care workers mutually taking responsibility *for* instead of *with* the client. This concept implies that all the care providers have to share the same conviction of what is best in a particular situation and then persuade the client of this - as opposed to there being a true dialogue.

This management dynamic also influences mutual communications between care workers. Care workers have commented that they no longer dare to admit that they 'also don't know'. This can lead to consultations where fictive solution strategies are agreed on, actions that people know will lead to little or no change but which exculpates them from being blamed for doing nothing. Cooperation can also be limited to 'referral': another – more expert in the area - service, must solve what one cannot solve oneself.

The acknowledgement of powerlessness

In reality, of course, the care service is often powerless – in terms of being able to solve problems – when confronted with certain situations. The cause of a problem often comes from outside of the client and his immediate environment, for instance poverty. Moreover, it is profoundly difficult to alter human behavior. Nevertheless, the care provision discourse implies a different reality: ideas such as participation, emancipation and empowerment point to a great capability of care services to change things – both individual and social –. Still, Margolin (1997) states that the care service does not succeed in substantially solving social problems. Apostel (1985) also calls the care service an essentially powerless – although endowed with powers – response to problematic situations. Margolin postulates that the care service cannot admit this fundamental impotence, because that would undermine the legitimacy of social work. Care provision must then be replaced by social action. But this proposition ignores the real support that people can experience from the care service and is ultimately unethical considering those persons who are unable to wait for social action (Apostel, 1985). Rather than reject care services for their powerlessness this element needs to be acknowledged as the basis of a participative care provision.

Towards an unknowing care provision

Participative care presumes a form of expertise that has space for 'not knowing' and 'not being able'. So the starting point when tackling a problem is knowing *from the outset* that one has at best a limited knowledge and expertise (Skrtic, 1999). This is in harmony with an acceptance of care provision as an uncertain and unpredictable business (Jordan, mentioned in Parton, 2000), that can in fact in itself reinforce a number of marginalization processes rather than prevent them. This idea *allows room to explore* – in discussion with other care workers and care receivers themselves – the most meaningful intervention in a particular case. This is a vision in which the object of research is the basis for a situation having been assessed as a problem rather than the problem itself. The respect for what constitutes a dignified human existence according to the personal view of children and adults is another starting point. This implies that both the motivations for and the impacts of an intervention are incorporated into the debate. It then becomes possible for a decision to involve reconsideration or redirection of a service's own intervention.

Motivation for such an approach is in practice extant but certainly not evident, for the obvious reason that it demands that the service is put into a vulnerable position.

Space for acknowledging 'not being able to solve a problem'

The Waasland Youth Care Networking research referred to the experience of care workers under great pressures from expectations concerning efficiency and management of problem situations. These expectations were primarily in a social context, but also came from care service demands voiced by the government - for example, stipulations for quality management - and colleagues, and from clients themselves when it came to problem-solving capacities.

As previously mentioned, the approach of care workers to these various expectations – solution capacity and participative care provision – shifts between a defensive and a reflective one. A defensive approach concentrates on the 'supply' and 'demand'. A reflective approach means exploring how these expectations can be handled critically in cooperation with parents and children, other care workers and between services.

So, within the same framework different practices have been developed according to whether the starting point is more a defensive or a reflective one. For example, a preliminary interview can be an instrument to learn as much as possible, to make the most incisive diagnosis and to control a situation; it can also be an instrument for dialogue with the children and adults in this particular situation. Confidentiality can also be used as a defensive tool to decelerate a communal reflection on the care provision yet precisely the opposite when it serves as a basis for augmenting this reflection. In concrete terms, this means that a participative approach cannot be elaborated without care workers being directly and individually addressed on their responsibility in the matter. The space which they get from their institutions, and from the government, is important just as is the notion that qualitative care provision owes a lot to the operating and personality of the individual care workers, rather than to the structure and the operating of institutions (Watson, 2003).

Bar-on states that care workers "must learn that the policies they and other service providers carry out are not inscribed in stone but are socially constructed, and so constantly subject to interpretation and discretion, particularly at field level (reference to Lipsky in Bar-on, 2002: 1010)." However, care workers often seem to accept their situation. "This behaviour is at least partly self-imposed and so can be changed from within (Bar-on, 2002, p. 1010).

The creation of a network as a platform for reflection

It is not easy to conduct the discussion on a space for the acknowledgment of a 'powerless' care service, not at least because it requires services and care workers putting themselves in a vulnerable position and putting their own operations in question. The demand for change can be threatening to the status quo, and, amongst other problems, can cause conflicts in power relationships. The possibly threatening nature of this demand makes individual workers or institutions almost unable to act since they could be seen as 'loose canons rocking the boat', with possible consequences for their position in the care service and their relations with other organizations (Williamson & Prosser, 2002).

Networking can deepen the foundations of this issue or shrink them. If a network aims to create space for reflection, however, the focus must not be on 'solving the problems of clients together' but on 'reflecting together' on the service's own supply: what support does or doesn't the network offer? And to whom? Who is it leaving out? Eventually, of course, it concerns political and ethical questions and the assumption of the mantle of common commitment.

Conclusion

The possibility of developing a care service network that would improve conditions for care receivers was the inspiration for the Waasland Youth Care Networking research. The study showed that not the improvement of organizations, but incorporation of committment and vision in the organization were the most important issues. There are two separate discourses running parallel - desire for control and desire for involvement. It is the responsibility of the care service and the care workers to position themselves with regard to these. A participative approach does not seem likely due to the tension between the pressure to 'manage and solve' on the one hand and an acknowledgement of the often fundamental powerlessness of care provision anticipated on the other hand. This acknowledgment does not imply that care services cannot make a meaningful contribution to the realization of a dignified human existence but refers to the importance of 'exploring' as opposed to 'knowing'. These different attitudes make reference to a reflective or defensive position regarding the diverse demands made on the care service. In practice, examples of both attitudes can be found. Networking also has the dual capacity to expand and shrink the space for reflection.

References

Apostel, L. (1985). Paradoxen van de welzijnszorg: Een driefrontenoorlog. In Seminarie en Laboratorium voor Jeugdwelzijn en Volwassenenvorming (Red.). *Interventierecht. Bijdragen tot de studiedag georganiseerd naar aanleiding van het emeritaat van Prof. Dr. G. De Bock op 5 oktober 1984* (pp. 29 – 48). Antwerpen: De Sikkel. (in Dutch)

Arendt, H. (1994). *Tussen verleden en toekomst. Vier oefeningen in politiek denken.* Leuven: Garant. (in Dutch)

Baldwin, M. (2001). Working together, learning together: co-operative Inquiry in the development of complex practice by teams of social workers. In P. Reason & Bradbury, H. (Eds.). *Handbook of action research. Participative inquiry and practice* (pp. 287–293). London – Thousand Oaks – New Delhi: Sage Publications.

Bar-on, A. (2002). Restoring power to social work practice. *British Journal of Social Work, 32,* 997 – 1014.

Bisschops, L. (2001). Beheerszucht en betrokkenheid in de jeugdzorg. De paradox van twee dominante trends. *Nederlands Tijdschrift voor Jeugdzorg, 3,* 124 – 130. (in Dutch)

De Wilde, C. (2003). *Het juridisch statuut van de minderjarige in de jeugdhulpverlening. Analyse van het huidig juridisch kader en eerste aanzet voor een effectieve rechtsbescherming van de minderjarige in de jeugdhulpverlening. Tussentijds rapport.* Brussel: Beleidsondersteuning Integrale Jeugdhulp. (in Dutch)

Degheldere, C., & Notredame, L., (1987). Welzijnsplanning: Zoeklicht op de welzijnsplanning in Vlaanderen. In H. Baert (ed.), *Welzijnsplanning* (pp. 63 – 93). Brussel: Koning Boudewijnstichting. (in Dutch)

Ellis, K., Davis, A & Rummery, K. (1999). Needs assesment, street-level bureaucracy and the new community care. *Social Policy & Administration, 33,* 262 – 280.

Hasenfeld, Y. (1987). Power in social work practice. *Social Service Review,* 469 – 483.

Lipsky, M. (1980). *Street-level bureaucracy.* New York: Russel Sage.

Margolin, L. (1997). *Under the cover of kindness: The invention of social work.* Charlottesville: University Press of Virginia Press.

Parmentier, S. (1998). Kansarmoede en rechtshulp. Drie uitdagingen op de drempel van de volgende eeuw. *Alert, 1,* 24–31. (in Dutch)

Parton, N. (2000). Some thoughts on the relationship between theory and practice in and for social work. *British Journal of Social Work, 4,* 449 – 463.

Proctor, E. K. (2002). Quality of care and social work research. *Social Work Research, 4,* 195-197.

Roose, R., & De Bie, M. (2003). From participative research to participative practice. A study in youth care. *Journal of Community & Applied Social Psychology, 6,* 475-485.

Roose, R. (2001). *Cliënten over formele hulpverlening.* Onuitgegeven rapport. Gent: Universiteit Gent.

Roose, R. (2003). Participatief werken in een jeugdbeschermingscontext. In M. Bouverne-De Bie et. al. (red.). *Armoede en participatie* (pp. 169 - 183). Gent: Academia Press. (in Dutch)

Skrtic, T. (1999). Learning disabilities as organizational pathologies. In G. R. Sternberg, & L. Spear-Swerling (eds.), *Perspectives on learning disabilities* (pp. 193-226). Colorado: Westview Press.

Sociale Interventie (2003). *Presentie (special issue, 12, No. 2)*. Den Haag: Elsevier Overheid. (in Dutch)

Tronto, J. (1993). *Moral boundaries: a political argument for an ethic of care*. New York: Routledge.

Van der Steege, M. (2003). *Gewoon goed hulpverlenen. Over de cliënt centraal, vraaggericht werken en cliëntenparticipatie in de jeugdzorg*. Utrecht: NIZW uitgeverij. (in Dutch)

Van Nijnatten, C., Hoogsteder, M., & Suurmond, J. (2001). Communication in care and coercion: Institutional interactions between family supervisors and parents. *British Journal of Social Work, 5,* 705 – 720.

Van Tilt, E. (2002). Integrale (jeugd)hulpverlening: een ba(a)nbrekend antwoord op een maatschappelijke nood? In R. Roose (red.), *Contactcomité van Organisaties voor Jeugdzorg. Jaarboek 2000 – 2001* (pp. 47-62). Gent: Academia Press. (in Dutch)

Verschelden, G., & Bouverne-De Bie, M. (2000). Jongeren aan het woord over hun behoeften aan zorg. *Alert, 5,* 20-31. (in Dutch)

Warmenhoven, O. (1973). *Prolegomena tot de andragologische propaedeuse*. Proefschrift. Amsterdam. (in Dutch)

Watson, D. (2003). Defining quality care for looked after children: Frontline workers' perspectives on standards and all that. *Child and Family Social Work, 8,* 67–77.

Williamson, G. R., & Prosser, S. (2002). Action research: Politics, ethics and participation. *Journal of Advanced Nursing, 40,* 587 – 593.

12

In the best interest of the child: Jewish and civic perspectives

Shlomo Romi & Israel Z. Gilat

Is "the child's best interest" the exclusive consideration of the court?

Each of us has fashioned a model through which we relate to the parent-child setting. Usually, our own model seems to be close to our ideal, and we become parents without any prior education or on-the-job training. It seems that when judges are asked to decide on parent-child issues, they do so using their own *idée fixe* regarding the way parenting should be, and to a lesser degree rely on the legal tools at their disposal, such as precedents, letters of request, or what is known as judicial logic.

The legal aspects of parent-child relations are complex (Cretney & Masson, 1997). When parents are in the process of divorce these relations move along two axes that at times intersect, at times touch, and to some degree also run parallel to each other. One axis is *the child,* and his or her rights and responsibilities. It is on this axis that a constant struggle takes place between the child who claims his rights and the parent who supervises and watches out for him. On this axis the tendency is to view the child as the one with the rights and parents as having only obligations, as those responsible for the child's needs. The second axis is *the struggle between the two parents over the child.* On this axis, one parent is the other's opponent, and the child is the object, not the subject. In most conflicts brought to court, the child is no more than a pawn in the chess game played out by the parents, aided by their attorneys. A parent who claims that he or she does not have to pay child support, a parent who wants to keep the child, or insists on determining the way the child will be educated, is not placing the child as his or her adversary and usually is not trying to cut down on what the child has coming, but rather is fighting the other parent for his or her rights (Glisson, 1994; Levi & Romi, 1998; Romi & Levi, 1998, 2000, 2003).

Nonetheless, there is a longstanding opinion in Israeli courts that parents' rights to their child are not independent but rather an "auxiliary authority" of sorts, one that the parent has in carrying out obligations toward the child. In other words, the conflict between two parents over their children is not an egotistical conflict over the parents' legal rights over their children, but rather an altruistic conflict between father and mother over who would better serve the child and the child's rights.

Judge of the High Court of Justice, Zilberg (1954) went so far as to write in his decision in *Steiner v. General Attorney*:

> In the test of the child's best interest, in my opinion, there is no escaping one of these two: either it is not a serious consideration or it is the one and only consideration. A compromise is not possible: it cannot be divided, and should not be mixed or merged with any other consideration. ... Therefore, the Israeli lawmaker was right in determining – and this, in our opinion is the true meaning of Section 3.B, that the best interest of children should be the *ultimate and decisive* (emphasis by the writers) consideration both when it conflicts with the right of custody in accordance with Section 3.A and when it conflicts with the letter of foreign laws...." (C.A. 209/54, 9 P.D. 241, 242).

Judge Zilberg considers the exclusivity of the best interest principle also in those cases where the conflict is between parents and Legislator. However, reading Section 3.B of the *Woman's Equal Rights Law* (1951), will prove Judge Zilberg's words to be emotional. A look at this law reveals that the Legislator's sole intention was to make men and women – father and mother – equal. It should be noted that in Judge Zilberg's verdict, several years before Section 25 of *Capacity and Guardianship Law* (1962) was enacted, there is a general statement regarding exclusive consideration of the best interest of the child. This statement is too general and does not clarify the position of a mother in a conflict with a father when the question is custody over a child who is younger than six years of age. When presented with a divorce agreement, what should a judge's attitude be? Should the judge not be convinced that this agreement reflects the best interest of the child in a manner that is "ultimate and decisive"? In addition, what is the position of the biological parents vis-à-vis other individuals, strangers, or distant relatives? Even the referral in Section 7 to "any court authorized to deal with personal status" was vague, and one could say that "judicial autonomy" was granted to each legal instance to interpret the child's best interest in its own way.

Section 25 of *Capacity and Guardianship Law* (1962) solved some of these problems. First, this Section established a framework in which the judge must consider the best interest of the child, which is when "the parents have not reached an agreement in accordance with Section 24, or have reached an agreement but the agreement was not executed." Thus, if the parents had reached an agreement, the judge is not obligated to doubt that the agreement does not meet the child's best interest. Judges have an inherent authority, or "a general authority for means of protection," in accordance with Section 68, and can disqualify such an agreement if, in their opinion, it does not serve the child's best interests. However, this authority is not obligatory but is left to the judge's discretion.

Second, the Legislator is not content with a nebulous declaration regarding "the child's best interest," but delineates several parameters, such as a preference to the mother, over the father, as custodian for a child up to six years of age, and the resultant total negation of such a priori preference for a child over the age of six. Again, if the child's best interest is the ultimate and decisive principle, what is the point of setting these parameters? Such a distinction does not appear in modern systems of justice. Third, although not explicit but generally implicit, there is no overall consideration of the child's best interest as an ultimate and decisive factor, except in the case of preferring one parent over the other. Thus, using the child's best interest as a guideline, the judge cannot prefer a third party to one of the parents.

In conclusion, both in theory and in practice, the child's best interest is not seen as an ultimate and decisive consideration, unless the case involves conflict between parents over custody of a child who is older than six years of age. However, in conflicts between parents and various social services, the child's best interest is not considered an ultimate and decisive consideration, but rather a counter-consideration, allowing the court to disregard parental rights over their children. If the child's best interest is maximal in a conflict between parents over their child, that is, where will the child be better off, in other conflicts this consideration is minimal, the question being whether the child's situation is bad enough to warrant removal from the legal custodian.

Furthermore, at times, conflicts between the parents are not decided according to the "maximal best interest of the child" but according to the "minimal best interest," for example, when a verdict is carried out by court implementation. In such a case, the verdict will be enforced not only if the guardian parent serves the maximal best interest of the child; on the contrary, it will not be enforced only if being with the guardian parent could lead to severe physical or mental damage. This is true also in cases of child kidnapping. The right of the parent from whom the child had been kidnapped (whether or not this parent had already been granted custody by the courts) is permanent and clear, and the "best interest of the child" might eliminate it only in such cases where there is proven real and immediate danger to the child. Currently this is stated explicitly in Article 13B of the *Hague Convention on International Child Abduction* (which was transformed to Israeli legislation in 1991); however, from the 1960s to the 1980s, when kidnappings were brought to the Israeli High Court of Justice as private petitions of *habeas corpus*, quite a few of the judges believed that the best interest of the child is an "ultimate and decisive" consideration even if this meant blatantly violating international law.

At times, placing the child's best interest at the center of conflicts between parents over their children, and concealing parental conflicts over the rights themselves, generated absurd responses. Thus, when the question arose whether parents can reach an agreement to authorize the rabbinical court (in accordance with the law) to discuss child custody, or whether this also requires the consent of the minor in question, the late Judge Heshin (1955) solved the problem with the following argument:

> It is without hesitation that we respond to this question in the affirmative. The father petitioned the rabbinical court because the parents, as stated above, have no rights of their own for custody over their offspring, and therefore the father sued for the girl. Hence the father, who is the girl's natural guardian, certainly agreed to the court's verdict. And in whose name did he agree if not the name of the minor? *He himself has no rights,* only obligations. The same holds true for the mother (H.C. 86/55 *Der'ei (Naum) v. Head of Execution* 9 P.D. 1938, 1944).

The arguments presented here, and others not included for lack of space, indicate the judicial point of view that parent-child relations are not based exclusively on the best interest of the child, but rather on another principle of parental guardianship of their children.

The origins of "the best interest of the child" in the idea of "parental guardianship"

It would seem, then, that "the best interest of the child" is not the be all and end all, and that the main principle prevalent in various judicial systems is "parental guardianship." If so, what is the principle of guardianship in and of itself, and how does the principle of "the best interest of the child" fit in?

We will state at the onset that up to modern times, the idea of "parental guardianship" was not the norm. Roman law adhered to *patria potestas* ("paternal sovereignty") over children, actually interpreted as *vitae necisque potestas* ("rule of life and death"), whereas medieval Germanic law regarded father and children as a domestic-agricultural unit in which the father had rights of sovereignty. Father and children "cohabited" in a "joint effort," although the father could dispossess his children. The children, too, had the right to leave the "cohabitation" setting and could express their own opinions independently. It is only in modern systems that the approach to the father has changed; he is no longer an omnipotent sovereign, a "director," or "cohabiter," and his status is based on an entirely new concept. The change in the definition of parental role was not sudden, but the result of a slow and gradual change. The birth of "parental guardianship" instead of the old approach is of great interest to those engaged in research of European legal history in various countries. As our main concern here is with the legal examples pertaining to parent-child relations, we will skip the stages of development in the various Western legal systems in the modern era, and limit ourselves to presenting European legal systems, especially Anglo-American, as these were interpreted in scholarly writings since the eighteenth century (Pollock & Maitland, 1968). According to these legal systems, parent-child relations are based on two tiers: (a) Parent-child relations are aimed, first and foremost, at meeting the child's best interest. (b) Parental obligations toward their parents are not voluntary and depend not only on parents' willingness.

The first tier, parent-child relations aimed at the child's best interest, means that parents' rights to their sons and daughters are nothing but conditions to ensure that they meet their obligations toward them. Hence, fulfilling obligations toward offspring is the be all and end all, and the parents' aim is to provide for the physical and mental needs of the children. What is the source of a parent's obligation to his or her child? According to the explanation in Blackstone's Commentaries (1969):

> The duty of parents to provide for the maintenance of their children, is a principle of natural law; an obligation, laid on them not only by nature herself, but by their own proper act, in bringing them into the world: for they would be in the highest manner injurious to their issue, if they only gave their children life, that they might afterwards see them perish. By begetting them, therefore, they have entered into a voluntary obligation, to endeavour, as far as in them lies, that the life which they have bestowed shall be supported and preserved. And thus the children will have a perfect right of receiving maintenance from their parents. (p. 452).

The explanation for the different role of the father concerning his sons' and daughters' property follows (Blackstone's Commentaries, 1969):

> The power of parents over their children is derived from the former consideration, their duty; this authority being given them, partly to enable the parent more effectually to perform his duty, and partly as a recompense for his care and trouble in the faithful discharge of it. A father has no other power over his child's *estate,* than as his trustee or guardian; for though he may receive the profits during the child's minority, yet he must account for them when he comes of age (p. 452).

The second tier is that parental obligation depends not only on the parent's willingness. The obligation is by no means voluntary, and a father cannot pass his children along to the supervision of others and thus release himself from his obligations toward them as we have seen in ancient legal systems, but rather is dependent on the State sovereign's will. (For Roman law see Jolowicz, 1965; Kirschenbaum, 1987; Schulz, 1969; Sohm, 1970; for Medieval Germanic law see Huebner, 1969; Schuster, 1979.)

According to modern European legal systems, a father's relation to his children is nothing but guardianship, and his responsibility for them is derived from the State sovereign. The parent's guardianship over his children is not contingent upon his good will, as is the guardianship of a person who is not the biological parent to become guardian of someone who is not his offspring. Paternal guardianship is mandated by law, and is referred to as "natural guardianship." In other words, the sovereign sees itself – according to these legal systems and through their judicial institutions, as the entity that has the primary responsibility for the children's welfare and wellness, and the parents are nothing more than his deputy, entrusted with caring for the children's needs and well-being (Bromley, 1971; Duncan, 1993; Eeklaar, 1993; Hoggett, 1987; Holdsworth, 1972). It was customary to view custodianship as the etymological parallel of "guardianship" and the parents as "natural guardians" (Eversley, 1937). However, in the United Kingdom this term is no longer in use as they find it evocative of mastery over land and belongings, and even the term "parental rights and obligations" has been changed there to "parental responsibility" (Cretney & Masson, 1997).

Establishing parental responsibility for the children was in the hands of the State sovereign, who was the only one to set the boundaries for the extent and quality of this responsibility. Initially (Pettit, 1957), many countries preferred the father as guardian and perceived him as sole guardian, a survival of the days when fathers ruled their children. The mother was an able guardian only in those cases where the father had died, had been exiled, or lost his mental capacities. However, at the end of the nineteenth century, English law established the mother's right to guardianship as equal to the father' (Pettit, 1957), and other European countries followed suit (Krause, 1983; Neuhaus, 1983). Researchers attributed this to the ideological influences of gender equality.

The State sovereign over the parents' guardianship, also holds true for the extent of their obligation toward their child. While former judiciary systems regarded child support as no more than a moral obligation that was dubiously enforceable, an obligation the father could shirk off at will, this is no longer the case. The law obligates the father to feed and support his sons and daughters (born within wedlock) up to the time they reach a predetermined age, and he cannot be prematurely released of this responsibility without sovereign approval. However, whereas former legal systems obligated a father to care for his grownup sons and daughters at the age when they could be self-sufficient yet continued to live under his roof, modern legal attitude is that a parent is not obligated, in any way, to care for his sons and daughters beyond maturity. The Legislator assumes that upon reaching maturity they are capable of supporting themselves.

Furthermore, according to these systems, the Legislator sees himself as bearing the primary responsibility for the children's welfare, and is the one authorized to determine the standards for this well-being. In most cases, the Legislator prefers material and mental considerations immediately relevant to the minor's development, and all but neglects (but does not nullify) unique class considerations such as spiritual, national, and religious ones; the father's opinion of the child is not a factor in this consideration (Bromley, 1971). Thus, for example, courts in the European system will not make the father's obligation contingent upon the child's obedience. Only in serious cases of rebelliousness does the law allow a father to turn to the courts and ask to be released of some of his obligations toward his child (Hoggett, 1987).

Accordingly, it would seem that under these legal systems the sovereign protects minors from their parents, and the parents cannot care for the minor if it is sovereign opinion that they might harm the child, whether intentionally or inadvertently. The court can refuse to grant the parents guardianship, either permanently or temporarily, if it believes that this guardianship may harm the child. Under this principle of protecting minors from their parents, the parents are not permitted to carry out certain transactions for the minor without prior court approval. At the same time, the Legislator contends that a parent can sue in the name of the minor and be sued, as the minor's representatives, if this does not contradict the minor's interests.

The best interest of the child in Israeli civil law

In the Roman legal system, "father rules" was, as described above, total and non- contestable, and the Roman Legislator would have been hard put to understand "the best interest of the child." Conversely, Germanic law could accept an explicit demand for "the best interest of the child" when the parents, and especially the father, was only running a "common household" with his children, a sort of as-you-will "cohabitation." This is not the case in Western legal systems that regard the parents as "guardians."

In Israel, where the legal system is Western, the *Capacity and Guardianship Law* (1962) does not fully define guardianship but determines it as a comprehensive definition. Furthermore, the law recognizes parents as "natural guardians" of their children, unlike court-appointed guardians. From an etymological point of view, the Greco-Hebrew word *Apotropsut* is a parallel word to guardianship, and the parents were viewed at "natural guardians." In Talmudic and rabbinical literature the term actually refers to a "trustee" who holds the property of another, to administer it for the benefit of that other person. Therefore the obligations of trustee are not outside the limits of the person who undertook the delegacy. It is only nowadays that *Apotropsut* has been differently interpreted, and had been separated dichotomously from the delegacy by Tedeschi (1978). Custody and delegacy serve the same purpose, except that custody creates legal status and delegacy does not, as it is obligatory.

If so, if parents are delegates, who is the sender? The answer would be the state and its various institutions. Hence, custodianship indicated parental subordination, and, in fact, the limits of parents' ability to care for their children. Parents cannot work downward toward their children if they have not been appointed by the State sovereignty, and have nothing more than the Legislator's concession to watch over their children. Not only does the sovereign establish the parents as custodians, it also establishes the way in which the parents will fulfill their mission, a way that will serve the best interests of the child. Thus, the Legislator has established on the one hand that the parent has the duty and the right to care for the needs of the minor, including his or her education, and on the other hand, the very same Legislator requires that the parent registers the child in a recognized educational institution and supervise his attendance there. Parents have practically no freedom in determining a child's education; in most cases they may choose from one of the recognized educational systems, sometimes limited to a geographical district as per the regulations of the educational administration. If so, consideration of the best interest of the child is not an exclusive, "ultimate and decisive" governing-principle, but rather changes according to the Legislator's winding policies and according to the interpretative policies of the judges appointed by the Legislator.

We would dare make an opposing argument (and one that is contrary to the opinions of other scholars, for instance Shaki, 1984 and Shamgar, 1993): parents are not only obligated to their children and responsible for them, but also have rights regarding the children. At least in the realm of relations between the minor and third parties, the decision of a parent in approving any legal action is that parent's right and such a decision binds the minor for many years after reaching legal adulthood. At least in one of the cases brought to the High Court of Justice (H.C. 709/79, *Amir Cohen v. The Minister of Defense*) the problem was raised in full acuteness: in order to be accepted to a military academy, the parents' minor signed an agreement with the security forces. Their signature committed the minor to serve an additional three years as a career soldier after his three years of compulsory military service. How binding is the signature? The legal answer is known, but here are the crucial words of Judge Cohen about the wide scope of guardianship:

> "Is it conceivable that a minor would commit himself – even with parental consent – to work for the owner of his contract as if he were a pierced-ear slave... and if a man sell his son to be a slave or his daughter to be a maidservant, could they not leave when they reach adulthood, even as could the Hebrew slaves?"

Metaphorically, relations between parents and children are constructed of a peel and the body within it. The peel is the custodianship – the concession, the sovereign's permission. The body within is the principle of "the best interests of the child." The best interest of the child is not an absolute, definitive idea, but rather changes according to the sovereign's policies. Other than a few general parameters, the Legislator does not provide any guidance as to what it perceives as the best interest of the child and what it does not perceive as such. Out of the considerable number of verdicts pertaining to the best interests of the child, it is clear that there are values that should not be considered such as matters of religion or nationalism. In addition, "guilt factors" should not be considered ("Who's to blame for everything falling apart?") and certainly no long-term considerations should be allowed (e.g., which parent would give the child a better chance of being accepted to a university-level computer training program or to a drama and fashion college?). According to the law, what remains are the barest material and emotional considerations, all pertaining to the very present – where will the child be better off at the moment? The reason for limiting the number of possible values to be considered could be that verdicts regarding child custody and support are, for the most part, recurring and can be changed on occasion as circumstances change. At times long-term, value-laden considerations were brought to the High Court of Justice in *habeas corpus* pleas, as it seemed that in the case of the High Court, any judgment would be nonrecurring due to the special circumstances.

Parental guardianship granted by the State and its institutions may, at times, cast a shadow over the child's rights. For example, the Legislator does not require that a guardian for court be appointed for each minor whose case is discussed in the legal proceedings regarding the conflict between the child's parents, nor is one required when an agreement regarding the child is being drawn. The assumption is, therefore, that as guardians, parents want the best for their child and are free of thoughts and calculations that might hurt the child or his interests. Even the right for "freedom of education," loosely based on Israel's Proclamation of Independence was recently interpreted by the Honorable Judge Or as "intended to guarantee freedom and choice in education", so that parents can choose between the various educational directions. However, in and of itself, the "right for the freedom of education" does not include the State's obligation to provide one form of education or another" (H.C. 1554/95, *GILAT Association v. Minister of Education* P.D. (3)2, 27).

Experts and psychological opinions

Civil courts often use expert opinion in their attempts to establish child custody. This usually involves engaging mental-health experts, among them psychologists, social workers, and psychiatrists, who conduct a specific diagnostic assessment of a type that could not be conducted by the courts. This assessment, which will be described below, includes addressing the child's world and that of the divorcing parents and the relevant environment. It focuses on the inner-psychological world, at times hidden, of the participants, and the findings are an essential foundation for court decisions. These experts can form a unique bridge between the out-of-court life and world of the child and parents and the arguments and their establishment as these are manifested in court (Romi & Levi, 1998, 2000, 2003; Levi & Romi, 1998).

Despite differences and ambivalence in the decision-making process and the guiding considerations for the custody of minors, we can point out several criteria accepted by most Western therapists and practitioners of law (Kaslow & Schwartz, 1987; Miller, 1993; Goldstein, Solnit & Freud, 1964,1979; Wall & Amadio, 1994; Wallerstein & Kelly, 1980). The court, the main client of the experts it appoints, expects the following:

The court, as the body that appointed the experts, expects to be presented with recommendations that can withstand meticulous legal scrutiny, and are least contestable. These recommendations should be such that the family can accept and live by, and be long lasting, or last until the family feels the need to review them and adjust them to changing circumstances. In conducting the assessment, experts are guided by the following principles:

Best interests of the child

This basic principle generally means that in cases of conflict between the child's needs and those of the adult, priority is given to those of the child. This principle is the underlying foundation of legislation to ensure the safety of the child during times of crisis, and it enables, among other things, separate legal representation for children. This principle also takes precedence over other legal principles. Thus, in contrast to the principle of public trials, legal cases involving minors are held in closed court and identifying disclosure is prohibited. Decisions and judgments on the subject of custody are always temporary and can be reconsidered with changing circumstances, in contrast to the principle of finality of judgment after appeals have been heard.

Security and consistency

The court prefers a setting that will ensure consistency and continuity of lifestyle and of primary relationships, such that are necessary for the normal development of children and of their feelings of stability, security, and protection.

The lesser of two evils

Frequently, in cases where no optimal solution can be found, the court is guided by seeking the lesser of two evils. The court then tries to find the option, which contains elements that are least harmful to the child.

The child's relations with the non-custodial parent and his/her family

The degree of readiness and openness to allow contact with the non-custodial parent and his/her extended family shows sensitivity to the needs of the child, and willingness to honor his needs and maintain the second parents' role in the child's life. The parent willing to allow this contact will usually be considered the preferable choice, an important criterion that could tip the scales in his/her favor.

Guidance for acting upon these principles is provided, as mentioned, by expert opinion. An interdisciplinary team of health care professional and mental health professionals is engaged to conduct their work over a relatively long period of time, to allow an in-depth study of all parties concerned and their environment. During this period, the team also supports and counsels the people they are evaluating. The evaluation process includes extended data gathering. In addition to observing the child and parents in various situations, team members meet professionals who touch upon the child's life (e.g., teachers and doctors). Team members must be objective and open, allowing each one of the parties to present themselves and their position, and to be examined respectfully and without prejudice. All information guided is held in strict confidentiality.

The best interest of the child in Jewish law

One of the anomalies of the State of Israel is the fact that two legal instances – civil and rabbinical – compete for jurisdiction over matters of personal status. An upshot of this is that the main issue over which most divorcing couples argue is the type of court to which they will present their case, with everything else often becoming secondary. This procedural struggle is echoed in rabbinical law codes and in studies conducted by practitioners of family law. The anomaly refers not only to the different personality make-up of those who sit in judgment and to the structural differences between the two instances, but also, and perhaps primarily, to the essential differences in the legal approaches. One source of tension between the two legal instances refers to the interpretation of the term "the best interest of the child."

Before continuing with the legal aspects, it is important to digress and explain the educational system, as this bears directly on all decisions. The Ministry of Education in Israel administers two parallel and equal Jewish educational systems – secular and religious. Unlike many Western countries where religious education is private, both systems are public, and the choice of school is up to the family. The curricula of both systems are supervised by the Ministry of Education, and both offer the same academic and vocational tracks. Although curricula differ in emphasis, with more religious studies taught in the religious schools, the systems are not exclusive, and a student may switch from one to the other. In addition, there are private religious schools, as well as state-run Arab schools.

The prevalent approach among *dayans* (religious judges of the rabbinical court) and among some scholars (e.g., Shifman, 1989) regarding "the best interest of the child" is that there is, indeed, formal equality between both judiciary systems regarding the supremacy and exclusivity of the principle of "the best interest of the child." Any difference between the judiciary systems as to the application of this rule in conflicts between parents over their children's custody and education, is a result of the changing interpretation given by the two systems to the term "best interest of the child." Hence, the best interest of the child is interpreted according to the underlying values of the system that employs it. One judiciary system sees religious and national values as its foundation, and another sees Western, humanistic, civic values as its guide (Shifman, 1989). Generally speaking, there is no absolute philosophical interpretation for the term "good" (in its superlative form "best," in our case), and it depends to a large degree on the value scale of the specific user (Bentham, 1950; Eduard, 1972).

On a practical level the difference is manifested as follows: while the judge sitting on a custody case – and the accompanying issues of learning and education – in civil court sees "the best interest of the child" as a series of psychological, immediate, and material considerations, (Gilat, 2000) the *dayan* in the rabbinical court envisions spiritual considerations and a view of the future, and gives them precedence over all others (Gilat, 1991-1992). Thus, according to Jewish law, it is in the best interest of a daughter to grow up in her mother's home so that "she may teach her modesty and good manners" (Gilat, 2000). However, it behooves a son – whose adult obligation is to worship God, study Torah, observe *mitzvahs* (Jewish religious edict), and earn a living as is men's wont – to be raised by his father who is the one fit to instruct him both in religious learning and in acquiring a profession. This explains why rabbinical courts prefer the religious parent and religious education to the non-religious parent and to secular education, an approach prevalent in rabbinical courts (Gilat, 2000). In their verdicts, the *dayans* emphasize their loyalty to the principle of best interest of the child and declare that they hold it to be a decisive, overriding consideration. However, in the same breath, using the same declarations and explanations, they reach conclusions that are diametrically opposed to those reached by Israeli civil courts applying the same principle (Gilat, 1990).

The weakness of this approach lies in its lack of justification, because, even if the rabbinical court is correct in terms of Jewish law in its preference of spiritual, ethical considerations of the type that are future-oriented, such as where the child will be better trained, this approach is not acceptable in civic judgment which interprets the best interest of the child as encompassing immediate material considerations. That being the case, how can one explain the overt struggle of rabbinical courts to avoid following civic judicial interpretation of the best interest of the child, if loosing the battle is a foregone conclusion?

Furthermore, why is the spiritual best interest of the child the end objective of the rabbinical court rather than immediate material ones, when both factors are important to a child's well-being?

It seems that in terms of Jewish law, the best interest of the child is not an overriding, exclusive super-principle. Although the best interest of the child is an important principle, common in Halakhic (Jewish legal) literature from the seventh century on, it is not the only one. Alongside the best interest of the child, even in its Halakhic interpretation, there is an additional, independent consideration, namely the religious one. The religious consideration is twofold: one part is the father's right to fulfill the *mitzvahs* (religious obligations) incumbent upon him as a father, which do not apply to anyone else, not even the child's mother. In such conflicts between two religious parents, the rivalry between them focuses to a large degree on the question of which parent has the right to educate the minor personally, or which has the right to determine the specific religious schooling the child will receive, in case the parents are in disagreement over this issue.

The other meaning of the religious consideration is more significant, and it involves keeping the child from prohibited actions or substances (e.g., desecrating the Sabbath or eating non-kosher foods). As we have indicated elsewhere (Gilat, 1991-1992, 2000), keeping a child from such actions or substances is not a task assigned particularly to the father, and it is one incumbent upon any Jew. If the child's father does not adhere to these edicts, it is the obligation of the mother or of any other Jew to do so for the minor, keeping him or her out of harm's way, in the religious sense. This obligation pertains not only to a 13-year-old boy who is a legal minor but, according to Jewish law is considered "adult" and obligated to fulfill *mitzvahs* as is every adult Jew and must be kept away but even young boys and girls who have not reached the age of obligations to fulfill religious tenets. (This refers to boys younger than 13 years of age and to girls younger than 12; Jewish law refers to them as "small." At 12 and 13, they have reached the age when they themselves are responsible for fulfilling *mitzvahs,* and are known as bar mitzvah or bat mitzvah, respectively.)

Conflicts surrounding "religious considerations" between parents who have separated, or are about to separate, are arbitrated in various judiciary instances. At times the conflict is based on difficult ideological differences, as when one parent has "found religion" and therefore left the partner who continues to adhere to his or her "secularism". In most cases, however, these "ideological" arguments are forced ones, and are part of a tactic that one parent chose against the other, either independently or under advice of counsel. The purpose of such rivalry is to impress upon the judge or the *dayan* that indeed there exists between the parents such ideological conflicts as cannot be reconciled, as any compromise might harm the child's mental development. For example, a child could not be educated in a religious setting if he or she is in custody of a parent who does not adhere to a religious lifestyle.

While civic judiciary instances may exhibit indifference toward the religious consideration, and view it as a mere appendage to the question of mental damage that will follow the decision, the *dayans* in rabbinical court accord it great importance. The rabbinical court will decide on matters of custody, learning, and education in favor of the religious parent, and in doing so will nullify the right of the "secular" parent to affect the minor's personality, learning, and education.

However, religious considerations are not limited to weighing the rights and obligations of the parents in and of themselves, but also involve the rights and obligations of the *dayan* himself. Thus, unlike judges who are to detach themselves from the rival parents and only seek the child's best interest, in religious consideration the *dayan* must detach himself from the child and from the rival parents and weigh his own religious obligation in determining the child's spiritual, religious future. If the *dayan* decides on a step that is not in accordance with religious law, he may find himself committing a religious sin, and such a sin may, at times, be irreparable. The *dayan* who is part of the team in such a conflict is under personal, religious obligation to make sure that the child will be educated in accordance with religious law, and most specifically, it is his responsibility to do all he can to avoid a situation where the child could sin or break religious edicts.

However, this type of consideration is not mentioned in rabbinical ruling, and is only implicit in a careful analysis of the facts in each case, as these facts are expressed in the verdict. Clearly, this concealment of the religious consideration does not indicate its absence, but rather the rabbinical court's fear of the High Court of Justice and its general handling of the best interest of the child issue, and particularly of High Court procedures where rabbinical courts appear as respondents. The "Stateliness" of the rabbinical court drives it to this concealment and to replacing the real reason with a reason that is anemic from a religious point of view, at times not always successful, at others downright groundless. Following are examples of two cases where custody was determined by the religious consideration.

In the first case, which appears in the rulings of the state-governed Israeli Rabbinical courts (Rabbinical appeal 5718/141) a couple had quarreled and maintained separate residences. The husband, referring to his wife's flawed religious practices, demanded that the children be given to him and that his 7-year-old son be transferred to a religious boarding school. The Rabbinical District Court decided that the boy should stay with his mother because the father does not want to keep him but rather intends to send him to an institute.

The Rabbinical Court of Appeals reversed the decision of the District Rabbinical Court (Rabbinical Appeal 5718/141) stating:

> ...the rule that the home of one of the parents is preferable to an institution has been recited and repeated in several verdicts in Israeli courts, and has become a permanent and decreed rule that no longer receives second thought. However, in our opinion, this matter should be clarified, and one should weigh... if, for example, one of the parents suggests entering a child to a boarding school that is part of a school that is not meant to be a shelter for abandoned children, but rather one to which respectable parents who live a proper family life send their children to be educated, ... the institute should be preferred to

the care of one of the parents.... and in this case, where the father wants to send the child to an institute where he will be educated according to the Torah, and *in accordance with the father's way* [emphasis ours], this too should be considered as if the son is with his father.

The second case (R.A. 5719/199) is one of a divorce agreement between parents. The agreement established the mother as custodian for the son. After the divorce the father demanded that the son be placed with him, because his ex-wife (mother of the boy) lived out of wedlock with a man.

Based on the best interest of the child, the court decreed that the boy be with his father and not with his mother, stating:

... family life, in wedlock in accordance to the Laws of Moses and Israel is among the most sacred things to the People of Israel, and is also accepted by those who do not observe tradition. Even the latter ... view family life outside of wedlock as a life of promiscuity and licentiousness. Whereas the appellant is living with a man out of wedlock, the father is entitled to demand that his young son not find himself on a permanent basis in a home where the laws and mores of Israel are blatantly violated (P.D.R. Vol 4 pp 335-336).

This, again, was a case where the moral consideration was the decisive argument in favor of the father, despite the previous agreement reached by the couple.

Discussion

There is a built-in paradox in the Israeli legal system: rabbinical courts are authorized to address conflict over custody according to Halakha (Jewish law). At the same time they are bound by the Legislator to consider the civic principles of "the best interest of the child."

These two judicial bodies are in perpetual struggle over authority regarding child custody, and more so, over forming the decisions themselves in issues of child custody. The rabbinical court comes under the direct scrutiny of the High Court and the indirect scrutiny of the civil courts in lower instances as we will presently show.

In the case of *Biares v. Rabbinical Court*, (H.C.7/83) the mother turned to the High Court of Justice against the rabbinical court. This court had delivered a short, unexplained verdict, when the evidence was not given in front of a full court, to remove the children from their mother to their father, in accordance with the father's demand. His demand was based on the fact that the woman had admitted to have been intimate with a non-Jewish man.

The decision reached by the rabbinic court was attacked and overruled by the High Court of Justice for a variety of procedural reasons. However, when addressing the claim made by the mother's attorney, as if the rabbinical court had made invalid religious considerations, such as giving a religious education, High Justice Baisky (Biares v. *Rabbinical Court*, (H.C.7/83) (1983) stated:

> There is no room for relating to the claim made by the appellant's attorney that the consideration of providing said children with religious education, or the consideration of removing them from the proximity of an undesirable person are not valid. All that could be said is that considerations of this kind may, under certain circumstances, have great, even dominant, bearing. However, what does this refer to? When the best interest of the children was examined and weighed from all possible aspects, and the judiciary instance reached a decision that among the complex of considerations these must be dominant, as in the case of a child who was brought up on religious values and attends a religious school, and the attempt of one of his parents to sway him away from these values may affect him mentally (p. 685).

Hence, according to Judge Baisky, children's religious education, in and of itself, is a minor consideration, and is therefore insignificant in the eyes of civic instances. However, what should be heavily weighed are the emotional aspects of moving from one type of educational philosophy to another. In this case it is possible that religious education would be a significant factor in assessing mental damage.

Based on the words of Judge Baisky, it is possible to understand his final conclusion regarding this case:

> We have not heard that the children had received religious education up to this point. With all the importance that should be attributed to religious values for those who adhere to them, another weighty consideration is the impact on the children of a sudden transition from a secular school to a religious one; ... this must be examined and considered, and it cannot be that this consideration only, disregarding all other worthy considerations, will be the decisive one that will determine who has custody. And when this is the only consideration, without investigating and looking into the entirety of the complex problems,... it cannot be said that the rule of the Legislator regarding the best interest of the child had been followed.

It should be mentioned that the position of the *dayan* in rabbinical court is unique when compared to the civic court, and points to the autonomy of religious considerations. The intent is that, unlike the consideration regarding the best interest of the child, where the judge is obligated to distance himself from the rivaling parents and see only the best interest of the minor, in the religious consideration, the *dayan* is obligated to distance himself from the minor and from his rival parents and weigh his religious duty in determining the spiritual and religious future of the child. If the *dayan* decides, regarding the child, on something that is opposed to religious values, he himself may be transgressing in a religious way. The *dayan* who sits in as part of the court in such a conflict is obligated, on a personal-religious level, to make sure that the young child receives a religious upbringing and education.

Summary

The various viewpoints regarding "the best interest of the child" as presented in the chapter highlight the gap on this issue between the two existent judiciary systems in Israel. At the same time, it would seem that this gap is becoming somewhat narrower. This movement is almost imperceptible, and is characterized by a de facto attitude without using expressions that give the impression of teaching religious law. The practical approach is an attempt to accept facts and not to seek new edicts that may be perceived as injurious to religion.

Acknowledgments

The authors would like to thank the Institute for Community Education and Research, School of Education and the Schnitzer Foundation for Research of Israeli Economy and Society of the Social Sciences Faculty, Bar-Ilan University, Israel, for their support.

References

Bentham, J. (1950). *The theory of legislation* (2nd ed.). London.
Biares v. Rabbinical Court, (H.C. 7/83) (1983) 1 P.D p. 673.
Blackstone, W. (1969). *Blackstone's commentaries,* Vol. II Tucker (Ed.), p. 452 (Rep. N.J, N.Y.).
Bromley, P. M. (1971). *Family law* (4th ed.), pp. 263-265. London.
Cohen, H (1979). H.C. 709/79, *Amir Cohen v. The Minister of Defense* 34 P.D. ii 467-474.
Cretney, S. M., & Masson, J. M. (1997). *Principles of family law* (6th ed.). London: Sweet & Maxwell.
Duncan, W. R. (1993). The constitutional protection of parental rights, *Parenthood in Modern Society,* 431-455.
Eduard, P. (Ed.) (1972). *The encyclopedia of philosophy* Vol. 3, p. 367-369. New York: (*The Good*).
Eekelaar, J. (1993). Are parents morally obliged to care for their children?" *Parenthood in Modern Society,* 51-64.
Eversley, W. P. (1937). *On domestic relations* (5th ed. Canada,), pp. 458-460.
Gilat, I. Z. (1990). Is "the benefit of the child" a major criterion according to Jewish Law in a parental conflict on custody of the child? *Bar-Ilan Law Studies, 8,* 297-349.
Gilat, I. Z. (1991-1992). The role of religious-Halakhic factors in custody and rearing disputes. *Dine' Israel: Annual of Jewish Law, 16,* 133-162.
Gilat, I. Z. (2000). *Relations between parents and children in Israeli and Jewish Law,* pp. 377-448. Tel Aviv: Choshen Lamishpat.
Glisson, C. (1994). The effect of services coordination teams on outcomes for children in State Custody. *Administration in Social Work, 18,* 1-23.
Goldstein, J., Freud, A., & Solnit, A. Z. (1964). *Behind the best interest of the child.* New York.
Goldstein, J., Freud, A., & Solnit, A. Z. (1979). *Before the best interests of the child.* New York: Free Press.
Heshin, S. Z. (1955). H.C. 86/55 *Der'ei (Naum) v. Head of Execution.* 9 P.D. 1938, 1944.
Hoggett, B. M. (1987). *Parents and children: The law of parental responsibility* (3rd ed.), pp. 7-17. London: Sweet and Maxwell.
Holdsworth, W. (1972). *A history of England law.* Burke (Ed.) Vol. V, p. 648. London.
Huebner, H. R. (1969). *A history of Germanic law.*(Rep. N.Y., 1969),657-670.
Jolowicz, H. F. (1965) *Historical introduction to the study of Roman Law,* pp. 118-120. (Rep Cambridge), 118-120.
Kaslow, F.W., & Schwartz, L.L. (1987) *The dynamics of divorce: A life cycle perspectives.* New York :Brunner/Mazel.
Kirschenbaum, A. (1987). *Sons, slaves and freemen in Roman commerce.* Jerusalem: Magnes Pub.

Krause, H. D. (1983). Creation of relationship of kinship. *The International Encyclopedia of Comparative Law,* Vol. 4, Chap. 6, para. 131. Tuebingen, Germany.

Levi, N., & Romi, S. (1998). Multi-disciplinary team for optimal placement of children in custody disputes: Critical necessity or luxury? *Sihot (Dialogue): Israel Journal of Psychotherapy,* 185-193 (in Hebrew).

Miller, G. (1993). The psychological best interests of the child. *Journal of Divorce and Remarriage, 19,* 21-36.

Neuhaus, P. H. (1983). Christian family law. *The International Encyclopedia of Comparative Law* Vol. IV, Chap. 11, para. 58. Tuebingen, Germany.

Pettit, P. (1957). Parental Control and Guardianship. *A century of family law 1857-1957,* Crane & Graveson (Eds.), pp. 56-87. London.

Pollock, F., & Maitland, F. W. (1968). *The history of the English Law* (2nd ed.), Vol. II, p. 438. Cambridge: Cambridge University Press.

Rabbinical appeal 5718/141(1958). P.D.R. Vol 4, p. 66.

Rabbinical appeal 5719/199 (1959). P.D.R. Vol 4, p. 74.

Romi, S., & Levi, N. (1998). What is the "preferred home" when the home doesn't exist anymore... dilemmas and criteria. *Society and Welfare Quarterly for Social Work, 18,* 384-406 (in Hebrew).

Romi, S., & Levi, N. (2000). A multi-disciplinary professional team to clarify the dilemmas in children's custody. In N. N. Singh, J. P. Leung & A. N. Singh (Eds.), *International research and practice in child and adolescent mental health* (pp. 357-379). Amsterdam: Elsevier.

Romi, S., & Levi, N. (2003). Children's custody assessment. *Encyclopedia of Psychological Assessment, 1,* 178-182. Thousand Oaks: Sage Publications.

Schuster, E. J. (1979). *The principles of German civil law,* pp. 546-556. Darmstadt, Germany.

Shaki, A. (1984). Main characteristics of the Law of Child Custody in Israel. *Law Review, 10,* 5-36.

Shamgar, M. (1993). *Ploni (minor) v. Ploni* C.A. 2266/93, 49, P.D.(1), p. 221.

Shifman, P. (1989). *Family law in Israel,* Part II, pp. 217-228. Jerusalem. Hebrew University.

Schulz, F. (1969). *Classical Roman Law* (Rep Oxford), pp. 142-161.

Sohm, R. (1970). *The Institutes, history and system of Roman Private Law* (Rep N.J.,N.Y.) pp. 479-488.

Tedeschi, G. (1978). *Legal essays,* pp. 334-369. Hebrew University, Jerusalem.

Wall, J. C., & Amadio, C. (1994). An integrated approach to child custody evaluation: Utilizing the "best interest" of the child and family systems frame works. *Journal of Divorce and Remarriage, 21,* 39-57.

Wallerstein, J. S., & Kelly, J. B. (1980). *Surviving the breakup.* New York: Basic Books.

Zilberg, M. (1954). C.A. 209/54 *Steiner v. General Attorney* 9 P.D. 241, 242.

13

Child maltreatment. Learning from tragedies – Lessons from child deaths

Christine Cocker

Introduction

Child murder or manslaughter is a permanent act with permanent consequences representing irrevocable damage to the notion of a parent as a trusting adult, carer and protector of a child. It represents something that is unthinkable to the majority of people – that a parent or carer would kill a child for whom they are responsible. Some of these children and their families will be known to child protection agencies, others will not (Bullock & Sinclair, 2002). This paper will highlight themes emerging from the research that has reviewed these serious cases where children have been killed.

What is a serious case review?

In England alone there are 150 different Local Authorities, all of whom are responsible for providing social services to children and families who live in their locality. Each of those Local Authorities must have an Area Child Protection Committee (ACPC). The ACPC is an inter-agency forum for agreeing how the different statutory and voluntary child care services and professional groups should co-operate to safeguard children and young people in any given locality. Membership and adherence to the policies and procedures produced by such committees is voluntary, as ACPC's are not currently located on a statutory footing, although this is set to change with the introduction of Local Safeguarding Boards (DFES, 2003).

Whenever a child dies of abuse or neglect, or has sustained a potentially life-threatening injury, suffered serious impairment of health and development or been subjected to particularly serious sexual abuse, then the Area Child Protection Committee must consider whether to conduct a case review. Such case reviews are called "Part 8 reviews" or Serious Case Reviews (Department of Health et al., 1999):

The purpose of a Serious Case Review is:

- to establish whether there are lessons learned about the way in which professionals and agencies work together to safeguard children;
- to identify what those lessons are, how they will be acted upon and what is expected to change as a result; and
- to improve inter-agency working.

These reviews can be undertaken by the ACPC in question or alternatively the ACPC can commission an external/independent organisation or individual to conduct the review. During the 19 years that The Bridge Child Care Development Service has been operating, it has undertaken more than 50 such reviews nationally.

Statistics kept on child deaths are fairly unreliable (Bullock & Sinclair, 2002, pp. 2-3). Browne and Lynch (1995) believe that it is still only possible to estimate the number of child abuse fatalities in a population due to problems of definition, recognition, misdiagnosis and data collection. The Department of Health estimates that there are 90 child deaths each year that are the subject of a full serious case review, although the most widely quoted statistic indicates that 'on average, between 1 to 2 children each week die as a result of abuse or neglect' (NSPCC, 2001). The difference in figures is because the link between serious case reviews and fatal child abuse is not straightforward. For example, there is variation in practice between ACPC's in their response to child death concerning whether a serious case review is undertaken, and there is also under-reporting of fatal child abuse to the Department of Health (Creighton, 2001; Wilczynski, 1994, cited in Bullock and Sinclair, 2002).

Key themes from research examining serious case reviews

Bullock and Sinclair (2002), in their Department of Health commissioned study, scrutinised 40 Serious Case Reviews, 20 conducted before and 20 after the introduction (updating) of the Department of Health guidance dictating how agencies involved in child protection should work together. ACPC chairs and report authors were interviewed in 20 cases.

In addition to Bullock and Sinclair's work, a handful of other studies have analysed a sample of serious case reviews submitted to the Department of Health (Falkov, 1996; Hill, 1990; James, 1994; Munro, 1996; and Reder & Duncan, 1999; Reder et al, 1993). When examining this literature, the most common themes identified in serious case reviews are as follows (Bullock & Sinclair, 2002):

- Limited inter-agency co-operation: One of the biggest criticisms is that each agency gives a different priority to the 'safeguarding children' agenda. Currently ACPC's do not have a statutory role (this is set to

change) and rely on the co-operation of member agencies to achieve their stated business aims and objectives. Issues of governance, accountability and resource allocation can also be raised;
- Poor communication between and within agencies;
- Inadequate links between social services and mental health services (Falkov, 1996; Reder and Duncan, 1999:145, The Bridge Child Care Development Service, 2001);
- Poor recording ;
- Inappropriate response to referrals ;
- Inadequate supervision;
- Failure to utilise cumulative information to assess risk factors;
- Lack of shared understanding of agency thresholds;
- Inadequate comprehensive family assessments: Macdonald, (2001) found that having a comprehensive assessment on a child's file was an exception rather than the norm; the exception was when the case was involved in Court proceedings;
- Absence of shared decision-making: this can also lead to errors in the professional decision-making process (Jowitt, 2003; Macdonald, 2001);
- Failure to plan a co-ordinated response: agencies do not always know what others are doing and often there is no baseline upon which to measure progress (or lack of it); and
- Lack of practice tools, especially for key decisions.

The existence of known indicators (some of this research is from USA studies)

According to Reder and Duncan (1999, pp. 2-3) early epidemiological studies identified some associated factors such as parents giving birth to children whilst young themselves and the young age of the children killed (Jason & Andereck, 1983; Oliver 1983; cited in Reder & Duncan, 1999).

A literature review by Hegar et al (1994) cited in Reder and Duncan (1999), showed that the severity of children's injuries is directly related to their age, and children in the first year of life are consistently reported as being most vulnerable, with a heightened risk into the second year (e.g., Durfee & Tilton-Durfee, 1995; Schlosser et al, 1992, cited in Reder & Duncan, 1999). An increased risk has been suggested for children living with non-biological fathers (Creighton, 1992; Scott, 1973, cited in Reder & Duncan, 1999), although female perpetrators outnumber males in most studies (e.g. Bourget & Bradford, 1990; Resnick, 1973, cited in Reder & Duncan, 1999). Unwanted children are also vulnerable and behaviour such as inconsolable crying can provoke unpremeditated violence (e.g. Kaplun & Reich, 1976; d'Orban, 1979; Greenland 1980; Husain & Daniel, 1984; Krugman, 1985; Korbin, 1987; cited in Reder & Duncan, 1999).

Physical abuse is the commonest cause of death, but a substantial number of fatal neglect cases also occur (e.g., Margolin 1990; Hicks & Gaughan, 1995 cited in Reder & Duncan, 1999). Schlosser et al. (1992), cited in Reder and Duncan, 1999, have identified an association with inadequate antenatal care and perinatal problems. Fatal abuse may be preceded by episodes of phyical abuse or other physical violence in the home (Hollander 1986; Sabotta & Davis, 1992 cited in Reder & Duncan, 1999), although many families in which children die are not known to statutory agencies (US advisory Board on Child Abuse and Neglect, 1995: Hicks & Gaughan, 1995; cited in Reder & Duncan, 1999). This last point is also supported by the findings of Bullock and Sinclair's study, although Bullock and Sinclair (2002) go on to comment that the existence of such indicators have limited predictive value when applied to the general population of vulnerable children.

> '...Macdonald (2001) concludes from her review of the research (that) the likelihood of abuse occurring will depend on the interplay of a range of factors and, 'it is not possible to say how significant a particular feature, characteristic or circumstance might be'. Even if the forecasts of future abuse were accurate, attempts to predict which of those children would be murdered or suffer serious injury are virtually impossible (Beaumont, 1999; Corby, 1996; Hagell, 1998; Harris-Hendricks, 1998; Little & Mount, 1999).'

(Bullock & Sinclair, 2002, pp. 17-18)

Potential risk factors

In order to avert serious child maltreatment where possible, practitioners must have a good understanding of potential areas of risk that may exist within families (for both parents and children), as well as know about common professional errors that can bias their work. The literature recognises the limitations in providing social workers with lists of risk factors and/or common errors as there is a danger in a list being interpreted as definitive, predictive and used as part of a mechanised assessment process instead of as an aid to reasoned and reflective thinking (Munro, 2002; Parton & Parton, 1989; Reder et al., 1993). Jeyarajah Dent (1998, p.4) summarises, "Risk assessment should not be a static task but rather a process which seeks to evaluate risk through a growing understanding of individual clients."

What constitutes 'dangerousness' within families

Within the UK there is a large quantity of literature available on child protection. This includes literature that specifically defines 'risk' and 'dangerousness' in relation to assessment (Carson, 1998; Greenland, 1987, Hagell, 1998; Jeyarajah Dent, 1998; MacDonald, 2001; Newman, Otvos, & Harris Hendriks, 1998). Munro (2002, p.63) contends that the language of risk that has permeated into child protection is a relatively recent development.

Hagell (1998) mentions difficulties in finding literature that adequately separates the concepts of 'risk' and 'dangerousness', as they are used interchangeably (Harris Hendriks & Newman, 1998). Munro (2002) also believes that the term 'risk' is ambiguous and confusing.

Carson (1998, p.6) defines risk as 'an occasion when two or more outcomes, whether beneficial or harmful, are possible'. In relation to child protection, 'risk in child protection can be justified whenever the value of the likely benefits sufficiently exceeds the seriousness of the possible harms....many risks, including some in child protection, will be dominated by avoidance of harm. There may be no option that does not involve some harm. The objective of those decisions is to minimise the loss' (Carson, 1998, pp. 91-92). Munro (2002) and Carson (1998) both refer to the time frames associated with risk assessments. Often in child protection the assessment is concentrated on the likelihood of immediate harm to the child. There is a danger that the longer-term risks to the child are ignored or underplayed.

Munro (2002, p. 105) contends that, 'The best predictor of future behaviour is past behaviour. Therefore, the main task in a risk assessment is investigating and assessing what has been or is happening in the family.' Hagell (1998, p. 57) found in her review of the research literature around the risks to children from their carers, that a number of factors could be identified which indicated an increased risk of violence from perpetrators:

- A record of previous violence;
- Level of previous offending of any type;
- Being male;
- Having a history of past mental illness, particularly if hospitalised;
- Personality disorder;
- Non-compliance (particularly with medication);
- Personal history of abuse and neglect;
- Cognitive distortions concerning the use of violence.

This list cannot be used as a checklist for dangerousness – but can help to indicate where social workers should be looking for evidence around past/present adult behaviour to support or deny concerns of violence. Hagell also notes the emerging consensus surrounding multiple, overlapping indicators being more successful predictors of dangerousness than single factors (1998, p.56).

The profiling of families within Bullock and Sinclair's (2002) sample group provides information concerning situational factors and attributes affecting individual members of the family. Some examples of these factors and attributes are:

- A history of care;
- Criminal records;
- Mental health problems;

- Domestic violence (chronic/serious as well as intermittent);
- Drug/alcohol abuse;
- Learning disability;
- Abusive backgrounds, detailing abuse and neglect;
- Poverty and poor housing;
- Unemployment;
- Frequent moves; and
- Frequent changes in adult relationships.

Bullock and Sinclair (2002) found several common situations among the children and families that formed their sample group:
- Young age of the children;
- Histories of emotional neglect and poor care;
- Parents' mental health problems; and
- Domestic violence.

These were not universal findings throughout the sample. Importantly, over 25% of the families were not known to Social Services. Other studies of serious case reviews have highlighted similar themes (Greenland, 1987; James, 1994; Owers, 1999).

However, these factors have limited predictive value (MacDonald, 2001; Munro, 2002) as child abuse is rarely related to a single cause, rather to the interplay of several factors in particular circumstances (Bullock & Sinclair, 2002; MacDonald, 2001). The benefit of an assessment that uses a multi-axial ecological framework is that greater account can be taken of the interrelationship between the child's needs, the needs and abilities of the parents and the situational factors (MacDonald, 2001; Reder & Duncan, 1999). The introduction of the Assessment Framework (Department of Health, 2000) in England should see some changes to the quality of assessments undertaken on children and families in need and/or in need of protection. The implementation of this framework is subject to ongoing evaluation to examine the effect on the quality of assessments undertaken, corresponding with interventions and outcomes achieved for children and families.

Cumulative error: what occurs when processes go wrong

A 'cumulative error' is a combination of single factors that would in themselves be relatively harmless. Such errors can and do interact and compound each other so that the risk of a disaster, such as a serious injury or death of a child is greatly multiplied. This is what Macdonald (2001) refers to as the interplay of different factors, as opposed to an isolated incident. Reder and Duncan (1999, p.139) describe how if each factor is at a marginal level of safety, the cumulative nature of a series of marginal risks will occasionally produce a runaway effect, resulting in a serious incident. Reder and Duncan (1999) illustrate 'cumulative error' using the Hillsborough football stadium tragedy in 1989 and the 'Herald of Free Enterprise' ferry disaster near Zeebrugge harbour in 1987. Not all child deaths fit this pattern.

Poor professional practice

Examples of poor professional practice that were highlighted most frequently in the 40 Serious Case Reviews examined by Bullock and Sinclair (2002, p.40) were:
- Poor interagency communication;
- Poor interagency joint working;
- Poor assessments undertaken by involved professionals;
- Ineffective decision-making;
- Poor recording of information; and
- Lack of information on significant males in the family.

In addition NCH - The Bridge would add:
- Not keeping the child at the focus of inquiries;
- Poor professional competence and;
- The 'rule of optimism' prevailing. We need to overcome the "rule of optimism" which is our wish to see the best in people and
- To see change, combined with our fear of imposing our own values on families as this can result in professional dangerousness.

Common professional errors in decision-making

Jones (2001, p.197) comments that, 'a criticism of current assessments is that they are frequently based upon unsystematic evaluations and are subject to bias, prejudice, or simply restricted in their scope by looking at one aspect of parenting while ignoring other important qualities.'

According to Macdonald (2001), assessments can be subject to psychological, cognitive and perceptual errors. These fundamental errors and biases can then affect the conclusions reached. Assessments can be biased by:
- Attending to the wrong data and ignoring other important data;
- Underestimating the significance of particular pieces of information and overestimating others; and
- Making errors in interpreting information and drawing conclusions from it.

Munro (2002, pp. 141-160) also acknowledges the impact of professional errors and divides these into 2 types:
- Inevitable errors given the fallibility of the knowledge and evidence base available at a certain time;
- Avoidable mistakes, which a competent professional would not have made.

Munro contends that, 'distinguishing the two types of error is essential for defining 'good practice' in child protection' (2002, p.141).

Macdonald (2001, pp. 227-248) identifies five areas of common errors. Where possible I will illustrate these using cases where fatal child abuse occurred.

1) Perceptual errors

Kimberly Carlisle (died 8.6.86 aged 5 years)

A Social Worker interviewed Kimberley Carlisle's family and was reassured all was well:

> 'I walked with the family to the door of the building, and watched as they walked across the road to where their car was parked. I still have a clear mental picture of the way in which they all walked across the road and got into the car, parents holding children by the hand, children leaping around in the car as they got in, laughing, shouting and playing happily with each other. It was almost an archetype for a happy family scene.' (A Child in Mind 1987 p. 108-110 quoted in Macdonald p. 242)

Kimberley's stepfather later killed her. The inquiry saw the social worker as having been "deceived" in this incident - but is there an error in assuming that abusing families don't have happy moments? The challenge for workers is how to ensure they 'read' a situation correctly, how much emphasis to give to one incident and not overplay other factors. In this complex work checks and balances should exist within the system of support available to workers to ensure this questioning occurs.

2) Perceptual/observational bias

This refers to a tendency to see things and people in a certain way, based either on what we are told about them beforehand or on the basis of certain characteristics. An example of this is the power of stereotypes.

Jasmine Beckford (died 5.7.84 aged 4 years)

With Jasmine Beckford,
> 'the Social Workers did not question the fact that they had not seen her for some months, and took the explanation ("she's with her grandmother") to be a positive indicator of the extended care one would expect to find from an African Caribbean grandmother, rather than a warning sign that all might not be well. What they did not do was visit the grandmother and check the validity of their conclusions.' (Macdonald, 2001, p.243)

3) Dominance of first impressions

One well-known point about first impressions is that initial views are highly resistant to change and they mould future information gathering to confirm any views professionals might hold rather than disprove them. This is of particular importance in assessments and also in group decision-making situations such as child protection conferences, where it can be difficult to change a course of action despite other conflicting information.

Neil Howlett (died 26.2.75 aged 2 years)

> 'The social worker for Neil Howlett decided at the first interview that he was not at risk from his mother, but that his brother – who was seen as the family scapegoat – was. This rather speedily formed judgement, based on an initial assessment, effectively pre-empted a full decision and formed the basis of a course of action which was to see Neil dead at the hands of his mother 4 months later. His brother had been taken into care. The inquiry report comments that the conclusion 'jumped to' by the social worker had been accepted uncritically by other staff, despite the fact that in the history of contact with the family, professional concern had always focussed on Neil.' (Macdonald, 2001, p.244).

4) Schemas and memory

Usually we only remember key points and not always all of these. If they are unfamiliar we may also re-interpret them to make them relevant to our context without realising that we may be changing the basic data.

Paul (died 7.3.93 aged 15 months)

The Paul Report has numerous examples of statements from professionals saying that the children in this family were, 'dirty, smelly but happy'. This dominant schema resulted in a failure to intervene that eventually resulted in Paul's death:

In July 92 a Social Worker and an Education Welfare Officer visited Paul's family. The social worker had already told the Education Welfare Officer that the 'concerns about hygiene are intractable, children never get washed. They wear their clothes until they rot" but "hygiene poses no medical problem for children'. The Education Welfare Officer records show the visit was recorded: 'house in completely chaotic state, clearly a warm and caring environment.'

But this is in direct contradiction of the evidence emerging from the chronology put together by the Bridge after the children had died as part of the serious case review, including the children being ostracised by other children at school because they were regarded as dirty and smelly. But this view was so strong that other professionals, despite their concerns seemed unwilling or unable to pursue any other possibility - they appeared to lack confidence to challenge the prevailing view. 'It was as though a collective inertia prevailed' (Bridge Child Care Development Service, 1995).

Macdonald rightly points out that in Paul's case, 'the professionals "reinterpreted" a host of warning signals with reference to this particular schema and others. These "filters" effectively "closed down" their receptivity to factors which should have triggered a more sceptical and investigative response.' (2001, p.247) However, she also cautions that hindsight is a 'dangerous principal for judging professional accountability' (2001, p.247).

5) Vagueness

Macdonald (2001) suggests that a failure to attend to detail, to be specific, and to quantify (i.e., provide examples of) or measure the extent of particular problems and/or causes for concern can cause two core problems which undermine the effectiveness of child protection work. Firstly, it leads to assessments that are not particularly helpful and may well be misleading, and secondly; it means that workers are not in a position to monitor progress and/or recognize change either for better or worse.

Comment

So why is this relevant for practice? The following quote from Hagell (1998, p.ix) encapsulates the key significance of how this information can inform best practice:

'...people are, and have to be, assessing danger in real world situations (in whatever terms this is referred to), that the literature should be able to contribute to and inform this practice, and that practice should be academically-based to improve standards and accuracy.'

Cross-cultural perspective

Two recent tragic cases of child death in England involving black children, have opened the debate about the role of culture in child protection. A number of studies quoted above note the poor recording of ethnicity of both parents and children in primary data, and this was exacerbated by limited reference to race or culture in the Serious Case Reviews included in their respective studies (Bullock & Sinclair, 2002; Reder & Duncan, 1999). So if race and culture are not recognised as significant factors within the Serious Case Review process, what does this say about how professional practice incorporates race and ethnicity within the assessment process? Is racism a further potential professional and situational risk factor to already vulnerable children?

Mistry and Chauhan (2003, p.34) comment that, 'the impact of race, culture and religion in child protection is hard to overestimate. And the absence of good, statistical evidence denies us the opportunity to identify gaps in service for black children and their families. It also prevents us improving professional practice in relation to these families.'

Victoria Climbie (died 25.2.2000 aged 8 years)

The death of Victoria, who was murdered by her Aunt and her Aunt's boyfriend in February 2000, sparked public outcry in the UK due to the nature and severity of abuse and neglect she endured prior to her death. The Consultant Paediatrician who treated Victoria on the last occasion Victoria was admitted to hospital just before she died said it was the worst case of child abuse she had ever seen.

Victoria was born in the Ivory Coast and travelled to Paris and then London with her Aunt in 1998-1999. During the eight months Victoria lived in the UK she was known to all the agencies empowered by the UK parliament to protect children from abuse and neglect, including three Local Authority housing departments, four Social Services Departments, two child protection teams of the Metropolitan Police Service, a specialist centre managed by the NSPCC (National Society for the Protection of Children against Cruelty) and she was admitted to two different hospitals because of suspected deliberate harm.

Lord Laming, who chaired the inquiry, stated in his report (2003, p.3), 'The suffering and death of Victoria was a gross failure of the system and was inexcusable'.

There are four major themes throughout his 108 recommendations:
1. A lack of good practice undertaken with this child.
2. A gross failure of the system to identify Victoria as a child in need of protection and to protect her
3. Widespread organisational malaise
4. Management issues. The Government's response to Lord Laming's report (Department for Education and Skills, Department of Health, Home Office, 2003; Treasury, 2003), refers to the changes deemed necessary, in order to break down agency barriers in an attempt to improve communication between professionals.

Issues of race in relation to Victoria

Neil Garnham, QC, Counsel to the Public Inquiry established to investigate the circumstances leading to and surrounding her death, (2003, p.12) stated that,

'assumption(s) based on race can be just as corrosive in its effect as blatant racism...racism can affect the way people conduct themselves in other ways. Fear of being accused of racism can stop people acting when otherwise they would. Assumptions that people of the same colour, but from different backgrounds, behave in similar ways can distort judgements.'

Lord Laming stated in his report into the death of Victoria Climbie (2003, p.345):

> "Victoria was a black child murdered by her two black carers. Many of the professionals with whom she came into contact during her life in this country were black. Therefore it is tempting to conclude that racism can have had no part to play in her case. But such a conclusion fails to recognise that racism finds expression in many other ways other than in direct application of prejudice."

This most recent public inquiry report was in my view a lost opportunity to comment on 'race' as an issue within child protection. Lord Laming used this latest public inquiry as an opportunity to comment on other aspects of the child protection system but has not chosen to address the challenges to the Child Protection system via institutionalised and other forms of racism. He talked about the effects of assumptions and the fear of workers being accused of racism, and that 'the basic requirement that children are kept safe is universal and cuts across cultural boundaries'. However, racism is a complex phenomenon. Within this case alone, the examination of internalised, institutional and inverted racism might have spearheaded wider debate in this area.

Ainlee Walker (died 7.1.02 aged 2 years)

The Local Authority concerned had known Ainlee and her family over a long period of time. The Serious Case Review written after her death highlights a number of the issues I have already highlighted:

- Poor communication between the agencies involved with Ainlee and her family;
- Staff failed to carry out an assessment of Ainlee's needs or determine the threat posed by her parents;
- Staff lacked the skill to deal with dangerous parents;
- Issues of supervision and training for inexperienced staff;
- Improve record keeping and the exchange of information between Child Protection agencies.

No comment was made in the Serious Case Review report about Ainlee's cultural background and the importance (or not) of this information regarding the assessment and services she received prior to her death.

The Newham ACPC report (2002, p.51) notes:
> "This was a violent and intimidating family, who treated all agencies with suspicion and mistrust and did all that they could to prevent

their involvement... it was extremely difficult to work with them and it is to the credit of many of the staff involved that they attempted to meet the needs of the children in the circumstances. However there was a lack of understanding and a lack of skills in working with dangerous families and a failure to recognise what was happening. Most of the records do not acknowledge that the family was frightening and there is no evidence that the effect they had was addressed in supervision."

At the time of Ainlee's death all agencies had withdrawn from working with the family (Mistry & Chauhan, 2003).

Chand (2003, p.31) notes a number of complexities in challenging people from minority ethnic backgrounds. In particular he identifies: the unwillingness or inability of staff to ask sensitive questions where these are necessary; professionals fear of being accused of racism; and professionals fear for their own safety when working with dangerous families. Can issues of race further compound levels of risk when working with dangerous families?

It is not that straightforward. Cultural factors neither explain nor condone acts of either omission or commission that places a child at risk of significant harm. However, the insidious nature of racism means that there are no quick and easy answers to effectively addressing this area within our practice. Solutions are complex.

There are particular issues in relation to potential racism within the social care arena within the UK. Social work has historically come under intense criticism from various media sources in the UK concerning the 'politically correct' position the media believes Social Work takes in relation to its core commitment to anti-discriminatory and anti-racist practice. However, this comes against the backdrop of another public inquiry into the racist murder of a black teenage boy called Stephen Lawrence over 10 years ago, this time examining the role of the Police in investigating the murder of this young man. The resulting report highlighted many recommendations for public services with regard to dealing with institutional racism (MacPherson, 1999). I do not believe that in the current political environment that any of us can be complacent about issues of race and racism and the effects of this on service users, professional staff and the communities in which we live and work. Professional debate needs to occur in this area.

Banks (2001, p.114) comments that:
"it is not so much the nature of difference between cultural groups that is an issue when assessing children and families from minority ethnic groups, but rather the response to the perception of difference by the assessing agencies and social workers, which may lead the process astray."

Banks identifies a need for cultural familiarity within the assessment process but warns against an over-reliance on cultural explanations. According to Banks (2001, p.114):
> 'familiarity is not necessarily synonymous with awareness or knowledge. Familiarity suggests a higher level of understanding born of engagement in the cultural experience of others outside a problem-centred assessment process.'

Ratna Dutt, director of the Race Equality Unit in the UK, said at the Public Inquiry into the death of Victoria Climbie (2002);
> 'There is some evidence to suggest that one of the consequences of an exclusive focus on 'culture' in work with black children and families, is [that] it leaves black and ethnic minority children in potentially dangerous situations, because the assessment has failed to address a child's fundamental care and protection needs'.

The danger is that the pendulum swings from a 'colour-blind' or assimilation approach regarding assessment to a situation where the emphasis is overly placed on culture and race to the extent that basic child protection issues are mixed. Mistry and Chauhan give a good example of this within their article, and criticism was made along similar lines of social workers involved in working with Tyra Henry (died 1.9.84 aged 22 months) and her family. A report on the case found that the white social workers from Lambeth council tended to be too trusting of the family because they were black (Batty, 2003). The challenge for us over this next period of time is to debate these issues more honestly within the child protection arena. Chand (2003, p.36) comments that, 'what is disheartening is that the examination of policies and practices by different organisations and professionals towards minority families in general only seems to come to the forefront when children like Victoria die. The report asserts that 'this was not an inquiry about racism' yet if issues of racism present themselves in the inquiry they should be properly examined or investigated.'

Conclusions

Child abuse and child neglect is a serious business, which inflicts misery and suffering on the lives of many children. In its most dangerous form it can result in terrible tragedy. Lord Laming's view is that it is doing the basic things well that saves children's lives. Whilst a number of similar issues are repeatedly raised throughout the literature in this area, the existence of known indicators to predict such tragedies outright is limited. It is important to remember this. However, we do have information about factors in perpetrators' backgrounds concerned with risk and dangerousness that has low/moderate predictive value. Studies reviewing serious case reviews also identify key themes that cut across many of the Part 8 and serious case review reports studied. In addition, understanding the risks or errors inherent within the professional decision-making process can assist in identifying potential areas of professional risk. Additional factors may also exist for children from ethnic minority families and there is a need for further debate within the child protection arena about how race and culture affects the assessment process and resulting professional intervention.

Considering the salutary lessons from all of this information is but one way to remind ourselves of the important nature of the work we undertake.

Currently in the UK there is no centralised service responsible for collectively reviewing the serious case reviews submitted annually to the Department of Health. Although such a review would not necessarily have a preventative element to its work, dissemination of the messages from serious case reviews remains important if local ACPC's are to learn the lessons from tragedies and truly change practice and ways of working with children within their local areas. This cannot occur in isolation and we are reliant on colleagues committed to undertaking research in this area in order to expand our knowledge regarding the causes of child abuse, effective interventions, and improving assessments and decision-making in this area.

References

Banks, N. (2001). Assessing children and families who belong to minority ethnic groups. *The Child's World* NSPCC, Leicester UK.

Batty, D. (2003). Catalogue of cruelty. *The Guardian Newspaper 27.1.2003* (http://society.guardian.co.uk/children/story/0,1074,563930,00.html).

Bridge Child Care Development Service (1995). *Paul: Death through neglect.* Islington: ACPC/The Bridge Publishing House.

Bridge Child Care Development Service (2001). *Childhood lost. Part 8 case review overview report D M.* London: Bridge Publishing House.

Browne, K., & Lynch, M. (1995). Fatal child abuse. *Child Abuse Review* IV, (Editorial).

Bullock, R., & Sinclair, R. (2002). *Learning from past experience – A Review of Serious case Reviews.* London: Department of Health HMSO.

Carson, D. (1998). Reducing the Riskiness of risk assessment. In R. Jeyarajah Dent (Ed.), *Dangerous care: Working to protect children.* London: Bridge Child Care Development Service.

Channer, Y., & Parton, N. (1989). Racism, cultural relativism and child protection. In Violence Against Children Study Group. *Taking child abuse seriously: Contemporary issues in child protection theory and practice (the State of Welfare Series).* London: Routledge.

Chand, A. (2003). Race' and the Laming Report on Victoria Climbie: Lessons for inter-professional policy and practice. *Journal of Integrated Care* 11(4).

Creighton, D. (2001). Childhood deaths reported to coroners: an investigation of the contribution of abuse and neglect. In NSPCC, *Out of sight,* op.cit.

Department of Health, Department of Education and Science and Welsh Office (1991). *Working together under the Children Act 1989.* London: HMSO.

Department of Health, Home Office and Department for Education and Employment (1999). *Working together to safeguard children: A guide to interagency working to safeguard and promote the welfare of children.* London: Stationery Office.

Department of Health, Department for Education and Employment, Home Office (2000). *Framework for the assessment of children in need and their families.* London: Stationery Office.

Department of Health, Social Services Inspectorate (2002). *Safeguarding children: A joint chief inspectors' report.* London: HMSO.

Department for Education and Skills, Department of Health, Home Office (2003). Keeping children safe: The government's response to the *Victoria Climbie inquiry report* and joint chief inspectors' report *Safeguarding Children.* London: HMSO.

Falkov, A. (1996). *A study of working together Part 8 reports: Fatal child abuse and parental psychiatric disorder.* London: Department of Health.

Greenland, C. (1987). *Preventing CAN deaths: An international study of deaths due to child abuse and neglect.* London: Tavistock.

Hagell, A. (1998). *Dangerous care: Reviewing the risk to children form their carers.* London: Policy Studies Institute.

Harris Hendriks, J., & Newman, M. (1998). Key messages from the research literature. In R. Jeyarajah Dent (Ed.), *Dangerous care: Working to protect children.* London: Bridge Child Care Development Service.

Hill, M. (1990). The manifest and latent lessons of child abuse inquiries. *British Journal of Social Work, 20,* 197-213.

James, G. (1994). *Study of working together Part 8 reports.* London: Department of Health.

Jeyarajah Dent, R. (Ed.) (1998). *Dangerous care: Working to protect children.* London: Bridge Child Care Development Service.

Jones, D. P. H. (2000). The assessment of parental capacity. In J. Horwath (Ed.), *The child's world: Assessing children in need – Reader.* England: NSPCC and University of Sheffield.

Jowitt, S. (2003). *Child neglect: Contemporary themes and issues.* London: the Bridge Publishing House.

Lord Laming (2003). *Victoria Climbié Inquiry Report.* London: TSO.

Macdonald, G. (2001). *Effective interventions for child abuse and neglect: An evidence-based approach to planning an evaluating interventions.* Chichester: Wiley.

MacPherson, W. (1999). *The Stephen Lawrence inquiry.* London: TSO.

Mistry, D., & Chauhan, S. (2003). Don't leave race on the side. *Community Care* 31 July – 6 August 2003.

Munro, E. (1996). Avoidable and unavoidable mistakes in child protection work. *British Journal of Social Work 26,* 793-808.

Munro, E. (2002). *Effective child protection.* London: Sage Publications.

Newham Area Child Protection Committee (2002). *Ainlee: Chapter 8 review.* London: Newham Area Child Protection Committee.

Newman, M., Otvos, B., & Harris Hendriks, J. (1998). Evaluating the risk to children. In R. Jeyarajah Dent (Ed.), *Dangerous care: Working to protect children.* London: Bridge Child Care Development Service.

NSPCC (2001). *Out of sight: Report on child deaths from abuse 1973-2000.* London: NSPCC.

Owers, M., Brandon, M., & Black, J. (1999). *Learning how to make children safer: An analysis for the Welsh Office of Serious Child Abuse Cases in Wales.* University of East Anglia: Welsh Office.

Parton, C., & Parton, N. (1989). Child protection, the law and dangerousness. In O. Stevenson (Ed.), *Child abuse: Public policy and professional practice.* Hemel Hempstead: Harvester Wheatsheaf.

Pritchard, C. (1992). Children's homicide as an indicator of effective child protection: A comparative study of Western European statistics. *British Journal of Social Work 22,* 663-684.

Reder, P., Duncan, S., & Gray, M. (1993). *Beyond blame: Child abuse tragedies revisited.* London: Routledge.

Reder, P., & Duncan, S. (1999). *Lost innocents: A follow-up study of fatal child abuse.* London and New York: Routledge.

Sanders, R., Colton, M., & Roberts, S. (1999). Child abuse fatalities and cases of extreme concern: Lessons from reviews. *Child Abuse and Neglect* 23, 3, 257-268.

Treasury (2003). *Every Child Matters.* London: HMSO.

UNICEF (2003). *A league table of child maltreatment deaths in rich nations. Innocenti Report Card No 5., September 2003.* Florence: UNICEF Innocenti Research Centre.

Wilczynski, P. (1994). The incidence of child homicide: How accurate are the official statistics? *Journal of Clinical Forensic Medicine, 1,* 61-66.

www.ingramcontent.com/pod-product-compliance
Ingram Content Group UK Ltd.
Pitfield, Milton Keynes, MK11 3LW, UK
UKHW021836140426
5217IPUK00021B/1477